The Theory of Business Enterprise

Thorstein Veblen

The Theory of Business Enterprise

Thorstein Veblen

- Preface
- 1: Introductory
- 2: The Machine Process
- 3: Business Enterprise
- 4: Business Principles
- 5: Value of Loan Credit
- 6: Modern Business Capital
- 7: Theory of Modern Welfare
- 8: Business Principles in Law and Politics
- 9: Cultural Incidence of Machine Process
- 10: Decay of Business Enterprise

Preface

In respect to its point of departure, the following inquiry into the nature, causes, utility, and further drift of business enterprise differs from other discussions of the same general range of facts. Any unfamiliar conclusions are due to this choice of a point of view, rather than to any peculiarity in the facts, articles of theory, or method of argument employed. The point of view is that given by the business man's work, — the aims, motives, and means that condition current business traffic. This choice of a point of view is itself given by the current economic situation, in that the situation plainly is primarily a business situation.

A much more extended and detailed examination of the ramifications and consequences of business enterprise and business principles would feasible, and should give interesting results. It might conceivably lead to something of a revision (modernization) of more than one point in the current body of economic doctrines. But it should apparently prove more particulary interesting if it were followed up at large in the bearing of this modern force upon cultural growth, apart from what is of immediate economic interest. This cultural bearing of business enterprise, however, belongs rather in the field of the sociologist than in that of the professed economist; so that the present inquiry, in its later chapters, sins rather by exceeding the legitimate bounds of economic discussion on this head than by falling short of them. In extenuation of this fault it is said that the features of general culture touched upon in these chapters bear too intimately on the economic situation proper to admit their being left entirely on one side.

Of the chapters included in the volume, the fifth, on Loan Credit, is taken without substantial change, from Volume IV of the Decennial Publications of the University of Chicago, where it appears as a monograph. The Theory of Business Enterprise by Thorstein Veblen 1904

Chapter One. Introductory

The material framework of modern civilization is the industrial system, and the directing force which animates this framework is business enterprise. To a greater extent than any other known phase of culture, modern Christendom takes its complexion from its economic organization. This modern economic organization is the "Capitalistic System" or "Modern Industrial System," so called. Its characteristic features, and at the same time the forces by virtue of which it dominates modern culture, are the machine process and investment for a profit.

The scope and method of modern industry are given by the machine. This may not seem to hold true for all industries, perhaps not for the greater part of industry as rated by the bulk of the output or by the aggregate volume of labor expended. But it holds true to such an extent and in such a pervasive manner that a modern industrial community cannot go on except by the help of the accepted mechanical appliances and processes. The machine industries -- those portions of the industrial system in which the machine process is paramount -- are in a dominant position; they set the pace for the rest of the industrial system. In this sense the present is the age of the machine process. This dominance of the machine process in industry marks off the present industrial situation from all else of its kind.

In a like sense the present is the age of business enterprise. Not that all industrial activity is carried on by the rule of investment for profits, but an effective majority of the industrial forces are organized on that basis. There are many items of great volume and consequence that do not fall within the immediate score of these business principles. The housewife's work, e.g., as well as some appreciable portion of the work on farms and in some handicrafts, can scarcely be classed as business enterprise. But those elements in the industrial world that take the initiative and exert a far-reaching coercive guidance in matters of industry go to their work with a view to profits on investment, and are guided by the principles and exigencies of business. The business man, especially the business man of wide and authoritative discretion, has become a controlling force in industry, because, through the mechanism of investments and markets, he controls the plants and processes, and these set the pace and determine the direction of movement for the rest. His control in those portions of the field that are not immediately under his hand is, no doubt, somewhat loose and uncertain; but in the long run his discretion is in great measure decisive even for these outlying portions of the field, for he is the only large self-directing economic factor. His control of the motions of other men is not strict, for they are not under coercion from him except through the coercion exercised by the exigencies of the situation in which their lives are cast; but as near as it may be said of any human power in modern times, the large business man controls the exigencies of life under which the community lives. Hence, upon him and his fortunes centres the abiding interest of civilized mankind.

For a theoretical inquiry into the course of civilized life as it runs in the immediate present, therefore, aud as it is running into the proximate future, no single factor in the cultural situation has an importance equal to that of the business man and his work.

This of course applies with peculiar force to an inquiry into the economic life of a modem community. In so far as the theorist aims to explain the specifically modern economic phenomena, his line of approach must be from the businessman's standpoint, since it is from that standpoint that the course of these phenomena is directed. A theory of the modern economic situation must be primarily a theory of business traffic, with its motives, aims, methods, and effects. The Theory of Business Enterprise by Thorstein Veblen 1904

Chapter Two. The Machine Process

In its bearing on modern life and modern business, the "machine process" means something more comprehensive and less external than a mere aggregate of mechanical appliances for the mediation of human labor. It means that, but it means something more than that. The civil engineer, the mechanical engineer, the navigator, the mining expert, the industrial chemist and mineralogist, the electrician, -- the work of all these falls within the lines of the modern machine process, as well as the work of the inventor who devises the appliances of the process and that of the mechanician who puts the inventions into effect and oversees their working. The scope of the process is larger than the machine.(1*) In those branches of industry in which machine methods have been introduced, many agencies which are not to be classed as mechanical appliances, simply, have been drawn into the process, and have become integral factors in it. Chemical properties of minerals, e.g., are counted on in the carrying out of metallurgical processes with much the same certainty and calculable effect as are the motions of those mechanical appliances by whose use the minerals are handled.

The sequence of the process involves both the one and the other, both the apparatus and the materials, in such intimate interaction that the process cannot be spoken of simply as an action of the apparatus upon the materials. It is not simply that the apparatus reshapes the materials; the materials reshape themselves by the help of the apparatus. Similarly in such other processes as the refining of petroleum, oil, or sugar; in the work of the industrial chemical laboratories; in the use of wind, water, or electricity, etc.

Wherever manual dexterity, the rule of thumb, and the fortuitous conjunctures of the seasons have been supplanted by a reasoned procedure on the basis of a systematic knowledge of the forces employed, there the mechanical industry is to be found, even in the absence of intricate mechanical contrivances. It is a question of the character of the process rater than a question of the complexity of the contrivances employed. Chemical, agricultural, and animal industries, as carried on by the characteristically modern methods and in due touch with the market, are to be included in the modern complex of mechanical industry.(2*)

No one of the mechanical processes carried on by the use of a given outfit of appliances is independent of other processes going on elsewhere. Each draws upon and presupposes the proper working of many other processes of a similarly mechanical character. None of the processes in the mechanical industries is self-sufficing. Each follows some and precedes other processes in an endless sequence, into which each fits and to the requirements of which each must adapt its own working. The whole concert of industrial operations is to be taken as a machine process, made up of interlocking detail processes, rather than as a multiplicity of mechanical appliances each doing its particular work in severalty. This comprehensive industrial process draws into its scope and turns to account all branches of knowledge that have to do with the material sciences, and the whole makes a more or less delicately balanced complex of sub-processes.(3*)

Looked at in this way the industrial process shows two well-marked general characteristics: (a) the running maintenance of interstitial adjustments between the several sub-processes or branches of industry, wherever in their working they touch one another in the sequence of industrial elaboration; and (b) an unremitting requirement of quantitative precision, accuracy in point of time and sequence, in the proper inclusion and exclusion of forces affecting the outcome, in the magnitude of the various physical characteristics (weight, size, density, hardness, tensile strength, elasticity, temperature, chemical reaction, actinic sensitiveness, etc.) of the materials handled as well as of the appliances employed. This requirement of mechanical accuracy and nice adaptation to specific uses has led to a gradual pervading enforcement of uniformity to a reduction to staple grades and staple character in the materials handled, and to a thorough standardizing of tools and units of measurement. Standard physical measurements are of the essence of the machine's regime.(4*)

The modern industrial communities show an unprecedented uniformity and precise equivalence in legally adopted weights and measures. Something of this kind would be brought about by the needs of commerce, even without the urgency given to the movement for uniformity by the requirements of the machine industry. But within the industrial field the movement for standardization has outrun the urging of commercial needs, and has penetrated every corner of the mechanical industries. The specifically commercial need of uniformity in weights and measures of merchantable goods and in monetary units has not carried standardization in these items to the extent to which the mechanical need of the industrial process has carried out a sweeping standardization in the means by which the machine process works, as well as in the products which it turns out.

As a matter of course, tools and the various structural materials used are made of standard sizes, shapes, and gauges. When the dimensions, in fractions of an inch or in millimetres, and the weight, in fractions of a pound or in grammes, are given, the expert foreman or workman, confidently and without reflection, infers the rest of what need be known of the uses to which any given item that passes under his hand may be turned. The adjustment and adaptation of part to part and of process to process has passed out of the category of craftsmanlike skill into the category of mechanical standardization. Hence, perhaps, the greatest, most wide-reaching gain in productive celerity and efficiency through modern methods, and hence the largest saving of labor in modern industry.

Tools, mechanical appliances and movements, and structural materials are scheduled by certain conventional scales and gauges; and modern industry has little use for, and can make little use of, what does not conform to the standard. What is not competently standardized calls for too much of craftsmanlike skill, reflection, and individual elaboration, and is therefore not available for economical use in the processes. Irregularity, departure from standard measurements in any of the measurable facts, is of itself a fault in any item that is to find a use in the industrial process, for it brings delay, it detracts from its ready usability in the nicely adjusted process into which it is to go; and a delay at any point means a more or less far-reaching and intolerable retardation of the comprehensive industrial process at large. Irregularity in products intended for industrial use carries a penalty to the nonconforming producer which urges him to fall into line and submit to the required standardization.

The materials and moving forces of industry are undergoing a like reduction to staple kinds, styles, grades, and gauge.(5*) Even such forces as would seem at first sight not to lend themselves to standardization, either in their production or their use, are subjected to uniform scales of measurement; as, e.g., water-power, steam, electricity, and human labor. The latter is perhaps the least amenable to standardization, but, for all that, it is bargained for, delivered, and turned to account on schedules of time, speed, and intensity which are continually sought to be reduced to a more precise measurement and a more sweeping uniformity.

The like is true of the finished products. Modern consumers in great part supply their wants with commodities that conform to certain staple specifications of size, weight, and grade. The consumer (that is to say the vulgar consumer) furnishes his hose, his table, and his person with supplies of standard weight and measure, and he can to an appreciable degree specify his needs and his consumption in the notation of the standard gauge. As regards the mass of civilized mankind, the idiosyncrasies of the individual consumers are required to conform to the uniform gradations imposed upon consumable goods by the comprehensive mechanical processes of industry. "Local color" it is said, is falling into abeyance in modern life, and where it is still found it tends to assert itself in units of the standard gauge.

From this mechanical standardization of consumable goods it follows, on the one hand, that the demand for goods settles upon certain defined lines of production which handle certain materials of definite grade, in certain, somewhat invariable forms and proportions; which leads to well-defined methods and measurements in the processes of production, shortening the average period of "ripening" that intervenes between the first raw stage of the product and its finished shape, and reducing the aggregate stock of goods necessary to be carried for the supply of current wants, whether in the raw or in the finished form.(6*) Standardization means economy at nearly all points of the process of supplying goods, and at the same time it means certainty and expedition at neatly all points in the business operations involved in meeting current wants. Besides this, the standardization of goods means that the interdependence of industrial processes is reduced to more definite terms than before the mechanical standardization came to its present degree of elaborateness and rigor. The margin of admissible variation, in time, place, form, and amount, is narrowed. Materials, to answer the needs of standardized industry, must be drawn from certain standard sources at a definite rate of supply. Hence any given detail industry depends closely on receiving its supplies from certain, relatively few, industrial establishments whose work belongs earlier in the process of elaboration. And it ma similarly depend on certain other, closely defined, industrial establishments for a vent of its own specialization and standardization product.(7*) It may likewise depend in a strict manner on special means of transportation.(8*)

Machine production leads to a standardization of services as well as of goods. So, for instance, the modern means of communication and the system into which these means are organized are also of the nature of a mechanical process, and in this mechanical process of service and intercourse the life of all civilized men is more or less intimately involved. To make effective use of the modern system of communication in any way or all of its ramifications (streets, railways, steamship lines, telephone, telegraph, postal service, etc.), men are required to adapt their needs and their motions to the exigencies of the process whereby this civilized method of intercourse is carried into effect. The service is standardized, and therefore the use of it is standardized also. Schedules of time, place, and circumstance rule throughout. The scheme of everyday life must be arranged with a strict regard to the exigencies of the process whereby this range of human needs is served, if full advantage is to be taken of this system of intercourse, which means that, in so far, one's plans and projects must be conceived and worked out in terms of those standard units which the system imposes.

For the population of the towns and cities, at least, much the same rule holds true of the distribution of consumable goods. So, also, amusements and diversions, much of the current amenities of life, are organized into a more or less sweeping process to which those who would benefit by the advantages offered must adapt their schedule of wants and the disposition of their time and effort. The frequency, duration, intensity, grade, and sequence are not, in the main, matters for the free discretion of the individuals who participate. Throughout the scheme of life of that portion of mankind that clusters about the centres of modern culture the industrial process makes itself felt and enforces a degree of conformity to the canon of accurate quantitative measurement. There comes to prevail a degree of standardization and precise mechanical adjustment of the details of everyday life, which presumes a facile and unbroken working of all those processes that minister to these standardized human wants.

As a result of this superinduced mechanical regularity of life, the livelihood of individuals is, over large areas, affected in an approximately uniform manner by any incident which at all seriously affects the industrial process at any point.(9*)

As was noted above, each industrial unit, represented by a given industrial "plant", stands in close relations of interdependence with other industrial processes going forward elsewhere, near or far away, from which it receives supplies -- materials, apparatus, and the like -- and to which it turns over its output of products and waste, or on which it depends for auxiliary work, such as transportation. The resulting concatenation of industries has been noticed by most modern writers. It is commonly discussed under the head of the division of labor. Evidently the prevalent standardization of industrial means, methods, and products greatly increases the reach of this concatenation of industries, at the same time that it enforces a close conformity in point of time, volume and character of the product, whether the product is goods or services.(10*)

By virtue of this concatenation of processes the modern industrial system at large bears the character of a comprehensive, balanced mechanical process. In order to an efficient working of this industrial process at large, the various constituent sub-processes must work in due coordination throughout the whole. Any degree of maladjustment in the interstitial coordination of this industrial process at large in some degree hinders its working. Similarity, any given detail process or any industrial plant will do its work to full advantage only when due adjustment is had between its work and the work done by the rest. The higher the degree of development reached by a given industrial community, the more comprehensive and urgent becomes this requirement of interstitial adjustment. And the more fully a given industry has taken on the character of a mechanical process, and the more extensively and closely it is correlated in its work with other industries that precede or follow it in the sequence of elaboration, the more urgent, other things equal, is the need of maintaining the proper working relations with these other industries, the greater is the industrial detriment suffered from any derangement of the accustomed working relations, and the greater is the industrial gain to be derived from a closer adaptation and a more facile method of readjustment in the event of a disturbance, -- the greater is also the chance for an effectual disturbance of industry at the particular point. This mechanical concatenation of industrial processes makes for solidarity in the administration of any group of related industries, and more remotely it makes for solidarity in the management of the entire industrial traffic of the community.

A disturbance at any point, whereby any given branch of industry fails to do its share in the work of the system at large, immediately affects the neighbouring or related branches which come before or after it in the sequence, and is transmitted through their derangement to the remoter portions of the system. The disturbance is rarely confined to the single plant or the single line of production first affected, but spreads in some measure to the rest. A disturbance at any given point brings more or less derangement to the industrial process at large. So that any maladjustment of the system involves a larger waste than simply the disabling of one or two members in the complex industrial structure.

So much is clear, that the keeping of the balance in the comprehensive machine process of industry is a matter of the gravest urgency if the productive mechanism is to proceed with its work in an efficient manner, so as to avoid idleness, waste, and hardship. The management of the various industrial plants and processes in due correlation with all the rest, and the supervision of the interstitial adjustments of the system, are commonly conceived to be a work of greater consequence to the community's well-being than any of the detail work involved in carrying on a given process of production. This work of interstitial adjustment, and in great part also the more immediate supervision of the various industrial processes, have become urgent only since the advent of the machine industry and in proportion as the machine industry has advanced in compass and consistency.

It is by business transactions that the balance of working relations between the several industrial units is maintained or restored, adjusted and readjusted, and it is on the same basis and by the same method that the affairs of each industrial unit are regulated. The relations in which any independent industrial concern stands to its employees, as well as to other concerns, are always reducible to pecuniary terms. It is at this point that the business man comes into the industrial process as a decisive factor. The organization of the several industries as well as the interstitial adjustments and discrepancies of the industrial process at large are of the nature of pecuniary transactions and obligations. It therefore rests with the business men to make or mar the running adjustments of industry. The larger and more close-knit and more delicately balanced the industrial system, and the larger the constituent units, the larger and more far-reaching will be the effect of each business move in the field.

NOTES:

1. Cf. Cooke Taylor, Modern Factory System, pp. 74-77.

2. Even in work that lies so near the fortuities of animate nature as dairying, stock-breeding, and the improvement of crop plants, a determinate, reasoned routine replaces the rule of thumb. By mechanical control of his materials the dairyman, e.g., selectively determines the rate and kind of the biological processes that change his raw material into finished product. The stock-breeder's aim is to reduce the details of the laws of heredity, as they apply within his field, to such definite terms as will afford him a technologically accurate routine of breeding, and then to apply this technological breeding process to the production of such varieties of stock as will, with the nearest approach to mechanical exactness and expedition, turn the raw materials of field and meadow into certain specified kinds and grades of finished product. The like is true of the plant-breeders. Agricultural experiment stations and bureaus, in all civilized countries, are laboratories working toward an effective technological control of biological factors, with a view to eliminating fortuitous, disserviceable, and useless elements from the processes of agricultural production, and so reducing these processes to a calculable, expeditious, and wasteless routine.

3. Cf. Sombart, Moderne Kapitalismus, vol. II, ch. III.

4. Twelfth Census (U.S.): "Manufactures," pt. I, p. xxxvi.

5.. E.g., lumber, coal, paper, wool and cotton, grain, leather, cattle for the packing houses. All these and many others are to an increasing extent spoken for, delivered, and disposed of under well-defined staple grades as to quality and dimensions, weight and efficiency.

6. Well shown in the case of wheat and flour; but the like is true as regards the stocks of other commodities carried by producers, jobbers, retailers, and consumers.

7. Well illustrated by the interdependence of the various branches of iron and steel production.

8. As seen, e.g., in the dependence of oil production or oil refining on the pipe lines and their management, or in the dependence of the prairie farmers on the railway lines, etc.

9. It may be noted in this connection, on the one hand, that a population which is in no degree habituated to the modern industrial process is unable to adapt its mode of life to the requirements of this method of supplying human wants, and so can derive but little benefit, and possibly great discomfort, from a forcible intrusion of the machine industry; as, for instance, many of the outlying barbarian peoples with whom the Western industrial culture is now enforcing a close contact. On the other hand, it is also true that even the most adequately trained modern community, among whom the machine industry is best at home, does not respond with fruitless alacrity to the demands and opportunities which this system holds out. The adaptation of habits of life and of ideals and aspirations to the exigencies of the machine process is not nearly complete, nor does the untrained man instinctively fall into line with it. Even the best-trained, severely disciplined man of the industrial towns has his seasons of recalcitrancy.

10. The dependence of one process upon the working of the others is sometimes very strict, as, for instance, in the various industries occupied with iron, including the extraction and handling of the ore and other raw materials. In other cases the correlation is less strict, or even very slight, as, e.g., that between the newspaper industry and lumbering, through the wood-pulp industry, the chief component of the modern newspaper being wood-pulp.

Chapter Three. Business Enterprise

The motive of business is pecuniary gain, the method is essentially purchase and sale. The aim and usual outcome is an accumulation of wealth.(1*) Men whose aim is not increase of possessions do not go into business, particularly not on an independent footing.

How these motives and methods of business work out in the traffic of commercial enterprise proper – in mercantile and banking business does not concern the present inquiry, except so far as these branches of business affect the course of industrial business in the stricter sense of the term. Nor is it necessary were to describe the details of business routine, whether in the mercantile pursuits or in the conduct of an industrial concern. The point of the inquiry is that characteristically modern business that is coextensive with the machine process described above and is occupied with the large mechanical industry. The aim is a theory of such business enterprise in outline sufficiently full to show in what manner business methods and business principles, in conjunction with the mechanical industry, influence the modern cultural situation. To save space and tedium, therefore, features of business traffic that are not of a broad character and not peculiar to this modern situation are left on one side, as being already sufficiently familiar for the purpose in hand.

In early modern times, before the regime of the machine industry set in, business enterprise on any appreciable scale commonly took the form of commercial business – some form of merchandising or banking. Shipping was the only considerable line of business which involved an investment in or management of extensive mechanical appliances and processes, comparable with the facts of the modern mechanical industry.(2*) And shipping was commonly combined with merchandising. But even the shipping trade of earlier times had much of a fortuitous character, in this respect resembling agriculture or any other industry in which wind and, weather greatly affect the outcome. The fortunes of men in shipping were on a more precarious footing than to-day, and the successful outcome of their ventures was less a matter of shrewd foresight and daily pecuniary strategy than are the affairs of the modern large business concerns in transportation or the foreign trade. Under these circumstances the work of the business man was rather to take advantage of the conjunctures offered by the course of the seasons and the fluctuations of demand and supply than to adapt the course of affairs to his own ends. The large business man was more of a speculative buyer and seller and less of a financiering strategist than he has since become.

Since the advent of the machine age the situation has changed. The methods of business have, of course, not changed fundamentally, whatever may be true of the methods of industry; for they are, as they had been, conditioned by the facts of ownership. But instead of investing in the goods as they pass between producer and consumer, as the merchant does, the business man now invests in the processes of industry; and instead of staking his values on the dimly foreseen conjunctures of the seasons and the act of God, he turns to the conjunctures arising from the interplay of the industrial processes, which are in great measure under the control of business men.

So long as the machine processes were but slightly developed, scattered, relatively isolated, and independent of one another industrially, and so long as they were carried on on a small scale for a relatively narrow market, so long the management of them was conditioned by circumstances in many respects similar to those which conditioned the English domestic industry of the eighteenth century. It was under the conditions of this inchoate phase of the machine age that the earlier generation of economists worked out their theory of the business man's part in industry. It was then still true, in great measure, that the undertaker was the owner of the industrial equipment, and that he kept an immediate oversight of the mechanical processes as well as of the pecuniary transactions in which his enterprise was engaged; and it was also true, with relatively infrequent exceptions, that an unsophisticated productive efficiency was the prime element of business success.(3*) A further feature of that precapitalistic business situation is that business, whether handicraft or trade, was customarily managed with a view to earning a livelihood rather than with a view to profits on investment.(4*)

In proportion as the machine industry gained ground, and as the modern concatenation of industrial processes and of markets developed, the conjunctures of business grew more varied and of larger scope at the same time that they became more amenable to shrewd manipulation. The pecuniary side of the enterprise came to require more unremitting attention, as the chances for gain or loss through business relatIons simply, aside from mere industrial efficiency, grew greater in number and magnitude. The same circumstances also provoked a spirit of business enterprise, and brought on a systematic investment for gain. With a fuller development of the modern closeknit and comprehensive industrIal system, the point of chief attention for the business man has shifted from the old-fashioned surveillance and regulation of a given industrial process, with which his livelihood was once bound up, to an alert redistribution of investments from less to more gainful ventures,(5*) and to a strategic control of the conjunctures of business through shrewd investments and coalitions with other business men.

As shown above, the modern industrial system is a concatenation of processes which has much of the character of a single, comprehensive, balanced mechanical process. A disturbance of the balance at any point means a differential advantage (or disadvantage) to one or more of the owners of the sub-processes between which the disturbance falls; and it may also frequently mean gain or loss to many remoter members in the concatenation of processes, for the balance throughout the sequence is a delicate one, and the transmission of a disturbance often goes far. It may even take on a cumulative character, and may thereby seriously cripple or accelerate branches of industry that are out of direct touch with those members of the concatenation upon which the initial disturbance falls. Such is the case, for instance, in an industrial crisis, when an apparently slIght initial disturbance may become the occasion of a widespread derangement. And such, on the other hand, is also the case when some favorable condition abruptly supervenes in a given industry, as, e.g., when a sudden demand for war stores starts a wave of prosperity by force of a large and lucrative demand for the products of certain industries, and these in turn draw on their neighbors in the sequence, and so transmit a wave of business activity.

The keeping of the industrial balance, therefore, and adjusting the several industrial processes to one another's work and needs, is a matter of grave and far-reaching consequence in any modern community, as has already been shown. Now, the means by which this balance is kept is business transactions, and the men in whose keeping it lies are the business men. The channel by which disturbances are transmitted from member to member of the comprehensive industrial system is the business relations between the several members of the system; and, under the modern conditions of ownership, disturbances, favorable or unfavorable, in the field of industry are transmitted by nothing but these business relations. Hard times or prosperity spread through the system by means of business relations, and are in their primary expression phenomena of the business situation simply. It is only secondarily that the disturbances in question show themselves as alterations in the character or magnitude of the mechanical processes involved. Industry is carried on for the sake of business, and not conversely; and the progress and activity of industry are conditioned by the outlook of the market, which means the presumptive chance of business profits.

All this is a matter of course which it may seem simply tedious to recite.(6*) But its consequences for the theory of business make it necessary to keep the nature of this connection between business and industry in mind. The adjustments of industry take place through the mediation of pecuniary transactions, and these transactions take place at the hands of the business men and are carried on by them for business ends, not for industrial ends in the narrower meaning of the phrase.

The economic welfare of the community at large is best served by a facile and uninterrupted interplay of the various processes which make up the industrial system at large; but the pecuniary interests of the business men in whose hands lies the discretion in the matter are not necessarily best served by an unbroken maintenance of the industrial balance. Especially is this true as regards those greater business men whose interests are very extensive. The pecuniary operations of these latter are of large scope, and their fortunes commonly are not permanently bound up with the smooth working of a given Sub-process in the industrial system. Their fortunes are rather related to the larger conjunctures of the industrial system as a whole, the interstitial adjustments, Or to conjunctures affecting large ramifications of the system. Nor is it at all uniformly to their interest to enhance the smooth working of the industrial system at large in so far as they are related to it. Gain may come to them from a given disturbance of the system whether the disturbance makes for heightened facility or for widespread hardship, very much as a speculator in grain futures may be either a bull or a bear. To the business man who aims at a differential gain arising out of interstitial adjustments or disturbances of the industrial system, it is not a material question whether his operations have an immediate furthering or hindering effect upon the system at large. The end is pecuniary gain, the means is disturbance of the industrial system, - except so far as the gain is sought by the old-fashioned method of permanent investment in some one industrial or commercial plant, a case which is for the present left on one side as not bearing on the point immediately in hand.(7*) The point immediately in question is the part which the business man plays in what are here called the interstitial adjustments of the industrial system; and so far as touches his transactions in this field it is, by and large, a matter of indifference to him whether his traffic affects the system advantageously or disastrously. His gains (or losses) are related to the magnitude of the disturbances that take place, rather than to their. bearing upon the welfare of the community.

The outcome of this management of industrial affairs through pecuniary transactions, therefore, has been to dissociate the interests of those men who exercise the discretion from the interests of the community. This is true in a peculiar degree and increasingly since the fuller development of the machine industry has brought about a closeknit and wide-reaching articulation of industrial processes, and has at the same time given rise to a class of pecuniary experts whose business is the strategic management of the interstitial relations of the system. Broadly, this class of business men, in so far as they have no ulterior strategic ends to serve, have an interest in making the disturbances of the system large and frequent, since it is in the conjunctures of change that their gain emerges. Qualifications of this proposition may be needed, and it will be necessary to return to this point presently.

It is, as a business proposition, a matter of indifference to the man of large affairs whether the disturbances which his transactions set up in the industrial system help or hinder the system at large, except in so far as he has ulterior strategic ends to serve. But most of the modern captains of industry have such ulterior ends, and of the greater ones among them this is peculiarly true. Indeed, it is this work of far-reaching business strategy that gives them full title to the designation, "Captains of Industry." This large business strategy is the most admirable trait of the great business men who with force and insight swing the fortunes of civilized mankind. And due qualification is accordingly to be entered in the broad statement made above. The captain's strategy is commonly directed to gaining control of some large portion of the industrial system. When such control has been achieved, it may be to his interest to make and maintain business conditions which shall facilitate the smooth and efficient working of what has come under his control, in case he continues to hold a large interest in it as an investor; for, other things equal, the gains from what has come under his hands permanently in the way of industrial plant are greater the higher and more uninterrupted its industrial efficiency.

An appreciable portion of the larger transactions in railway and "industrial" properties, e.g., are carried out with a view to the permanent ownership of the properties by the business men into whose hands they pass. But also in a large proportion of these transactions the business men's endeavors are directed to a temporary control of the properties in order to close out at an advance or to gain some indirect advantage; that is to say, the transactions have a strategic purpose. The business man aims to gain control of a given block of industrial equipment – as, e.g., given railway lines or iron mills that are strategically important – as a basis for further transactions out of which gain is expected. In such a case his efforts are directed, not to maintaining the permanent efficiency of the industrial equipment, but to influencing the tone of the market for the time being, the apprehensions of other large operators, or the transient faith of investors.(8*) His interest in the particular block of industrial equipment is, then, altogether transient, and while it lasts it is of a factitious character.

The exigencies of this business of interstitial disturbance decide that in the common run of cases the proximate aim of the business man is to upset or block the industrial process at some one or more points. His strategy is commonly directed against other business interests and his ends are commonly accomplished by the help of some form of pecuniary coercion. This is not uniformly true, but it seems to be true in appreciably more than half of the transactions in question. In general, transactions which aim to bring a coalition of industrial plants or processes under the control of a given business man are directed to making it difficult for the plants or processes in question to be carried on in severalty by their previous owners or managers.(9*) It is commonly a struggle between rival business men, and more often than not the outcome of the struggle depends on which side can inflict or endure the greater pecuniary damage. And pecuniary damage in such a case not uncommonly involves a setback to the industrial plants concerned and a derangement, more or less extensive, of the industrial system at large.

The work of the greater modern business men, in so far as they have to do with the ordering of the scheme of industrial life, is of this strategic character. The dispositions which they make are business transactions, "deals," as they are called in the business jargon borrowed from gaming slang. These do not always involve coercion of the opposing interests; it is not always necessary to "put a man in a hole" before he is willing to "come in on" a "deal." It may often be that the several parties whose business interests touch one another will each see his interest in reaching an amicable and speedy arrangement; but the interval that elapses between the time when a given "deal" is seen to be advantageous to one of the parties concerned and the time when the terms are finally arranged is commonly occupied with business manoeuvres on both or all sides, intended to "bring the others to terms." In so playing for position and endeavoring to secure the largest advantage possible, the manager of such a campaign of reorganization not infrequently aims to "freeze out" a rival or to put a rival's industrial enterprise under suspicion of insolvency and "unsound methods," at the same time that he "puts up a bluff" and manages his own concern with a view to a transient effect on the opinions of the business community. Where these endeavors occur, directed to a transient derangement of a rival's business or to a transient, perhaps specious, exhibition of industrial capacity and earning power on the part of one's own concern, they are commonly detrimental to the industrial system at large; they act temporarily to lower the aggregate serviceability of the comprehensive industrial process within which their effects run, and to make the livelihood and the peace of mind of those involved in these industries more precarious than they would be in the absence of such disturbances. If one is to believe any appreciable proportion of what passes current as information on this head, in print and by word of mouth, business men whose work is not simply routine constantly give some attention to manoeuvring of this kind and to the discovery of new opportunities for putting their competitors at a disadvantage. This seems to apply in a peculiar degree, if not chiefly, to those classes of business men whose operations have to do with railways and the class of securities called "industrials." Taking the industrial process as a whole, it is safe to say that at no time is it free from derangements of this character in any of the main branches of modern industry. This chronic state of perturbation is incident to the management of industry by business methods and is unavoidable under existing conditions. So soon as the machine industry had developed to large proportions, it became unavoidable, in the nature of the case, that the business men in whose hands lies the conduct of affairs should play at cross-purposes and endeavor to derange industry. But chronic perturbation is so much a matter of course and prevails with so rare interruptions, that, being the normal state of affairs, it does not attract particular notice.

In current discussion of business, indeed ever since the relation of business men to the industrial system has seriously engaged the attention of economists, the point to which attention has chiefly been directed is the business man's work as an organizer of comprehensive industrial processes. During the later decades of the nineteenth century, particularly, has much interest centred, as there has been much provocation for its doing, on the formation of large industrial consolidations; and the evident good effects of this work in the way of heightened serviceability and economies of production are pointed to as the chief and characteristic end of this work of reorganization. So obvious are these good results and so well and widely has the matter been expounded, theoretically, that it is not only permissible, but it is a point of conscience, to shorten this tale by passing over these good effects as a matter of common notoriety. But there are other features of the case, less obtrusive and less attractive to the theoreticians, which need more detailed attention than they have commonly received.

The circumstances which condition the work of consolidation in industry and which decide whether a given move in the direction of a closer and wider organization of industrial processes will be practicable and will result in economies of production, — these circumstances are of a mechanical nature. They are facts of the comprehensive machine process. The conditions favorable to industrial consolidation on these grounds are not created by the business men. They are matters of "the state of industrial arts," and are the outcome of the work of those men who are engaged in the industrial employments rather than of those who are occupied with business affairs. The inventors, engineers, experts, or whatever name be applied to the comprehensive class that does the intellectual work involved in the modern machine industry, must prepare the way for the man of pecuniary affairs by making possible and pitting in evidence the economies and other advantages that will follow from a prospective consolidation.

But it is not enough that the business man should see a chance to effect economies of production and to heighten the efficiency of industry by a new combination. Conditions favorable to consolidation on these grounds must be visible to him before he can make the decisive business arrangements; but these conditions, taken by themselves, do not move him. The motives of the business man are pecuniary motives, inducements in the way of pecuniary gain to him or to the business enterprise with which he is identified. The end of his endeavors is, not simply to effect an industrially advantageous consolidation, but to effect it under such circumstances of ownership as will give him control of large business forces or bring him the largest possible gain. The ulterior end sought is an increase of ownership, not industrial serviceability. His aim is to contrive a consolidation in which he will be at an advantage, and to effect it on the terms most favorable to his own interest.

But it is not commonly evident at the outset what are the most favorable terms that he can get in his dealings with other business men whose interests are touched by the proposed consolidation, or who are ambitious to effect some similar consolidation of the same or of competing industrial elements for their own profit. It rarely happens that the interests of the business men whom the prospective consolidation touches all converge to a coalition on the same basis and under the same management. The consequence is negotiation and delay. It commonly also happens that some of the business men affected see their advantage in staving off the coalition until a time more propitious to their own interest, or until those who have the work of consolidation in hand can be brought to compound with them for the withdrawal of whatever obstruction they are able to offer.(10*) Such a coalition involves a loss of independent standing, or even a loss of occupation, to many of the business men interested in the deal. If a prospective industrial consolidation is of such scope as to require the concurrence or consent of many business interests, among which no one is very decidedly preponderant in pecuniary strength or in strategic position, a long time will be consumed in the negotiations and strategy necessary to define the terms on which the several business interests will consent to come in and the degree of solidarity and central control to which they will submit.

It is notorious, beyond the need of specific citation, that the great business coalitions and industrial combinations which have characterized the situation of the last few years have commonly been the outcome of a long-drawn struggle, in which the industrial ends, as contrasted with business ends, have not been seriously considered, and in which great shrewdness and tenacity have commonly been shown in the staving off of a settlement for years in the hope of more advantageous terms. The like is true as regards further coalitions, further consolidations of industrial processes which have not been effected, but which are known to be feasible and desirable so far as regards the mechanical circumstances of the case. The difficulties in the way are difficulties of ownership, of business interest, not of mechanical feasibility.

These negotiations and much of the strategy that leads up to a business consolidation are of the nature of derangements of industry, after the manner spoken of above. So that business interests and manoeuvres commonly delay consolidations, combinations, correlations of the several plants and processes, for some appreciable time after such measures have become patently advisable on industrial grounds. In the meantime the negotiators are working at cross-purposes and endeavoring to put their rivals in as disadvantageous a light as may be, with the result that there is chronic derangement, duplication, and misdirected growth of the industrial equipment while the strategy is going forward, and expensive maladjustment to he overcome when the negotiations are brought to a close.(11*)

Serviceability, industrial advisability, is not the decisive point. The decisive point is business expediency and business pressure. In the normal course of business touching this matter of industrial consolidation, therefore, the captain of industry works against, as well as for, a new and more efficient organization. He inhibits as well as furthers the higher organization of industry.(12*) Broadly, it may be said that industrial consolidations and the working arrangements made for the more economical utilization of resources and mechanical contrivances are allowed to go into effect only after they are long overdue.

In current economic theory the business man is spoken of under the name of "entrepreneur" or "undertaker," and his function is held to be the coordinating of industrial processes with a view to economics of production and heightened serviceability. The soundness of this view need not be questioned. It has a great sentimental value and is useful in many ways. There is also a modicum of truth in it as an account of facts. In common with other men, the business man is moved by ideals of serviceability and an aspiration to make the way of life easier for his fellows. Like other men, he has something of the instinct of workmanship. No doubt such aspirations move the great business man less urgently than many others, who are, on that account, less successful in business affairs. Motives of this kind detract from business efficiency, and an undue yielding to them on the part of business men is to be deprecated as an infirmity. Still, throughout men's dealing with one another and with the interests of the community there runs a sense of equity, fair dealing, and workmanlike integrity; and in an uncertain degree this bent discountenances gain that is got at an undue cost to others, or without rendering some colorable equivalent. Business men are also, in a measure, guided by the ambition to effect a creditable improvement in the industrial processes which their business traffic touches. These sentimental factors in business exercise something of a constraint, varying greatly from one person to another, but not measurable in its aggregate results. The careers of most of the illustrious business men show the presence of some salutary constraint of this kind. Not infrequently an excessive sensitiveness of this kind leads to a withdrawal from business, or from certain forms of business which may appeal to a vivid fancy as peculiarly dishonest or peculiarly detrimental to the community.(13*) Such grounds of action, and perhaps others equally genial and equally unbusinesslike, would probably be discovered by a detailed scrutiny of any large business deal. Probably in many cases the business strategist, infected with this human infirmity, reaches an agreement with his rivals and his neighbors in the industrial system without exacting the last concession that a ruthless business strategy might entitle him to. The result is, probably, a speedier conclusion and a smoother working of the large coalitions than would follow from the unmitigated sway of business principles.(14*)

But the sentiment which in this way acts in constraint of business traffic proceeds on such grounds of equity and fair dealing as are afforded by current business ethics; it acts within the range of business principles, not in contravention of them; it acts as a conventional restraint upon pecuniary advantage, not in abrogation of it. This code of business ethics consists, after all, of mitigations of the maxim, Caveat emptor. It touches primarily the dealings of man with man, and only less directly and less searchingly inculcates temperance and circumspection as regards the ulterior interests of the community at large. Where this moral need of a balance between the services rendered the community and the gain derived from a given business transaction asserts itself at all, the balance is commonly sought to be maintained in some sort of pecuniary terms; but pecuniary terms afford only a very inadequate measure of serviceability to the community.

Great and many are the items of service to be set down to the business man's account in connection with the organization of the industrial system, but when all is said, it is still to be kept in mind that his work in the correlation of industrial processes is chiefly of a permissive kind. His furtherance of industry is at the second remove, and is chiefly of a negative character. In his capacity as business man he does not go creatively into the work of perfecting mechanical processes and turning the means at hand to new or larger uses. That is the work of the men who have in hand the devising and oversight of mechanical processes. The men in industry must first create the mechanical possibility of such new and more efficient methods and correlations, before the business man sees the chance, makes the necessary business arrangements, and gives general directions that the contemplated industrial advance shall go into effect. The period between the time of earliest practicability and the effectual completion of a given consolidation in industry marks the interval by which the business man retards the advance of industry. Against this are to be offset the cases, comparatively slight and infrequent, where the business men in control push the advance of industry into new fields and prompt the men concerned with the mechanics of the case to experiment and exploration in new fields of mechanical process.

When the recital is made, therefore, of how the large consolidations take place at the initiative of the business men who are in control, it should be added that the fact of their being in control precludes industrial correlations from taking place except by their advice and consent. The industrial system is organized on business principles and for pecuniary ends. The business man is at the centre; he holds the discretion and he exercises it freely, and his choice falls out now On one side, now on the other. The retardation as well as the advance is to be set down to his account.

As regards the economies in cost of production effected by these consolidations, there is a further characteristic feature to be noted, a feature of some significance for any theory of modern business. In great measure the saving effected is a saving of the costs of business management and of the competitive costs of marketing products and services, rather than a saving in the prime costs of production. The heightened facility and efficiency of the new and larger business combinations primarily affect the expenses of office work and sales, and it is in great part only indirectly that this curtailment and consolidation of business management has an effect upon the methods and aims of industry proper. It touches the pecuniary processes immediately, and the mechanical processes indirectly and in an uncertain degree. It is of the nature of a partial neutralization of the wastes due to the presence of pecuniary motives and business management, – for the business management involves waste wherever a greater number of men or transactions are involved than are necessary to the effective direction of the mechanical processes employed. The amount of "business" that has to be transacted per unit of product is much greater where the various related industrial processes are managed in severalty than where several of them are brought under one business management. A pecuniary discretion has to be exercised at every point of contact or transition, where the process or its product touches or passes the boundary between different spheres of ownership. Business transactions have to do with ownership and changes of ownership. The greater the parcelment in point of ownership, the greater the amount of business work that has to be done in connection with a given output of goods or services, and the slower, less facile, and less accurate on the whole, is the work. This applies both to the work of bargain and contract, wherein pecuniary initiative and discretion are chiefly exercised, and to the routine work of accounting, and of gathering and applying information and misinformation.

The standardization of industrial processes, products, services, and consumers, spoken of in an earlier chapter, very materially facilitates the business man's work in reorganizing business enterprises on a larger scale; particularly does this standardization serve his ends by permitting a uniform routine in accounting, invoices, contracts, etc., and so admitting a large central accounting system, with homogeneous ramifications, such as will give a competent conspectus of the pecuniary situation of the enterprise at any given time.

The great, at the present stage of development perhaps the greatest, opportunity for saving by consolidation, in the common run of cases, is afforded by the ubiquitous and in a sense excessive presence of business enterprise in the economic system. It is in doing away with unnecessary business transactions and industrially futile manoeuvring on the part of independent firms that the promoter of combinations finds his most telling opportunity. So that it is scarcely an over-statement to say that probably the largest, assuredly the securest and most unquestionable, service rendered by the great modern captains of industry is this curtailment of the business to be done, this sweeping retirement of business men as a class from the service and the definitive cancelment of opportunities for private enterprise.

So long as related industrial units are under different business managements, they are, by the nature of the case, at cross-purposes, and business consolidation remedies this untoward feature of the industrial system by eliminating the peCuniary element from the interstices of the system as far as may be. The interstitial adjustments of the industrial system at large are in this way withdrawn from the discretion of rival business men, and the work of pecuniary management previously involved is in large part dispensed with, with the result that there is a saving of work and an avoidance of that systematic mutual hindrance that characterizes the competitive management of industry. To the community at large the work of pecuniary management, it appears, is less serviceable the more there is of it. The heroic role of the captain of industry is that of a deliverer from an excess of business management. It is a casting out of business men by the chief of business men.(15*)

The theory of business enterprise sketched above applies to such business as is occupied with the interstitial adjustments of the system of industries. This work of keeping and of disturbing the interstitial adjustments does not look immediately to the output of goods as its source of gain, but to the alterations of values involved in disturbances of the balance, and to the achievement of a more favorable business situation for some of the enterprises engaged. This work lies in the middle, between commercial enterprise proper, on the one hand, and industrial enterprise in the stricter sense, on the other hand. It is directed to the acquisition of gain through taking advantage of those conjunctures of business that arise out of the concatenation of processes in the industrial system.

In a similar manner commercial business may be said to be occupied with conjunctures that arise out of the circumstances of the industrial system at large, but not originating in the mechanical exigencies of the industrial processes. The conjunctures of commercial business proper are in the main fortuitous, in so far that they are commonly not initiated by the business men engaged in these commercial pursuits. Commercial business, simply as such, does not aim to guide the course of industry.

On the other hand, the large business enterprise spoken of above initiates changes in industrial organization and seeks its gain in large part through such alterations of value levels as take place on its own initiative. These alterations of the value levels, of course, have their effect upon the output of goods and upon the material welfare of the community; but the effect which they have in this way is only incidental to the quest of profits.

But apart from this remoter and larger guidance of the course of industry, the business men also, and more persistently and pervasively, exercise a guidance over the course of industry in detail. The production of goods and services is carried on for gain, and the output of goods is controlled by business men with a view to gain. Commonly, in ordinary routine business, the gains come from this output of goods and services. By the sale of the output the business man in industry "realizes" his gains. To "realize" means to convert salable goods into money values. The sale is the last step in the process and the end of the business man's endeavor.(16*) When he has disposed of the output, and so has converted his holdings of consumable articles into money values, his gains are as nearly secure and definitive as the circumstances of modern life admit. It is in terms of price that he keeps his accounts, and in the same terms he computes his output of products. The vital point of production with him is the vendibility of the output, its convertibility into money values, not its serviceability for the needs of mankind. A modicum of serviceability, for some purpose or other, the output must have if it is to be salable. But it does not follow that the highest serviceability gives the largest gains to the business man in terms of money, nor does it follow that the output need in all cases have other than a factitious serviceability. There is, on the one hand, such a possibility as overstocking the market with any given line of goods, to the detriment of the business man concerned, but not necessarily to the immediate disadvantage of the body of consumers. And there are, on the other hand, certain lines of industry, such as many advertising enterprises, the output of which may be highly effective for its purpose but of quite equivocal use to the community. Many well-known and prosperous enterprises which advertise and sell patent medicines and other proprietary articles might be cited in proof.

In the older days, when handicraft was the rule of the industrial system, the personal contact between the producer and his customer was somewhat close and lasting. Under these circumstances the factor of personal esteem and disesteem had a considerable play in controlling the purveyors of goods and services. This factor of personal contact counted in two divergent ways: (1) producers were careful of their reputation for workmanship, even apart from the gains which such a reputation might bring; and (2) a degree of irritation and ill-will would arise in many cases, leading to petty trade quarrels and discriminations on other grounds than the gains to be got, at the same time that the detail character of dealings between producer and consumer admitted a degree of petty knavery and huckstering that is no longer practicable in the current large-scale business dealings. Of these two divergent effects resulting from close personal relations between producer and consumer; the former seems on the whole to have been of preponderant consequence. Under the system of handicraft and neighborhood industry, the adage that "Honesty is the best policy" seems on the whole to have been accepted and to have been true. This adage has come down from the days before the machine's regime and before modern business enterprise. Under modern circumstances, where industry is carried on on a large scale, the discretionary head of an industrial enterprise is commonly removed from all personal contact with the body of customers for whom the industrial process under his control purveys goods or services. The mitigating effect which personal contact may have in dealings between man and man is therefore in great measure eliminated. The whole takes on something of an impersonal character. One can with an easier conscience and with less of a sense of meanness take advantage of the necessities of people whom one knows of only as an indiscriminate aggregate of consumers. Particularly is this true when, as frequently happens in the modern situation, this body of consumers belongs in the main to another, inferior class, so that personal contact and cognizance of them is not only not contemplated, but is in a sense impossible. Equity, in excess of the formal modicum specified by law, does not so readily assert its claims where the relations between the parties are remote and impersonal as where one is dealing with one's necessitous neighbors who live on the same social plane. Under these circumstances the adage cited above loses much of its axiomatic force. Business management has a chance to proceed on a temperate and sagacious calculation of profit and loss, untroubled by sentimental considerations of human kindness or irritation or of honesty.

The broad principle which guides producers and merchants, large and small, in fixing the prices at which they offer their wares and services is what is known in the language of the railroads as "charging what the traffic will bear."(17*) Where a given enterprise has a strict monopoly of the supply of a given article or of a given class of services this principle applies in the unqualified form in which it has been understood among those who discuss railway charges. But where the monopoly is less strict, where there are competitors, there the competition that has to be met is one of the factors to be taken account of in determining what the traffic will bear; competition may even become the most serious factor in the case if the enterprise in question has little or none of the character of a monopoly. But it is very doubtful if there are any successful business ventures within the range of the modern industries from which the monopoly element is wholly absent.(18*) They are, at any rate, few and not of great magnitude. And the endeavor of all such enterprises that look to a permanent continuance of their business is to establish as much of a monopoly as may be. Such a monopoly position may be a legally established one, or one due to location or the control of natural resources, or it may be a monopoly of a less definite character resting on custom and prestige (good–will). This latter class of monopolies are not commonly classed as such; although in character and degree the advantage which they give is very much the same as that due to a differential advantage in location or in the command of resources. The end sought by the systematic advertising of the larger business concerns is such a monopoly of custom and prestige. This form of monopoly is sometimes of great value, and is frequently sold under the name of good–will, trademarks, brands, etc. Instances are known where such monopolies of custom, prestige, prejudice, have been sold at prices running up into the millions.(19*)

The great end of consistent advertising is to establish such differential monopolies resting on popular conviction. And the advertiser is successful in this endeavor to establish a profitable popular conviction, somewhat in proportion as he correctly apprehends the manner in which a popular conviction on any given topic is built up.(20*) The cost, as well as the pecuniary value and the magnitude, of this organized fabrication of popular convictions is indicated by such statements as that the proprietors of a certain well–known household remedy, reputed among medical authorities to be of entirely dubious value, have for a series of years found their profits in spending several million dollars annually in advertisements. This case is by no means unique.

It has been said,(21*) no doubt in good faith and certainly with some reason, that advertising as currently carried on gives the body of consumers valuable information and guidance as to the ways and means whereby their wants can be satisfied and their purchasing power can be best utilized. To the extent to which this holds true, advertising is a service to the community. But there is a large reservation to be made on this head. Advertising is competitive; the greater part of it aims to divert purchases, etc., from one channel to another channel of the same general class.(22*) And to the extent to which the efforts of advertising in all its branches are spent on this competitive disturbance of trade, they are, on the whole, of slight if any immediate service to the community. Such advertising, however, is indispensable to most branches of modern industry; but the necessity of most of the advertising is not due to its serving the needs of the community nor to any aggregate advantage accruing to the concerns which advertise, but to the fact that a business concern which falls short in advertising fails to get its share of trade. Each concert must advertise, chiefly because the others do. The aggregate expenditure that could advantageously be put into advertising in the absence of competition would undoubtedly be but an inconsiderable fraction of what is actually incurred, and necessarily incurred under existing circumstances.(23*)

Not all advertising is wholly competitive, or at least it is not always obviously so. In proportion as an enterprise has secured a monopoly position, its advertising loses the air of competitive selling and takes on the character of information designed to increase the use of its output independently. But such an increase implies a redistribution of consumption on the part of the customers.(24*) So that the element of competitive selling is after all not absent in these cases, but takes the form of competition between different classes of wares instead of competitive selling of different brands of the same class of wares.

Attention is here called to this matter of advertising and the necessity of it in modern competitive business for the light which it throws on "cost of production" in the modern system, where the process of production is under the control of business men and is carried on for business ends. Competitive advertising is an unavoidable item in the aggregate costs of industry. It does not add to the serviceability of the output, except it be incidentally and unintentionally. What it aims at is the sale of the output, and it is for this purpose that it is useful. It gives vendibility, which is useful to the seller, but has no utility to the last buyer. Its ubiquitous presence in the costs of any business enterprise that has to do with the production of goods for the market enforces the statement that the "cost of production" of commodities under the modern business system is cost incurred with a view to vendibility, not with a view to serviceability of the goods for human use.

There is, of course, much else that goes into the cost of competitive selling, besides the expenses of advertising, although advertising may be the largest and most unequivocal item to be set down to that account. A great part of the work done by merchants and their staff of employees, both wholesale and retail, as well as by sales-agents not exclusively connected with any one mercantile house, belongs under the same head. Just how large a share of the costs of the distribution of goods fairly belongs under the rubric of competitive selling can of course not be made out. It is largest, on the whole, in the case of consumable goods marketed in finished form for the consumer, but there is more or less of it throughout. The goods turned out on a large scale by the modern industrial processes, on the whole, carry a larger portion of such competitive costs than the goods still produced by the old-fashioned detail methods of handicraft and household industry; although this distinction does not hold hard and fast. In some extreme cases the cost of competitive selling may amount to more than ninety per cent. of the total cost of the goods when they reach the consumer. In other lines of business, commonly occupied with the production of staple goods, this constituent of cost may perhaps fall below ten per cent of the total. Where the average, for the price of finished goods delivered to the consumers, may lie would be a hazardous guess.(25*)

It is evident that the gains which accrue from this business of competitive selling and buying bear no determinable relation to the services which the work in question may render the community. If a comparison may be hazarded between two unknown and indeterminate quantities, it may perhaps be said that the gains from competitive selling bear something more of a stable relation to the service rendered than do the gains derived from speculative transactions or from the financiering operations of the great captains of industry. It seems at least safe to say that the converse will not hold true. Gains and services seem more widely out of touch in the case of the large-scale financiering work. Not that the work of the large business men in reorganizing and consolidating the industrial process is of slight consequence; but as a general proposition, the amount of the business man's gains from any given transaction of this latter class bear no traceable relation to any benefit which the community may derive from the transaction.(26*)

As to the wages paid to the men engaged in the routine of competitive selling, as salesmen, buyers, accountants, and the like, — much the same holds true of them as of the income of the business men who carry on the business on their own initiative. Their employers pay the wages of these persons, not because their work is productive of benefit to the community, but because it brings a gain to the employers. The point to which the work is directed is profitable sales, and the wages are in some proportion to the efficiency of this work as counted in terms of heightened vendibility.

The like holds true for the work and pay of the force of workmen engaged in the industrial processes under business management. It holds, in a measure, of all modern industry that produces for the market, but it holds true, in an eminent degree, of those lines of industry that are more fully under the guidance of modern business methods. These are most closely in touch with the market and are most consistently guided by considerations of vendibility. They are also, on the whole, more commonly carried on by hired labor, and the wages paid are competitively adjusted on grounds of the vendibility of the product. The brute serviceability of the output of these industries may be a large factor in its vendibility, perhaps the largest factor; but the fact remains that the end sought by the business men in control is a profitable sale, and the wages are paid as a means to that end, not to the end that the way of life may be smoother for. the ultimate consumer of the goods produced.(27*)

The outcome of this recital, then, is that wherever and in so far as business ends and methods dominate modern industry the relation between the usefulness of the work (for other purposes than pecuniary gain) and the remuneration of it is remote and uncertain to such a degree that no attempt at formulating such a relation is worth while. This is eminently and obviously true of the work and gains of business men, in whatever lines of business they are engaged. This follows as a necessary consequence of the nature of business management.

Work that is, on the whole, useless or detrimental to the community at large may be as gainful to the business man and to the workmen whom he employs as work that contributes substantially to the aggregate livelihood. This seems to be peculiarly true of the bolder flights of business enterprise. In so far as its results are not detrimental to human life at large, such unproductive work directed to securing an income may seem to be an idle matter in which the rest of the community has no substantial interests. Such is not the case. In so far as the gains of these unproductive occupations are of a substantial character, they come out of the aggregate product of the other occupations in which the various classes of the community engage. The aggregate profits of the business, whatever its character, are drawn from the aggregate output of goods and services; and whatever goes to the maintenance of the profits of those who contribute nothing substantial to the output is, of course, deducted from the income of the others, whose work tells substantially.

There are, therefore, limits to the growth of the industrially parasitic lines of business just spoken of. A disproportionate growth of parasitic industries, such as most advertising and much of the other efforts that go into competitive selling, as well as warlike expenditure and other industries directed to turning out goods for conspicuously wasteful consumption, would lower the effective vitality of the community to such a degree as to jeopardize its chances of advance or even its life. The limits which the circumstances of life impose in this respect are of a selective character, in the last resort. A persistent excess of parasitic and wasteful efforts over productive industry must bring on a decline. But owing to the very high productive efficiency of the modern mechanical industry, the margin available for wasteful occupations and wasteful expenditures is very great. The requirements of the aggregate livelihood are so far short of the possible output of goods by modern methods as to leave a very wide margin for waste and parasitic income. So that instances of such a decline, due to industrial exhaustion, drawn from the history of any earlier phase of economic life, carry no well−defined lesson as to what a modern industrial community may allow itself in this respect.

While it is in the nature of things unavoidable that the management of industry by modern business methods should involve a large misdirection of effort and a very large waste of goods and services, it is also true that the aims and ideals to which this manner of economic life gives effect act forcibly to offset all this incidental futility. These pecuniary aims and ideals have a very great effect, for instance, in making men work hard and unremittingly, so that on this ground alone the business system probably compensates for any wastes involved in its working. There seems, therefore, to be no tenable ground for thinking that the working of the modern business system involves a curtailment of the community's livelihood. It makes up for its wastefulness by the added strain which it throws upon those engaged in the productive work.

NOTES:

1. The ulterior ground of efforts directed to the accumulation of wealth is discussed at some length in the Theory of the Leisure Class, ch. II. and V, and the economic bearing of the business man's work is treated in a paper on "Industrial and Pecuniary Employments," in the Proceedings of the thirteenth annual meeting of the American Economic Association. Cf. also Marshall, Principles of Economics (3d ed.), bk. I. ch. III, bk. IV. ch. XII, bk. V. ch. IV, bk. VII. ch. VII and VIII; Bagehot, Economic Studies, especially pp. 53 et seq.; Walker, Wages Question, ch. XIV; and more especially Sombart, Moderne Kapitalismus, vol. I. ch. I, VIII, XIV, XV; Marx, Kapital, bk. I. ch. IV; Schmoller, Grundriss, bk. II. ch. VII.

2. It is significant that joint-stock methods of organization and management — that is to say, impersonally capitalistic methods — are traceable, for their origin and early formulation, to the shipping companies of early modern times. Cf. K. Lehmann, Die geschichtliche Entwickelung des Aktienrechts bis zum Code de Commerce. The like view is spoken for by Ehrenberg, Zeitglter der Fugger; see vol. II. pp. 325 et seq. 3. Cf. Cantillon, Essai sur le Commerce, 1e partie, ch. III, VI, IX, XIV, XV, Wealth of Nations, bk. I; Bucher, Enstehung der Volks wirtschaft (3d ed.), ch. IV and V; Sombart, Kapitalismus, Vol. I bk. I.

4. Sombart, vol. I. ch. IV-VIII; Ashley, Economic History and Theory, bk. II, ch. VI, especially pp. 389-397.

5. Cf. Marshall, Principles of Economics, on the "Law of Substitution," e.g. bk. VI. ch. I. The law of substitution implies freedom of investment and applies fully only in so far as the investor in question is not permanently identified with a given industrial plant or even with a given line of industry. It requires great facility in shifting from one to another point of investment. It is therefore only as the business situation has approached the modern form that the law of substitution has come to be of considerable importance to economic theory; for a theory of business, such as business was in mediaeval and early modern times, this law need scarcely have been formulated.

6. See Sombart, Kapitalismus, vol. 1. chap. VIII.

7. It is chiefly the passive owner of stock and the like that holds permanently to a given enterprise, under the fully developed modem business conditions. The active business man of the larger sort is not in this way bound to the glebe of the given business concern.

8. Cf. testimony of J.B. Dill, Report of the Industrial Commission, vol. I. pp. 1078, 1080-1085; "Digest of Evidence," p., 77. also testimony of various witnesses on stock speculation and corporate management, and particularly the special report to the Commission, on "Securities of Industrial Combinations and Railroads," vol. XIII., especially pp. 920-922.

9. The history of the formation of any one of the great industrial coalitions of modem times will show how great and indispensable a factor in the large business is the invention and organization of difficulties desired to force rival enterprises to come to terms. E.g. the manoeuvres preliminary to the

formation of the United States Steel Corporation, particularly the movements of the Carnegie Company, show how this works on a large scale. Cf. E.S. Meade, Trust Finance, pp. 204–217. Report of the Industrial Commission, vol. XIII., "Review of Evidence," pp. v–vii, with the testimony relating to this topic. The pressure which brings about a new adjustment (coalition) is commonly spoken of as "excessive competition."

10. Cf., e.g., the accounts of the formation of the United States Steel Corporation or the Shipbuilding Company.

11. Witness the rate wars and the duplications of inefficient track and terminal equipment among the railways, and the similar duplications in the iron and steel industry. The system of railway terminals in Chicago, e.g., is an illuminated object–lesson of systematic ineptitude.

12. The splendid reach of this inhibitory work of the captain of industry, as well as of his aggressive work of consolidation, is well shown, for instance, in the history and present position of the railway industry in America. It is and has for a long term of years been obvious that a very comprehensive unification or consolidation, in respect of the mechanical work to be done by the railway system, is eminently desirable and feasible, – consolidation of a scope not only equalling, but far out reaching, the coalitions which have lately been effected or attempted. There is no hazard in venturing the assertion that several hundreds of men who are engaged in the mechanical work of railroading, in one capacity and another, are conversant with feasible plans for economizing work and improving the service by more comprehensive and closer correlation of the work; and it is equally obvious that nothing but the diverging interests of the business men concerned hinders these closer and larger feasible correlations from being put into effect. It is easily within the mark to say that the delay which railway consolidation has suffered up to the present, from business exigencies as distinct from the mechanical circumstances of the case, amounts to an average of at least twenty years. Ever since railroading began in this country there has been going on a process of reluctant consolidation, in which the movements of the business men in control have tardily followed up the opportunities for economy and efficient service which the railroad industry has offered. And their latest and boldest achievements along this line, as seen from the standpoint of mechanical advisability, have been foregone conclusions since a date so far in the past as to be forgotten, and taken at their best they fall short to–day by not less than some fifty per cent. of their opportunities. Cf. Report of the Industrial Commission, vol. XIX., "Transportation," especially pp. 304–348.

Like other competitive business, but more particularly such business as has to do with the interstitial adjustments of the industrial system, the business of railway consolidation is of the nature of a game, in which the end sought by the players is their own pecuniary gain and to which the industrial serviceability of the outcome is incidental only. This is recognized by popular opinion and is made much of by popular agitators, who take the view that when once the game between the competing business interests has been played to a finish, in the definitive coalition of the competitors under one management, then the game will go on as a somewhat one–sided conflict between the resulting monopoly and the community at large.

So again, as a further illustration, it is and from the outset has been evident that the iron–ore beds of northern Wisconsin, Michigan, and Minnesota ought, industrially speaking, to have been worked as one collective enterprise. There are also none but business reasons why practically all the ore beds and iron and steel works in the country are not worked as one collective enterprise. It is equally evident that such correlations of work as are permitted by the business coalitions already effected in this field have resulted in a great economy of production, and that the failure to carry these coalitions farther means an annual waste running up into the millions. Both the economies so effected and the waste so incurred are to be set down to the account of the business manners who have gone so far and have failed to go farther. The like is obvious as regards many other branches of industry and groups of industries.

13. Illustrative instances will readily suggest themselves. Many a business man turns by preference to something less dubious than the distilling of whiskey or the sale of deleterious household remedies. They prefer not to use deletrious adulterants, even within the limits of the law. They will rather use wool than shoddy at the same price. The officials of a railway commonly prefer to avoid wrecks and manslaughter, even if there is no pecuniary advantage in choosing the more humane course. More than that, it will be found true that the more prosperous of the craft, especially, take pride and pains to make the service of their roads or the output of their mills as efficient, not simply as the pecuniary advantage of the concern demands, but as the best pecuniary results will admit. Instances are perhaps not frequent, but they are also not altogether exceptional, where a prosperous captain of industry will go out of his way to heighten the serviceability of his industry even to a degree that is of doubtful pecuniary expediency for himself. Such aberrations are, of course, not large; and if they are persisted in to any very appreciable extent the result is, of course, disastrous to the enterprise. The enterprise in such a case falls out of the category of business management and falls under the imputation of philanthropy.

14. The captains of the first class necessarily are relatively exempt from these unbusinesslike scruples.

15. See Report of the Industrial Commission. vol. I., Testimony of J.W. Gates, pp. 1029–1039; S. Dodd, pp. 1049–1050; N.B. Rogers, p. 1068; vol. XIII, C.M. Schwab, pp. 451, 459, H.B. Butler, p. 490; L.R. Hopkins, pp. 346, 347; A.S. White, pp. 254, 256.

16. Cf. Marx, Kapital, bk. I, pt. II.

17. The economic principle of "charging what the traffic will bear" is discussed with great care and elaboration by R. T. Ely, Monopolies and Trusts, ch. III, "The Law of Monopoly Price." Cf., for illustration of the practical working of this principle, testimony of C.M. Schwab, Report of the Industrial Commission, vol. XIII. pp. 453–455.

18. "Monopoly" is here used in that looser sense which it has colloquially, not in the strict sense of an exclusive control of the supply, as employed, e g., by Mr Ely in the volume cited above. This usage is the more excusable since Mr. Ely finds that a "monopoly" in the strict sense of the definition practically does not occur in fact. Cf. Jenks, The Trust Problem, ch. IV.

19. E.g. the prestige value of Ivory Soap.

20. Cf. W.D. Scott, The Theory of Advertising; J. L. Mahin, The Commercial Value of Advertising, pp. 4–6, 12–13, 15; E. Fogg–Meade, "The Place of Advertising in Modern Business," Journal of Political Economy, March 1901; Sombart, vol. II. ch. XX–XXI; G. Tarde, Psychologie Economique, vol. I. pp. 187–190. The writing and designing of advertisements (letterpress, display, and illustrations) has grown into a distinct calling; so that the work of a skilled writer of advertisements compares not unfavorably, in point of lucrativeness, with that of the avowed writers of popular fiction.

The psychological principles of advertising may be formulated somewhat as follows: A declaration of fact, made in the form and with the incidents of taste and expression to which a person is accustomed, will be accepted as authentic and will be acted upon if occasion arises, in so far as it does not conflict with opinions already accepted. The acceptance of an opinion seems to be almost entirely a passive matter. The presumption remains in favor of an opinion that has once been accepted, and an appreciable burden of proof falls on the negative. A competent formulation of opinion on a given point is the chief factor in gaining adherents to that opinion, and a reiteration of the statement is the chief factor in carrying conviction. The truth of such a formulation is a matter of secondary consequence, but a wide and patent departure from known fact generally weakens its persuasive effect. The aim of the advertiser is to arrest attention and then present his statement in such a manner that it is easily assimilated into the habits of thought of the person whose conviction is to be influenced. When this is effectually done a reversal of the conviction so established is a matter of considerable difficulty. The tenacity of a view once accepted in this way is evidenced, for instance, by the endless number and variety of testimonials to the merits of well-advertised but notoriously worthless household remedies and the like.

So acute an observer as Mr Sombart is still able to hold the opinion that "auf Schwindel ist dauerud noch nie ein Unternehmen begrundet worden" (Kopitalismus, vol. II. p. 376). Mr Sombart has not made acquaintance with the adventures of Elijah the Restorer, nor is he conversant with American patent-medicine enterprise. With Mr. Sombart's view may be contrasted that of Mr L.F. Ward, an observer of equally large outlook and acumen:

"The law of mind as it operates in society as an aid to competition and in the interest of the individual is essentially immoral. It rests primarily on the principle of deception. It is an extension to other human beings of the method applied to the animal world by which the latter was subjected to man. This method was that of the ambush and the snare. Its ruling principle was cunning. Its object was to deceive, circumvent, ensnare, and capture. Low animal cunning was succeeded by more refined kinds of cunning. The more important of these go by the names of business shrewdness, strategy, and diplomacy, none of which differ from ordinary cunning in anything but the degree of adroitness by which the victim is outwitted. In this way social life is completely honeycombed with deception." "The Psychologic Basis of Social Economics," Ann. of Am. Acad., vol. III. pp. 83 84 [475-476].

21. Fogg-Meade, "Place of Advertising in Modern Business," pp. 218, 224-236.

22. Advertising and other like expedients for the sale of goods aim at changes in the "substitution values" of the goods in question, not at an enhancement of the aggregate utilities of the available output of goods.

23. Cf. Jenks, The Trust Problem, pp. 21-28; Report of the Industrial Commission, vol. XIX. pp. 611-612.

24. Cf. Bohm-Bawerk, Positive Theory of Capital, bk. III, ch. V, VII-IX, on the value of alternative and complementary goods.

25. Where competitive selling makes up a large proportion of the aggregate final cost of the marketed product, this fact is likely to show itself in an exceptionally large proportion of good-will in the capitalization of the concerns engaged in the given line of business; as, e.g., the American Chicle Company.

26. Cf. Ed. Hahn, Die Wirtschaft der Welt am Ausgang des XIX Jahrhunderts. – "In unserem heutigen Wirtsehaftsleben ist der Gewinn durch den Zuwachs der Produktion, mit dem fruhere Jahrhunderte rechneten, ganz und gar zuruckgedrangt, er ist unwesentlich geworden."

27. It might, therefore, be feasible to set up a theory to the effect that wages are competitively proportioned to the vendibility of the product; but there is no cogent ground for saying that the wages in any department of industry, under a business regime, are proportioned to the utility which the output has to any one else than the employer who sells it. When it is further taken into account that the vendibility of the product in very many lines of production depends chiefly on the wastefulness of the goods (cf. Theory of the Leisure Class, ch. V), the divergence between the usefulness of the work and the wages paid for it seems wide enough to throw the whole question of an equivalence between work and pay out of theoretical consideration. Cf., however, Clark, The Distribution of Wealth, especially ch. VII. and XXII.

Chapter 4. Business Principles

The physical basis of modern business traffic is the machine process, as described in Chapter II. It is essentially a modern fact, – late and yet in its early stages of growth, especially as regards its wider sweep in the organization of the industrial system. The spiritual ground of business enterprise, on the other hand, is given by the institution of ownership. "Business principles" are corollaries under the main proposition of ownership; they are principles of property, – pecuniary principles. These principles are of older date than the machine industry, although their full development belongs within the machine era. As the machine process conditions the growth and scope of industry, and as its discipline inculcates habits of thought suitable to the industrial technology, so the exigencies of ownership condition the growth and aims of business, and the discipline of ownership and its management inculcates views and principles (habits of thought) suitable to the work of business traffic.

The discipline of the machine process enforces a standardization of conduct and of knowledge in terms of quantitative precision, and inculcates a habit of apprehending and explaining facts in terms of material cause and effect. It involves a valuation of facts, things, relations, and even personal capacity, in terms of force. Its metaphysics is materialism and its point of view is that of causal sequence.(1*) Such a habit of mind conduces to industrial efficiency, and the wide prevalence of such a habit is indispensable to a high degree of industrial efficiency under modern conditions. This habit of mind prevails most widely and with least faltering in those communities that have achieved great things in the machine industry, being both a cause and an effect of the machine process.

Other norms of standardization, more or less alien to this one, and other grounds for the valuation of facts, have prevailed elsewhere, as well as in the earlier phases of the Western culture. Much of this older standardization still stands over, in varying degrees of vigor or decay, in that current scheme of knowledge and conduct that now characterizes the Western culture. Many of these ancient norms of thought which have come down from the discipline of remote and relatively primitive phases of the cultural past are still strong in the affections of men, although most of them have lost greatly in their power of constraint. They no longer bind men's convictions as they once did. They are losing their axiomatic character. They are no longer self-evident or self-legitimating to modern common sense, as they once were to the common sense of an earlier time.

These ancient norms differ from the modern norms given by the machine in that they rest on conventional, ultimately sentimental grounds; they are of a putative nature. Such are, e.g., the principles of (primitive) blood relationship, clan solidarity, paternal descent, Levitical cleanness, divine guidance, allegiance, nationality. In their time and under the circumstances which favored their growth these were, all and several, powerful factors in controlling human conduct and shaping the course of events. In their time each of these institutional norms served as a definitive ground of authentication for such facts as fell under its particular scope, and the scope of each was very wide in the day of its best vigor. As time has brought change of circumstances, the facts of life have gradually escaped from the constraint of these ancient principles; so that the dominion which they now hold over the life of civilized men is relatively slight and shifty.

It is among these transmitted institutional habits of thought that the ownership of property belongs It rests on the like general basis of use and wont. The binding relation of property to its owner is of a conventional, putative character. But while these other conventional norms cited above are in their decline, this younger one of the inherited institutions stands forth without apology and shows no apprehension of being crowded into the background of sentimental reminiscence.

In absolute terms the institution of ownership is ancient, no doubt; but it is young compared with blood-relationship, the state, or the immortal gods. Especially is it true that its fuller development is relatively late. Not until a comparatively late date in West European history has ownership come to be emancipated from all restrictions of a non-pecuniary character and to stand in a wholly impersonal position, without admixture of personal responsibility or class prerogative.(2*) Freedom and inviolability of contract has not until recently been the unbroken rule. Indeed, it has not even yet been accepted without qualification and extended to all items owned. There still are impediments in the way of certain transfers and certain contracts, and there are exemptions in favor of property held by certain privileged persons, and especially by certain sacred corporations. This applies particularly to the more backward peoples; but nowhere is the "cash nexus" free from all admixture of alien elements. Ownership is not all-pervading and all-dominant, but it pervades and dominates the affairs of civilized peoples more freely and widely than any other single ground of action, and more than it has ever done before. The range and number of relations and duties that are habitually disposed of on a pecuniary footing are greater than in the past, and a pecuniary settlement is final to a degree unknown in the past. The pecuniary norm has invaded the domain of the older institutions, such as blood-relationship, citizenship, or the church, so that obligations belonging under the one or the other of these may now be assessed and fulfilled in terms of a money payment, although the notion of a pecuniary liquidation seems to have been wholly remote from the range of ideas – habits of thought – on which these relations and duties were originally based.

This is not the place for research into the origin and the primitive phases of ownership, nor even for inquiry into the views of property current in the early days of the Western culture. But the views current on this head at present – the principles which guide men's thinking and roughly define the right limits of discretion in pecuniary matters – this common-sense apprehension of what are the proper limits, rights, and responsibilities of ownership, is an outgrowth of the traditions, experiences, and speculations of past generations. Therefore some notice of the character of these traditional views and the circumstances out of which they have arisen in the recent past is necessary to an understanding of the part which they play in modern life.(3*) The theory of property professed at a given time and in a given cultural region shows what is the habitual attitude of men, for the time being, on questions of ownership; for any theory that gains widespread and uncritical acceptance must carry a competent formulation of the deliverances of common sense on the matter with which it deals. Otherwise it will not be generally accepted. And such a commonplace view is in its turn an outcome of protracted experience on the part of the community.

The modern theories of property run back to Locke,(4*) or to some source which for the present purpose is equivalent to Locke; who, on this as on other institutional questions, has been proved by the test of time to be a competent spokesman for modern culture in these premises. A detailed examination of how the matter stood in the theoretical respect before Locke, and whence, and by what process of selection and digestion, Locke derived his views, would lead too far afield. The theory is sufficiently familiar, for in substance it is, and for the better part of two centuries has been, held as an article of common sense by nearly all men who have spoken for the institution of property, with the exception of some few and late doubters.(5*)

This modern European, common-sense theory says that ownership is a "Natural Right." What a man has made, whatsoever "he hath mixed his labor with," that he has thereby made his property. It is his to do with it as he will. He has extended to the object of his labor that discretionary control which in the nature of things he of right exercises over the motions of his own person. It is his in the nature of things by virtue of his having made it. "Thus labor, in the beginning, gave a right of property." The personal force, the functional efficiency of the workman shaping material facts to human use, is in this doctrine accepted as the definitive, axiomatic ground of ownership; behind this the argument does not penetrate, except it be to trace the workman's creative efficiency back to its ulterior source in the creative efficiency of the Deity, the "Great Artificer." With the early spokesmen of natural rights, whether they speak for ownership or for other natural rights, it is customary to rest the case finally on the creator's discretionary dispositions and workmanlike efficiency. But the reference of natural rights back to the choice and creative work of the Deity has, even in Locke, an air of being in some degree perfunctory; and later in the life-history of the natural-rights doctrine it falls into abeyance; whereas the central tenet, that ownership is a natural right resting on the productive work and the discretionary choice of the owner, gradually rises superior to criticism and gathers axiomatic certitude. The Creator presently, in the course of the eighteenth century, drops out of the theory of ownership.

It may be worth while to indicate how this ultimate ground of ownership, as conceived by modern common sense, differs from the ground on which rights of the like class were habitually felt to rest in mediaeval times. Customary authority was the proximate ground to which rights, powers, and privileges were then habitually referred. It was felt that if a clear case of devolution from a superior could be made out, the right claimed was thereby established; and any claim which could not be brought to rest on such an act, or constructive act, of devolution was felt to be in a precarious case. The superior from whom rights, whether of ownership or otherwise, devolved held his powers by a tenure of prowess fortified by usage; the inferior upon whom given rights and powers devolved held what fell to his lot by a tenure of service and fealty sanctioned by use and wont. The relation was essentially a personal one, a relation of status, of authority and subservience. Hereditary standing gave a presumption of ownership, rather than conversely. In the last resort the chain of devolution by virtue of which all rights and powers of the common man pertained to him was to be traced back through a sequence of superiors to the highest, sovereign secular authority, through whom in turn it ran back to God. But neither in the case of the temporal sovereign nor in that of the divine sovereign was it felt that their competence to delegate or devolve powers and rights rested on a workmanlike or creative efficiency. It was not so much by virtue of His office as creator as it was by virtue of His office as suzerain that the Deity was felt to be the source and arbiter of human rights and duties. In the course of cultural change, as the medieval range of ideas and of circumstances begins to take on a more modern complexion, God's creative relation to mundane affairs is referred to with growing frequency and insistence in discussions of all questions of this class; but for the purpose in hand His creative relation to human rights does not supersede His relation of sovereignty until the modern era is well begun. It may be said that God's tenure of office in the medieval conception of things was a tenure by prowess, and men, of high and low degree, held their rights and powers of Him by a servile tenure. Ownership in this scheme was a stewardship. It was a stewardship proximately under the discretion of a secular lord, more remotely under the discretion of the divine Overlord. And the question then pressing for an answer when a point of competency or legitimacy was raised in respect of any given human arrangement or institution was not, What hath God wrought? but, What hath God ordained?

This medieval range of conceptions first began to break down and give place to modern notions in Italy, in the Renaissance. But it was in the English-speaking communities that the range of ideas upon which rests the modern concept of natural rights first gathered form and reached a competent expression. This holds true with respect to the modern doctrines of natural rights as contrasted with the corresponding ancient doctrines. The characteristically modern traits of the doctrine of natural rights are of English derivation. This is peculiarly true as regards the natural right of ownership. The material, historical basis of this English right of ownership, considered as a habit of thought, is given by the modern economic factors of handicraft and trade, in contrast with the medieval institutions of status and prowess. England, as contrasted with the Continent, during modern times rapidly substituted the occupation of the merchant and the ubiquitous free artisan as the tone-giving factors of her everyday life, in place of the prince, the soldier, and the priest. With this change in the dominant interests of everyday life came a corresponding change in the discipline given by the habits of everyday life, which shows itself in the growth of a new range of ideas as to the meaning of human life and a new ground of finality for human institutions. New axioms of right and truth supplant the old as new habits of thought supersede the old.

This process of substitution, as a struggle between rival concepts of finality in political theory, reached a dramatic climax in the revolution of 1688. As a battle of axioms the transition comes to a head in the controversy between John Locke and Sir Robert Filmer. Filmer was the last effective spokesman of the medieval axiom of devolution. Locke's tracing of natural rights, the right of property among the rest, back to the workmanlike performance of the Creator, marks the form in which, at the point of transition, the modern view pays its respects to the superseded axiom of devolution and takes leave of it.

The scope given to the right of ownership in later modern times is an outgrowth of the exigencies of mercantile traffic, of the prevalence of purchase and sale in a "money economy." The habits of thought enforced by these exigencies and by the ubiquitous and ever recurring resort to purchase and sale decide that ownership must naturally, normally, be absolute ownership, with free and unqualified discretion in the use and disposal of the things owned. Social expediency may require particular limitations of this full discretion, but such limitations are felt to be exceptional derogations from the "natural" scope of the owner's discretion.

On the other hand, the metaphysical ground of this right of ownership, the ultimate fact by virtue of which such a discretionary right vests in the owner, is his assumed creative efficiency as a workman; he embodies the work of his brain and hand in a useful object, – primarily, it is held, for his own personal use, and, by further derivation, for the use of any other person to whose use he sees fit to transfer it. The workman's force, ingenuity, and dexterity was the ultimate economic factor, – ultimate in a manner patent to the common sense of a generation habituated to the system of handicraft, how ever doubtful such a view may appear in the eyes of a generation in whose apprehension the workman is no longer the prime mover nor the sole, or even chief, efficient factor in the industrial process. The free workman, master of his own motions and with discretion as to what he would turn his efforts to, if to anything, had by Locke's time become an habitual fact in the life of the English community to such a degree that free labor, of the character of handicraft, was accepted uncritically as the fundamental factor in all human economy, and as the presumptive original fact in industry and in the struggle for wealth. So settled did this habit of thought become that no question was entertained as to the truth of the assumption.

It became a principle of the natural order of things that free labor is the original source of wealth and the basis of ownership. In point of historical fact, no doubt, such was not the pedigree of modern industry or modern ownership; but the serene, undoubting assumption of Locke and his generation only stands out the more strongly and unequivocally for this its discrepancy with fact. It is all the more evidently a competent expression of the trend which English common sense was following at this time, since this doctrine of a "natural" right of property based on productive labor carries all before it, in the face of the facts. In this matter English thought, or rather English common sense, has led; and the advanced Continental peoples have followed the English lead as the form of economic organization exemplified by the English-speaking communities has come to prevail among these Continental peoples.

Such a concept belongs to the regime of handicraft and petty trade, and it is from, or through, the era of handicraft that it has come down to the present.(6*) It fits into the scheme of handicraft, and it is less fully in consonance with the facts of life in any other situation than that of handicraft. Associated with the system of handicraft, as its correlate, was the system of petty trade; and as the differentiation of occupations was carried to a high degree, purchase and sale came to prevail very generally, and the community acquired a commercial complexion and commercial habits of thought. Under these circumstances the natural right of ownership came to comprise an extreme freedom and facility in the disposal of property. The whole sequence of growth of this natural right is, of course, to be taken in connection with the general growth of individual rights that culminated in the eighteenth-century system of Natural Liberty. How far the English economic development is to be accounted the chief or fundamental factor in the general growth of natural rights is a question that cannot be taken up here. The outcome, so far as it immediately touches the present topic, was that by the time of the industrial revolution a fairly consistent standardization of economic life had been reached in terms of workmanship and price. The writings of Adam Smith and his contemporaries bear witness to this. And this eighteenth-century standardization stands over as the dominant economic institution of later times.(7*) Such, in outline, seem to be the historical antecedents and the spiritual basis of the modern institution of property, and therefore of business enterprise as it prevails in the present.(8*)

This sketch of the genesis of the modern institution of property and of modern business principles may seem dubious to those who are inclined to give it a more substantial character than that of a habit of thought, − that is to say, those who still adhere to the doctrine of natural rights with something of the eighteenth−century naivete. But whatever may be accepted as the ulterior grounds of that cultural movement which culminated in the system of Natural Liberty, it is plain that the industrial and commercial experience of western Europe, and primarily of England, from the fifteenth to the eighteenth century, had much to do with the outcome of the movement in so far as natural liberty touches economic matters. It is as an outcome of this recently past phase of economic development that we have incorporated in the law, equity, and common sense of to−day, these peculiarly free and final property rights and obligations, that is to say, those peculiar principles that control current business and industry. We owe to the eighteenth century a very full discretion and free swing in all pecunIary matters. It has given freedom of contract, together with security and ease of credit engagements, whereby the competitive order of business has been definitively installed.(9*)

The subject−matter about which this modern pecuniary discretion turns, with all its freedom and inviolability of contract, is money values. Accordingly there underlies all pecuniary contracts. an assumption that the unIt of money value does not vary. Inviolability of contracts involves this assumption. It is accepted unquestioningly as a point of departure in all business transactions. In the making and enforcement of contracts it is a fundamental point of law and usage that money does not vary.(10*) Capitalization as well as contracts are made in its terms, and the plans of the business men who control industry look to the money unit as the stable ground of all their transactions. Notoriously, business men are jealous of any attempt to change the value or lessen the stability of the money unit, which goes to show how essential a principle in business traffic is the putative invariability of the money unit.(11*)

Usage fortified by law decides that when prices vary the variation is held to occur in the value of the vendible commodities, not in the value of the money unit, since money is the standard of value. There is, of course, no intention here to question the position, familiar to all economists, that fluctuations in the course of prices may as well be due to variation on the part of the money metals as to a variation on the part of the articles whose prices fluctuate. In so far as the distinction so made between variations in the one or the other member of a value ratio has a meaning − which it is not always clear that it has − it does not touch the argument. It is a matter of common notoriety, which has also had the benefit of reiterated statistical proof, that, as measured, for instance, in terms of livelihood or of labor, the value of money has varied incontinently throughout the course of history.

But in the routine of business throughout the nineteenth century the assumed stability of the money unit has served as an axiomatic principle, in spite of facts which have from time to time shown the falsity of that assumption.(12*)

The all−dominating issue in business is the question of gain and loss. Gain and loss is a question of accounting, and the accounts are kept in terms of the money unit, not in terms of livelihood, nor in terms of the serviceability of the goods, nor in terms of the mechanical efficiency of the industrial or commercial plant. For business purposes, and so far as the business man habitually looks into the matter, the last term of all transactions is their outcome in money values. The base line of every enterprise is a line of capitalization in money values. In current business practice, variations from this base line are necessarily rated as variations on the part of the other factors in the case, not as variations of the base line. The business man judges of events from the standpoint of ownership, and ownership runs in terms of money.(13*)

Investments are made for profit, and industrial plants and processes are capitalized on the basis of their profit−yielding capacity. In the accepted scheme of things among business men, profits are included as intrinsic to the conduct of business. So that, in place of the presumption in favor of a simple pecuniary stability of wealth, such as prevails in the rating of possessions outside of business traffic, there prevails within the range of business traffic the presumption that there must in the natural course of things be a stable and orderly increase of the property invested. Under no economic system earlier than the advent of the machine industry does profit on investment seem to have been accounted a normal or unquestionably legitimate source of gain. Under the agrarian-manorial regime of the Middle Ages it was not felt that the wealth of the large owners must, as a matter of course, increase by virtue of the continued employment of what they already had in hand − whatever may be the historical fact as regards the increase of wealth in their hands. Particularly, it was not the sense of the men of that time that wealth so employed must increase at any stated, "ordinary" rate per time unit. Similarly as regards other traffic in those days, even as regards mercantile ventures. Gain from investment was felt to be a fortuitous matter, not reducible to a stated rate. This is reflected, e.g., in the tenacious protests against the taking or paying of interest and in the ingenious sophistries by which the payment of interest was defended or explained away. Only under more settled commercial relations during the era of handicraft did the payment of interest gradually come to be accepted into full legitimacy. But even then gains from other business employments than mercantile traffic were apparently viewed as an increase due to productive labor rather than as a profit on investment.(14*) In industrial pursuits, as distinct from mercantile traffic proper, profits apparently come to figure as a regular and ordinary incident only when the industries come to be carried on on a mercantile basis by relatively large employers working with hired labor.

This orderly increase is, of course, taken account of in terms of the money unit. The "ordinary" rate of profits in business is looked upon as a matter of course by the body of business men. It is part of their common-sense view of affairs, and is therefore a normal phenomenon.(15*) Gain, they feel, is normal, being the purpose of all their endeavors; whereas a loss or a shrinkage in the values invested is felt to be an untoward accident which does not belong in the normal course of business, and which requires particular explanation. The normality, or matter-of-course character, of profits in the modern view is well shown by the position of those classical economists who are inclined to include "ordinary profits" in the cost of production of goods.

The precise meaning of "ordinary profits" need not detain the argument. It may mean net average profits, or it may mean something else. The phrase is sufficiently intelligible to the business community to permit the business men to use it without definition and to rest their reasoning about business affairs on it as a secure and stable concept; and it is this commonplace resort to the term that is the point of interest here.

At any given time and place there is an accepted ordinary rate of profits, more or less closely defined, which, it is felt, should accrue to any legitimate and ordinarily judicious business venture. However shifty the definition of this rate of profits may be, in concrete, objective terms, it is felt by the men of affairs to be of so substantial and consistent a character that they habitually capitalize the property engaged in any given business venture on the basis of this ordinary rate of profits. Due regard being had to any special advantages and drawbacks of the individual case, any given business venture or plant is capitalized at such a multiple of its earning-capacity as the current ordinary rate of profits will warrant.(16*)

Proceeding on the common-sense view built up out of this range of habits of thought with respect to normal profits and price phenomena, the business community holds that times are ordinary or normal so long as the accepted or reasonable rate of profits accrues on the accustomed capitalization; whereas times are good or brisk if the rate of gain is accelerated, and hard or dull if profits decline. This is the meaning of the phrases, "brisk times" and "dull times," as currently used in any business community.

Under the exigencies of the quest of profits, as conditioned by the larger industry and the more sweeping business organization of the last few decades, the question of capital in business has increasingly become a question of capitalization on the basis of earning-capacity, rather than a question of the magnitude of the industrial plant or the cost of production of the appliances of industry. From being a sporadic trait, of doubtful legitimacy, in the old days of the "natural" and "money" economy, the rate of profits or earnings on investment has in the nineteenth century come to take the central and dominant place in the economic system.

Capitalization, credit extensions, and even the productiveness and legitimacy of any given employment of labor, are referred to the rate of earnings as their final test and substantial ground. At the same time the "ordinary rate of profits" has become a more elusive idea. The phenomenon of a uniform rate of profits determined by competition has fallen into the background and lost something of its matter-of-fact character since competition in the large industry has begun to shift from the position of a stable and continuous equilibration to that of an intermittent, convulsive strain in the service of the larger business men's strategy. The interest of the business community centres upon profits and upon the shifting fortunes of the profit-maker, rather than upon accumulated and capitalized goods. Therefore the ultimate conditioning force in the conduct and aims of business is coming to be the prospective profit-yielding capacity of any given business move, rather than the aggregate holdings or the recorded output of product.

But this latest development in the field of industrial business has not yet come to control the field. It is rather an inchoate growth of the immediate present than an accomplished fact even of the recent past, and it can be understood only by reference to those conditions of the recent past out of which it comes. Therefore it is necessary to turn back to a further consideration of the old-fashioned business traffic as it used to go on by the competitive method before the competitive order began seriously to be dislocated and take on an intermittent character, as well as to a consideration of that resort to credit which has, in large part, changed the competitive system of business from what it was at the beginning of the nineteenth century to what it has become at its close.

NOTES:

1. See ch. IX.

2. Cf. e.g. E. Jenks, Law and Politics in the Middle Ages, ch. VI and VII.

3. "It has been said that the science of one age is the common sense of the next. It might with equal truth be said that the equity of one age becomes the law of the next. If positive law is the basis of order, ideal right is the active factor in progress." - H.S. Foxwell, Introduction to Menger's Right to the Whole Produce of Labor, p. XI. Cf. the entire passage.

4. See the essay, of Civil Government, ch. V.

5. Apart from the familiar historical materials for the study of the growth of national rights, including the right of property, there are a number of late writings that may be consulted; e.g. Jellinek, Declaration of the Rights of Man and of the Citizen; Ritchie, Natural Rights; Bonar, chapters relating to this topic in Philosophy and Political Economy; Hoffding, History of Modern Philosophy, vol. I; Albee, History of English Utilitarianism; and, lately come to hand, Scherger, Evolution of Modern Liberty. These and other writers treat of natural rights and the law of nature chiefly in other bearings than that of ownership; while the legal writers treat the subject from the legal rather than the de facto standpoint. It is also not unusual to spend attention chiefly on the pedigree of the doctrines rather than on the genesis and growth of the concepts. An endeavor at a genetic account of the modern concepts of ownership is found in Jenks, Law and Politics in the Middle Ages, so also in Cunningham, Western Civilization in its Economic Aspects.

6. What appears to be necessary to the development of such a sentiment is that neither slavery nor the machine system shall be present in sufficient force to give a pronounced bias to the community's habits of thought, at the same time that each member of the community, or each minor group of persons, habitually carries on its own work at its own discretion and for its own ends. Such a situation may or may not involve handicraft as that term is specifically understood. A presumption of similar import, but less pronounced and less defined, seems to prevail in an uncertain degree among many peoples on a low stage of culture. The tenet, accordingly, has some claim to stand as an egression of "natural" right, even when "natural" is taken in

an evolutionary sense.

7. Taken by and large, the standardization of conduct, knowledge, and ideals Current in the eighteenth century, and consonant with the eighteenth-century economic situation, is in the last analysis reducible to terms of workmanlike efficiency rather than terms of material cause and effect. This leaning to personal, workmanlike efficiency as an ultimate term shows itself even in the science of that time, e.g. in the quasi-personal character imputed to the so-called "natural laws" which then largely occupied scientific speculation; similarly in the Romantic literature and political philosophy.

8. As late as the close of the sixteenth century English law and usage in the matter of loans for interest and other contracts of a pecuniary character were in a less advanced state, admitted a less full and free discretion, than the corresponding development on the Continent; but from about that time the English rapidly gains on the Continental community in the habitual acceptance and application of these "business principles," and it has since then held the lead in this respect. Cf. Ashley, Economic History, vol. II. ch. VI.

9. Cf. Sombart, Kapitalismus, vol. II. ch. II.

10. On the putative stability of the money unit, cf. W.W. Carlile, The Evolution of Modern Money, pt. II. ch. IV.

11. Economists are in the habit of speaking of money as a medium of exchange, a "great wheel" for the circulation of goods. In the same connection business traffic is spoken of as a means of obtaining goods suitable for consumption, the end of all purchase and sale being consumable goods, not money values. It may be true in some profound philosophical sense that money values are not the definitive term of business endeavor, and that the business man seeks through the mediation of money to satisfy his craving for consumable goods. Looking at the process of economic life as a whole and taking it in its rationalized bearing as a collective endeavor to purvey goods and services for the needs of collective humanity, the office of the money unit – money transactions, exchange, credit, and all the rest that make up the phenomena of business – is perhaps justly rated as something subsidiary, serving to facilitate the distribution of consumable goods to the consumers, the Consumption of goods being the objective point of all this traffic. Such is the view of this matter given by the rationalistic, normalizing speculations of the eighteenth-century philosophers; and such is, in substance, the view spoken for by those economists who still consistently remain at the standpoint of the eighteenth century. The contention need neither be defended nor refuted here, since it does not seriously touch the facts of modern business. Within the range of business transactions this ulterior end does not necessarily come into view, at least not as a motive that guides the transactions from day to day. The matter is not so conceived in business transactions, it does not so appear on the face of the negotiable instruments, it is not in this manner that the money unit enters into the ruling habits of thought of business men.

12. Still, latterly, in the traffic of some of the more wide-awake business men, account is practically taken of the variations of the unit of value. What may be the future effects of habitual and incontinent variations of the unit, such as prevail in the present, is of course impossible to foretell. These variations seem due mainly to the extensive prevalence of credit relations; and the full development of credit relations in business is apparently a matter of the future rather than of the recent past, in spite of the great improvements that have been made in the use of credit. The modern conventional imputation of stability to the money unit dates back to the regime of a "money economy," such as prevailed under the circumstances of handicraft and the earlier huckstering commerce, and it holds its place in the developed "credit economy" largely as a survival of this more elementary past phase of economic life.

13. The conventional acceptance of the money unit as an invariable measure of value and standard of wealth is of very ancient derivation. (Cf. Carlile, Evolution of Modern Money, pt. II. ch. I; Ridgeway, Origin of Metallic Currency and Weight Standards, ch. I, II) Its present-day consequences are also of

first-rate importance, as will be indicated in a later chapter.

14. Cf., e.g., Mun, England's Treasure, particularly ch. II; Ashley, Economic History and Theory, bk. II. ch. VI. pp. 391-397. This, essentially handicraft, presumption is reflected even in the classical economists, who feel a moral necessity of explaining profits on some basis of productivity, or even of workmanship in some sophisticated sense. The whole discussion of the doctrine of Wages of Superintendence will serve to illustrate the case; the point is well shown in Mr Davidson's article on "Earnings of Management" in Palgrave's Dictionary of Political Economy.

15. The "ordinary" rate, of course, differs in detail from one line of business to another, as well as from place to place.

16. This statement applies with greater aptness to the business situation of England during the earlier three-quarters of the nineteenth century, and to the American situation of the third quarter of the century, than it does to the situation of the last decade. Qualifications required by the later phases of business development will be noted presently.

Chapter Five. The Use of Loan Credit

Credit serves two main uses in the regular course of such business as is occupied with the conduct of industry. - (a) that of deferred payments in the purchase and sale of goods - book accounts, bills, checks, and the like belong chiefly under this head; and (b) loans or debts - notes, stock shares, interest-bearing securities, deposits, call loans, etc., belong chiefly here. These two categories of credit extension are by no means clearly distinct. Forms of credit which commonly serve the one purpose may be turned to the other use; but the two uses of credit are, after all, broadly distinguishable. For many purposes of economic theory such a distinction might not be serviceable, or even practicable; it is here made merely for present use. It is chiefly with credit of the latter class, or rather with credit in so far as it is turned to use for the latter purpose, that this inquiry is concerned.

Suppose due credit arrangements have already been made - in the way of investments in stocks, interest-bearing securities and the like - such as to place the management of the industrial equipment in competent hands. This supposition is not a violent one, since a condition roughly approximating to this prevails in any quiescent period of industry when there is no appreciable depression. Under these "normal" conditions, the capital invested in any given industrial venture is turned over within a certain, approximately definite, length of time. The length of time occupied by the turnover may vary from one establishment to another, but in any given case the length of the turnover is one of the important factors that determine the chances of gain for the business concern in question. Indeed, if the general conditions of the trade and of the market are given, the two factors which determine the status and value of a given sound concern, as seen from the business man's standpoint, are the magnitude of the turnover and the length of time it occupies.

The business man's object is to get the largest aggregate gain from his business. It is manifestly for his interest, as far as may be, to shorten the process out of which his earnings are drawn,(1*) or, in other words, to shorten the period in which he turns over his capital. If the turnover consumes less than the time ordinarily allowed in the line of industry in which he is engaged, he gains more than the current rate of profits in that line of business, other things equal; whereas he loses if the turnover takes more than the normal time. This fact is forcibly expressed in the maxim, "Small profits and quick returns." There are two chief means of shortening the interval of the turnover, currently resorted to in industrial business. The first is the adoption of more efficient, time-saving industrial processes. Improvements of industrial plant and industrial processes having this in view are gaining in importance in the later developments of business, since a closer attention is now given to the time element in investments, and great advances have been made in this direction.(2*) A second expedient for accelerating the rate of turnover is the competitive pushing of sales, through larger and more urgent advertising and the like. It is needless to say that this means of accelerating business also receives due attention at the hands of modern business men.

But the magnitude of the turnover, "the volume of business," is of no less consequence than its rapidity. It is, of course, a trite commonplace that the earnings of any industrial business are a joint function of the rate of turnover and the volume of business.(3*) The business man may reach his end of increased earnings by either the one or the other expedient, and he commonly has resource to both if he can. His means of increasing the magnitude of the turnover is a resort to credit and a close husbanding of his assets. He is under a constant incentive to increase his liabilities and to discount his bills receivable. Indebtedness in this way comes to serve much the same purpose, as regards the rate of earnings, as does a time-saving improvement in the processes of industry.(4*) The effect of the use of credit on the part of a business man so placed is much the same as if his capital had been turned over a greater number of times in the year. It is accordingly to his interest to extend his credit as far as his standing and the state of the market will admit.(5*)

But on funds obtained on credit the debtor has to pay interest, which, being deducted from the gross earnings of the business, leaves, as net gain due to his use of credit, only the amount by which the increment of gross earnings exceeds the interest charge. This sets a somewhat elastic limit to the advantageous use of loan credit in business. In ordinary times, however, and under capable management, the current rate of business earnings exceeds the rate of interest by an appreciable amount; and in times of ordinary prosperity, therefore, it is commonly advantageous to employ credit in the way indicated. Still more so in brisk times, when opportunities for earnings are many and promise to increase. To turn the proposition about, so as to show the run of business motives in the case: whenever the capable business manager sees an appreciable difference between the cost of a given credit extension and the gross increase of gains to be got by its use, he will seek to extend his credit. But under the regime of competitive business whatever is generally advantageous becomes a necessity for all competitors. Those who take advantage of the opportunities afforded by credit are in a position to undersell any others who are similarly placed in all but this respect. Speaking broadly, recourse to credit becomes the general practice, the regular course of competitive business management, and competition goes on on the basis of such a use of credit as an auxiliary to the capital in hand. So that the competitive earning capacity of business enterprises comes currently to rest on the basis, not of the initial capital alone, but of capital plus such borrowed funds as this capital will support.

The competitive rate of earnings is brought to correspond with this basis of operation; the consequence being that under such competitive employment of credit the aggregate earnings of an enterprise resting on a given initial capital will be but slightly larger than it might have been if such a general recourse to credit to swell the volume of business did not prevail. But since such use of credit prevails generally, a further consequence is that any concern involved in the open business competition, which cannot or does not take recourse to credit to swell its volume of business, will be unable to earn a "reasonable" rate of profits. So that the general practice drives all competitors to the use of the same expedient; but since the advantage to be derived from this expedient is a competitive advantage only, the universality of the practice results in but a slight, if any, increase of the aggregate earnings of the business community. Borrowed funds afford any given business concern a differential advantage as against other competitors; but it is, in the main, a differential advantage only. The competitive use of such funds in extending business operations may, incidentally, throw the management of some portion of the industrial process into more competent or less competent hands. So far as this happens, the credit operations in question and the use of the borrowed funds may increase or diminish the output of industry at large, and so may affect the aggregate earnings of the business community. But, apart from such incidental shifting of the management of industry to more competent (or less competent) hands, this competitive use of borrowed funds has no aggregate effect upon earnings or upon the industrial output.

The current or reasonable rate of profits is, roughly, the rate of profits at which business men are content to employ the actual capital which they have in hand.(6*) A general resort to credit extension as an auxiliary to the capital in hand results, on the whole, in a competitive lowering of the rate of profits, computed on capital plus credit, to such a point as would not be attractive to a business man who must confine himself to the employment of capital without credit extension. On an average, it may be said, the aggregate earnings of the aggregate capital with credit extension are but slightly greater than the aggregate earnings of the same capital without credit extension would be in the absence of a competitive use of credit extension. But under modern conditions business cannot profitably be done by any one of the competitors without the customary resort to credit. Without the customary resort to credit a "reasonable" return could not be obtained on the investment.

To the extent to which the competitive recourse to credit is of the character here indicated – to the extent to which it is a competitive bidding for funds between competent managers – it may be said that, taken in the aggregate, the funds so added to business capital represent no material capital or "production goods." They are business capital, only. they swell the volume of business, as counted in terms of price, etc., but they do not directly swell the volume of industry, since they do not add to the aggregate material apparatus of industry, or alter the character of the processes employed, or enhance the degree of efficiency with which industry is managed.

The "buoyancy" which a speculative inflation of values gives to industrial business may indirectly increase the material output of industry by enhancing the intensity with which the industrial process is carried on under the added stimulus; but apart from this psychological effect the expansion of business capital through credit extension has no aggregate industrial effect. This secondary effect of credit inflation may be very considerable and is always present in brisk times. It is commonly obvious enough to be accounted the chief characteristic of a period of "prosperity." For a theory of industry this indirect effect of credit inflation would be its main characteristic, but for a theory of business it occupies the place of a corollary only.

To the view set forth above, – that borrowed funds do not increase the aggregate industrial equipment, – the objection may present itself that all funds borrowed represent property owned by some one (the lender or his creditors), and transferred, in usufruct, by the loan transaction to the borrower; and that these funds can, therefore, be converted to productive uses, like any other funds, by drawing into the industrial process, directly or indirectly, the material items of wealth whose fluent form these funds are.(7*) The objection fails at two points: (a) while the loans may be covered by property held by the lender, they are not fully covered by property which is not already otherwise engaged; and even if such were the case, it would (b) not follow that the use of these funds would increase the technical (material) outfit of industry.

As to the first point (a): Loans made by the financial houses in the way of deposits or other advances on collateral are only to a fractional extent covered by liquid assets;(8*) and anything but liquid assets is evidently beside the point of the present question. An inconsiderable fraction of these loans is represented by liquid assets. The greater part of the advances made by banking houses, for instance, rest on the lender's presumptive ability to pay eventually, on demand or at maturity, any claims that may in the course of business be presented against the lender on account of the advances made by him. It is a business truism that no banking house could at a moment meet all its outstanding obligations.(9*) A necessary source of banking profits, e.g., is a large excess of the volume of business over reserves.

As to (b): Another great part of the basis of such loans is made up of invested funds and collateral held by the lender. These at the same time are much of the basis on which rests the lender's presumptive ability to pay claims presented. But these investments, in industry or real estate, in interest-bearing securities and collateral of whatever description, represent future income of the lender's debtors (as, e.g., government and municipal securities), or property which is already either engaged in the industrial process or tied up in forms of wealth (as, e.g., real estate) which do not lend themselves to industrial uses. Loans obtained on property which has no present industrial use, which cannot in its present form or under existing circumstances be employed in the processes of industry (as, e.g., speculative real estate), or loans on property which is already engaged in the industrial process (as, e.g., stocks, industrial plant, goods on hand, real estate in use),(10*) represent, for the purpose in hand, nothing more substantial than a fictitious duplication of material items that cannot be drawn into the industrial process. Therefore such loans cannot, at least not directly, swell the aggregate industrial equipment or enhance the aggregate productivity of industry; for the items which here serve as collateral are already previously in use in industry to the extent to which they can be used. Property of these kinds – what is already in use in industry and what is not of use for industrial purposes – may be "coined into means of payment," and so may be made to serve as additional pecuniary (business) capital, but such property is mechanically incapable of serving as additional material (industrial) capital. To a very considerable extent the funds involved in these loans, therefore, have only a pecuniary (business) existence, not a material (industrial) one; and, so far as that is true, they represent, in the aggregate, only fictitious industrial equipment. Even such inconsiderable portion of them, however, as represents metallic reserves also adds nothing to the effective material apparatus of industry; since money as such, whether metallic or promissory, is of no direct industrial effect; as is evident from the well-known fact that the absolute quantity of the precious metals in use is a matter of no consequence to the conduct of either business or industry, so long as the quantity neither increases nor decreases by an appreciable amount. Nummus nummum non parit.

So that all advances made by banking houses or by other creditors in a like case, – whether the advances are made on mortgage, collateral or personal notes, in the form of deposits, note issues, Or. what not; whether they are taken to represent the items of property covered by the collateral, the cash reserves of the banks, or the general solvency of the creditor or debtor, – all these "advances" go to increase the "capital" of which business men have the disposal; but for the material purposes of industry, taken in the aggregate, they are purely fictitious items.(11*) Cash loans (such as savings-bank deposits (12*) and the like) belong in the same category. All these advances afford the borrower a differential advantage in bidding against other business men for the control and use of industrial processes and materials, they afford him a differential advantage in the distribution of the material means of industry; but they constitute no aggregate addition to the material means of industry at large. Funds of whatever character are a pecuniary fact, not an industrial one; they serve the distribution of the control of industry only, not its materially productive work.

Loan credit in excess of what may serve to transfer the management of industrial materials from the owner to a more competent user – that is to say, in so far as it is not, in effect, of the nature of a lease of industrial plant – serves, on the whole, not to increase the quantity of the material means of industry nor, directly, to enhance the effectiveness of their use; but, taken in the aggregate, it serves only to widen the discrepancy between business capital and industrial equipment. So long as times are brisk this discrepancy ordinarily goes on widening through a progressive extension of credit. Funds obtained on credit are applied to extend the business; competing business men bid up the material items of industrial equipment by the use of funds so obtained; the value of the material items employed in industry advances; the aggregate of values employed in a given undertaking increases, with or without a physical increase of the industrial material engaged; but since an advance of credit rests on the collateral as expressed in terms of value, an enhanced value of the property affords a basis for a further extension of credit, and so on.(13*)

Now, the base line of business transactions is the money value (market or exchange value, price) of the items involved, not their material efficiency. The value of the money unit is by conventional usage held to be invariable, and the lenders perforce proceed on this assumption, so long as they proceed at all.(14*) Consequently, any increase of the aggregate money values involved in the current industrial business enterprises will afford a basis for an extension of loans, indistinguishable from any other block of capitalized values, even if the increase of capitalized values is due to credit advances previously made on the full cash value of the property hypothecated, The extension of loans on collateral, such as stock and similar values involved in industrial business, has therefore in the nature of things a cumulative character. This cumulative extension of credit through the enhancement of prices goes on, if otherwise undisturbed, so long as no adverse price phenomenon obtrudes itself with sufficient force to convict this cumulative enhancement of capitalized values of imbecility. The extension of credit proceeds on the putative stability of the money value of the capitalized industrial material, whose money value is cumulatively augmented by this extension itself. But the money value of the collateral is at the same time the capitalized value of the property, computed on the basis of its presumptive earning-capacity. These two methods of rating the value of collateral must approximately coincide, if the capitalization is to afford a stable basis for credit; and when an obvious discrepancy arises between the outcome given by the two ratings, then a rerating will be had in which the rating on the basis of earning-capacity must be accepted as definitive, since earnings are the ground fact about which all business transactions turn and to which all business enterprise converges. A manifest discrepancy presently arises in this way between the aggregate nominal capital (capital plus loans) engaged in business, on the one hand, and the actual rate of earning-capacity of this business capital, on the other hand; and when this discrepancy has become patent a period of liquidation begins.

To give a readier view of the part played by loan credit in this discrepancy between the business capital and the earning-capacity of industrial concerns, it will be in place to indicate more summarily what are the factors at play.

The earnings of the business community, taken as a whole, are derived from the marketable output of goods and services turned out by the industrial process – disregarding such earnings as accrue to one concern merely at the cost of another. The effective industrial capital, from the use of which this output, and therefore these earnings, arise, is the aggregate of capitalized material items actually engaged in industry. The business capital, on the other hand, is made up of this capitalized industrial material taken as a fund of values, plus good-will, plus whatever funds are obtained on credit by using this capitalized industrial material as collateral, plus funds obtained on other, non-industrial, property used as collateral. Through the competitive use of funds obtained on credit, as spoken of above, the nominal value of the capitalized industrial material is cumulatively augmented so as to make it approximately equal to its original capitalization plus whatever funds are obtained on credit of all kinds. On this basis of an expanded collateral a further extension of credit takes place, and the funds so obtained are incorporated in the business capital and turned to the like competitive use, and so on.(15*) Capital and earnings are counted in terms of the money unit. Counted in these terms, the earnings (industrial output) are also increased by the process of iflation though credit, since the competitive Use of funds spoken of acts to bid up prices of whatever products are used in industry, and of whatever speculative property is presumed to have some eventual industrial use. But the nominal magnitude (value) of the earnings is not increased in as large a ratio as that of the business capital; since the demand whereby the values of the output are regulated is not altogether a business demand (for productive goods), but is in great part, and indeed in the last resort mainly, reducible to a consumptive demand for finished goods.(16*)

Looking at credit extension and its use for purposes of capital as a whole, the outcome which presents itself most strikingly at a period of liquidation is the redistribution of the ownership of industrial property incident to the liquidation. The funds obtained on credit are in great measure invested competitively in the same aggregate of material items that is already employed in industry apart from the use of loan credit, with the result that the same range of items of wealth are rated at a larger number of money units. In these items of wealth – which, apart from the use of credit, are owned by their nominal owners – the creditors, by virtue of the credit extension, come to own an undivided interest proportioned to the advances which they have made. The aggregate of these items of property comes hereby to be potentially owned by the creditors in approximately the proportion which the loans bear to the collateral plus the loans. The outcome of credit extension, in this respect, is a situation in which the creditors have become potential owners of such a fraction of the industrial equipment as would be represented by the formula: (17*) loans/capitalization (=collateral + loans) In a period of liquidation this potential ownership on the part of the creditors takes effect to the extent to which the liquidation is carried through.(18*)

The precise measure and proportion in which the industrial property of the business community passes into the hands of the creditors in a period of liquidation can, of course, not be specified; it depends on the degree of shrinkage in values, as well as on the degree of thoroughness with which the liquidation is carried out, and perhaps on other still less ascertainable causes, among which is the degree of closeness of organization of the business community. It is, however, through the shrinkage of market values of the output and the industrial plant that the transfer of ownership to the creditor class takes place. In case no shrinkage of values took place, no such general transfer of ownership to the creditors as a class would become evident.

In point of fact, the shrinkage commonly supervenes, in the course of modern business, when a general liquidation comes; although it is conceivable that the period of acute liquidation and its attendant shrinkage of values need not supervene. Such would probably be the case in the absence of competitive investment in industrial material on a large scale. Secondary effects, such as perturbations of the rate of interest, insolvency, forced sales, and the like, need scarcely be taken up here, although it may be well to keep in mind that these secondary effects are commonly very considerable and farreaching, and that they may in specific instances very materially affect the outcome.

The theoretical result of this summary sketch of loan credit so far seems to be: (a) an extension of loan credit beyond that involved in the transference of productive goods from their owners to more competent users is unavoidable under the regime of competitive business – credit expansion is normally in some degree "abnormal" or "excessive"; (b) such a use of credit does not add to the aggregate of industrially productive equipment nor increase its material output of product, and therefore it does not add materially to the aggregate gross earnings obtained by the body of business men engaged in industry, as counted in material terms of wealth or of permanent values;(19*) (c) it diminishes the aggregate net profits obtained by the business men engaged in industry, as counted in such terms, in that it requires them to pay interest, to creditors outside the industrial process proper, on funds which, taken as an aggregate, represent no productive goods and have no aggregate productive effect; (d) there results an overrating of the aggregate capital engaged in industry, compared with the value of the industrial equipment at the starting-point, by approximately the amount of the aggregate deposits and loans on collateral; (e) the overrating swells the business capital, thereby raises the valuation of collateral, and gives rise to a further extension of credit, with further results of a like nature; (f) commonly beginning at some point where the extension of credit is exceptionally large in proportion to the material substratum of productive goods, or where the discrepancy between nominal capital and earning-capacity is exceptionally wide, the overrating is presently recognized by the creditor and a settlement ensues; (g) on the consequent withdrawal of credit a forced rerating of the aggregate capital follows, bringing the nominal aggregate into approximate accord with the facts of earning-capacity; (h) the shrinkage which takes place in reducing the aggregate rating of business capital from the basis of capital goods plus loans to the basis of capital goods alone, takes place at the expense of debtors and nominal owners of industrial equipment, in so far as they are solvent; (i) in the period of liquidation the gain represented by the credit inflation goes to the creditors and claimants of funds outside the industrial process proper, except that so much as is cancelled in bad debts is written off; (j) apart from secondary effects, such as heightened efficiency of industry due to inflated values, changes of the rate of interest, insolvency, etc., the main final outcome is a redistribution of the ownership of property whereby the creditor class, including holders and claimants of funds, is benefited.

Since the modern industrial situation began to take form, there have been two principal forms of credit transactions current in the usage of the business community for the purpose of investment: the old-fashioned loan, the usage of which has come down from an earlier, day. and the stock share, whereby funds are invested in a joint stock company or corporation. The latter is a credit instrument, so far as touches the management of the property represented, in that (in earlier usage at least) it effects a transfer of a given body of property from the hands of an owner who resigns discretion in its control to a board of directors who assume the management of it. In addition to these two methods of credit relation there has, during the late-modern industrial period, come into extensive use a third class of expedients, viz. debentures of one form and another - bonds of various tenor, preferred stock, preference shares, etc., ranging, in point of technical character and degree of liability, from something approaching the nature of a bill of sale to something not readily distinguishable in effect from a personal note. The typical (latest and most highly specialized) instrument of this class is the preferred stock. This is in form a deed of ownership and in effect an evidence of debt. It is typical of a somewhat comprehensive class of securities in use in the business community, in the respect that it sets aside the distinction between capital and credit. In this respect, indeed, preferred stock, more adequately perhaps than any other instrument, reflects the nature of the "capital concept" current among the up-to-date business men who are engaged in the larger industrial affairs.

The part which debenture credit, nominal and virtual, plays in the financing of modern industrial corporations is very considerable, and the proportion which it bears in the capitalization of these corporations apparently grows larger as time passes and shrewder methods of business gain ground. In the field of the "industrials" proper, debenture credit has not until lately been employed with full effect. It seems to be from the corporation finance of American railway companies that business men have learned the full use of an exhaustive debenture credit as an expedient for expanding business capital. It is not an expedient newly discovered, but its free use, even in railway finance, is relatively late. Wherever it prevails in an unmitigated form, as with some railway companies, and latterly in many other industrial enterprises, it throws the capitalization of the business concerns affected by it into a peculiar, characteristically modern, position in relation to credit. When carried out thoroughly it places virtually the entire capital, comprising the whole of the material equipment, on a credit basis. Stock being issued by the use of such funds as will pay for printing the instruments, a road will be built or an industrial plant established by the use of funds drawn from the sale of bonds; preferred stock or similar debentures will then be issued, commonly of various denominations, to the full amount that the property will bear, and not infrequently somewhat in excess of what the property will bear. When the latter case occurs, the market quotations of the securities will, of course, roughly adjust the current effective capitalization to the run of the facts, whatever the nominal capitalization may be. The common stock in such a case represents "goodwill," and in the later development it usually represents nothing but "good-will."[20*] The material equipment is covered by credit instruments debentures. Not infrequently the debentures cover appreciably more than the value of the material equipment, together with such property as useful patent rights or trade secrets; in such a case the good-will is also, to some extent, covered by debentures, and so serves as virtual collateral for a credit extension which is incorporated in the business capital of the company. In the ideal case, where a corporation is financed with due perspicacity, there will be but an inappreciable proportion of the market value of the company's good-will left uncovered by debentures. In the case of a railway company, for instance, no more should be left uncovered by debentures than the value of the "franchise," and probably in most cases not that much actually is uncovered.

Whether capitalized good-will (including "franchise" if necessary) is to be rated as a credit extension is a nice question that can apparently be decided only on a legal technicality. In any case so much seems clear - that good-will is the nucleus of capitalization in modern corporation finance. In a well financed, flourishing corporation, good-will, indeed, constitutes the total remaining assets after liabilities have been met, but the total remaining assets may not nearly equal the total market value of the company's good-will; that is to say, the material equipment (plant, etc.) of a shrewdly managed concern is hypothecated at least once, commonly more than once, and its immaterial properties (good-will), together with the evidences of its indebtedness, may also to some extent be drawn into the hypothecation.[21*]

What has just been said of the part borne by good-will and debentures in the capitalization of corporations should be taken in connection with what was said above (pp. 100-104) as to the nature of the securities offered as collateral in procuring a credit extension. The greater part of the securities used as collateral, and so "coined into means of payment," are evidences of debt, at the first remove or farther from their physical basis, instruments of credit recording a previous credit extension.

In the earlier period of growth of this debenture financiering in industry, as, e.g., in the railroad financiering of the third quarter of the nineteenth century, the process of expansion by means of debenture credit, in any given case, was worked out gradually, over a more or less extended period of time. But as the possibilities of this expedient have grown familiar to the business community, the time consumed in perfecting the structure of debentures in each case has been reduced; until it is now not unusual to perfect the whole organizztion, with its load of debentures, at the inception of a corporate enterprise. In such a case, when a corporation starts with a fully organized capital and debt, the owners of the concern are also its creditors; they are, at the start, the holders of both common and preferred stock, and probably also of the bonds of the company – so adding another increment of confusion to the relation between modern capital and credit, as seen from the old-fashioned position as to what capitalization and its basis should be.

This syncopated process of expanding capital by the help of credit financiering, however, is seen at its best in the latter-day reorganizations and coalitions of industrial corporations; and as this class of transactions also illustrate another interesting and characteristically modern feature of credit financiering, the whole matter may best be set out in the way of a sketch of what takes place in a case of coalition of industrial corporations on a large scale such as recent industrial history has made familiar.

The avowed end of these latter-day business coalitions is economy of production and sale and an amicable regulation of intercorporate relations. So far as bears on the functioning of credit in the attendant business transactions, the presence or absence of these purposes, of course, does not affect the course of events or the outcome. These avowed incentives do not touch the credit operations involved. On the other hand, the need of large credit in consummating the deal, as well as the presumptive gains to be drawn from the credit relations involved, offer inducements of their own to men who are in a position to effect such a coalition. Inducements of this kind seem to have been of notable effect in bringing on some of the recent operations of this class.

Credit operations come into these transactions mainly at two points: in the "financing" of the deal, and in the augmentation of debentures; and at both of these points there is a chance of gain on the one hand to the promoter (organizer) and the credit house which finances the operation, and on the other hand to the stockholders. The gain which accrues to the two former is the more unequivocal, and this seems in some cases to be the dominant incentive to effect the reorganization. The whole operation of reorganization may, therefore, best be taken up from the point of view of the promoter, who is the prime mover in the matter.

A reorganization of industrial concerns on a large scale, such as are not uncommon at the present time, involves a campaign of business strategy, engaging, it is said, abilities and responsibilities of a very high order. Such a campaign of business strategy, as carried out by the modem captains of industry, runs, in the main, on credit relations, in the way of financial backing, options, purchases, leases, and the issuance and transfer of stock and debentures. In order to carry through these large "deals," in the first place, a very substantial basis of credit is required, either in the hands of the promoter (organizer) himself or in the hands of a credit house which "finances" the organization for him.

The strategic use of credit here involved is, in effect, very different from the old-time use of loan credit in investments. In transactions of this class the time element, the credit period, is an inconspicuous factor at the most; it plays a very subordinate and uncertain part. The volume of credit at the disposal of a given strategist is altogether the decisive point, as contrasted with the lapse of time over which the incident credit extension may run. The usefulness of the credit extension is not measured in terms of time, nor are the gains which accrue to the creditor in the case proportioned to the length of time involved.

This follows from the peculiar nature of the work which these great captains of industry have in hand, and more remotely, therefore, from the peculiar character of the earnings which induce them to undertake the work. Their work, though it is of the gravest consequence to industry, is not industrial business, in that it is not occupied with anything like the conduct of a continuous industrial process. Nor is it of the same class as commercial business, or even banking business, in that there is no investment in a continued sequence of transactions. It differs also from stock and produce speculation, as that is currently conceived,(22*) in that it does not depend on the lapse of time to bring a change of circumstances; although it has many points of similarity with stock speculation. In its details this work resembles commercial business, in that it has to do with bargaining; but so does all business, and this peculiar work of the trust promoter differs from mercantile business in the absence of continuity. Perhaps its nearest business analogue is the work of the real estate agent.

The volume of credit involved is commonly very great; whereas the credit period, the lapse of time, is a negligible factor. Indeed, if an appreciable credit period intervenes, that is a fortuitous circumstance. The time element in these credit operations is in abeyance, or at the best, it is an indeterminate magnitude. Hence the formula shown above (p. 95, n. 3) is practically not applicable to business of this class. So far as bears upon the credit operations involved in these transactions of the large finance, the question about which interest turns is almost exclusively the volume of the turnover; its velocity is a negligible quantity. Such strategic use of credit is not confined to the business of making or marring industrial coalitions. It is habitually to be met with in connection with stock (and produce) speculation, and ramifications of the like use of credit run through the dealings of the business community at large in many directions; but it rarely attains the magnitude in the service of stock speculation which it reaches in the campaign incident to a trust-making deal. The form of credit extension employed in these transactions with indeterminate time also varies. The older and more familiar form is that of the call loan, together with the stock exchange transactions for which call loans are largely used. Here the time element is present, especially in form; but the credit period is somewhat indeterminate, as is also the gain that accrues to the creditor from the transaction; although the creditor's gain here continues to be counted at a (variable) rate per cent. per time-unit. The strategic use of credit in the affairs of the large business finance has much in common with the call loan. Indeed, the call loan in set form is often resorted to as a valuable auxiliary recourse, although the larger arrangements for financing such a campaign of business strategy are not usually put in the form of a call loan. The arrangement between the promoter and the financial agent is commonly based on a less specific stipulation as to collateral, and the payment for credit obtained takes even less, if any, account of the length of the credit period. In financing a campaign of coalition the credit house that acts as financial agent assumes, in effect, an even less determinate credit responsibility. Here, too, the gains accruing to the creditor are no longer, even nominally, counted per cent. per time-unit, but rather in the form of a bonus based mainly on the volume of the turnover, with some variable degree of regard to other circumstances.

Answering to the essentially timeless character of the gains accruing to the financial agent, the earnings of the promoter engaged in transactions of this class are also not of the nature of profits per cent. per time-unit, but rather a bonus which commonly falls immediately into the shape of a share in the capitalization of the newly organized concern. Much of the increment of capital, or capitalization, that goes to the promoter is scarcely distinguishable from an increase of the liabilities of the new corporation (e.g. preferred stock); and the remainder (e.g. common stock) has also some of the characteristics of a credit instrument. It is worth noting that the cost of reorganization, including the bonus of the promoter and the financial agent, is, in the common run of cases, added to the capitalization; that is to say, as near as this class of transactions may be spoken of in terms borrowed from the old-fashioned business terminology, what answers to the "interest" due the creditor on the credit extension involved is incorporated in the "capital" of the debtor, without circumlocution or faltering.(23*)

The line between credit and capital, or between debt and property, in the values handled throughout these strategic operations of coalition, remains somewhat uncertain. Indeed, the old-fashioned concepts of "debt" and "property," or "liabilities" and "assets," are not fairly applicable to the facts of the case – except, of course, in the way of a technical legal distinction. The old-fashioned law and legal presumptions and the new-fashioned facts and usages are parting company, at this point as well as at some others in the affairs of modern business.

When such a large transaction in the reorganization of industrial concerns has been completed, the values left in the hands of the former owners of the concerns merged in the new coalition are only to a fractional and uncertain extent of the nature of material goods. They are in large part debentures, and much of the remainder is of a doubtful character. A large proportion of the nominal collective capital resulting in such cases is made up of the capitalized good-will of the concerns merged.(24*) This good-will is chiefly a capitalization of the differential advantages possessed by the several concerns as competitors in business, and is for the most part of no use for other than competitive business ends. It has for the most part no aggregate industrial effect. The differential advantages possessed by business concerns as competitors disappear when the competitors are merged, in the degree in which they cease to compete with rival bidders for the same range of business. To this aggregate defunct good-will of the consolidated concerns (which in the nature of things can make only an imaginary aggregate) is added something in the way of an increment of good-will belonging to the new corporation as such;(25*) and the whole is then represented, approximately, by the common stock issued. The nominal capital of the concerns merged (in good part based on capitalized goodwill) is aggregated, after an appraisement which commonly equalizes the proportion of each by increasing the nominal shares of all. This aggregate is covered with common and preferred stock, chiefly preferred, which is a class of debentures issued under the form of capital. The stock, common and preferred, goes to the owners of the concerns merged, and to the promoter and the financial agent, as indicated above. In case bonds are issued, these likewise go to the former owners, in so far as they do not replace outstanding liabilities of the concerns merged.

"Capital" in the enlightened modern business usage means "capitalized presumptive earning-capacity," and in this capitalization is comprised the usufruct of whatever credit extension the given business concern's industrial equipment and good-will will support.(26*) By consequence the effectual capitalization (shown by the market quotations) as contrasted with the nominal capital (shown by the par value of the stock of all descriptions) fluctuates with the fluctuations of the prevalent presumption as to the solvency and earning-capacity of the concern and the good faith of its governing board.

When the modern captain of industry reorganizes and consolidates a given range of industrial business concerns, therefore, and gives them a collective form and name as an up-to-date corporation, the completed operation presents, in syncopated form and within a negligible lapse of time, all that intricate process of cumulative augmentation of business capital through the use of credit which otherwise may come gradually in the course of business competition. At the same time it involves a redistribution of the ownership of the property engaged in industry, such as otherwise occurs at a period of liquidation. The result is, of course, not the same at all points, but the equivalence between the two methods of expanding business capital and distributing the gains is close in some respects. The resemblances and the differences between the two processes, so far as relates to credit, are worth noticing. The trust-maker is in some respects a surrogate for a commercial crisis.

When credit extension is used competitively in the old-fashioned way for increasing the business of competing concerns, as spoken of above (pp. 94-100, 109-114), the expansion of business capital through credit operations occupies a period of some duration, commonly running over an interval recognized as a period of speculative advance or "rising prosperity." The expansion of capitalized values then takes place more or less gradually through a competitive enhancement of the prices of industrial equipment and the like. The creditors then commonly come in for their resulting share in the industrial equipment only at the period of liquidation, with its attendant shrinkage of values. In the timeless credit transactions involved in the modern reorganizations of industrial business, on the other hand, the creditors' claim takes effect without an appreciable lapse of time, a liquidation, or a shrinkage of values.

The whole process of credit extension, augmentation of business capital, and distribution of proceeds is reduced to a very simple form. The credit extension is effected in two main forms: (a) the "financing" undertaken by the credit house in conjunction with the promoter, and (b) the issuance of debentures. The bonus of the financing house and promoter, as well as the debentures, are all included in the recapitalization, together with an increment of good-will and any other incidental items of expense or presumptive gain. The resulting collective capitalization (assets and liabilities) is then distributed to the several parties concerned in the transaction. The outcome, so far as touches the present argument, being that when the operation is completed the ownership of the recapitalized industrial equipment, with whatever other property is involved, appears distributed between the former owners, the promoter, and the credit house which financed the operation. But, by virtue of the debentures distributed, the former owners, together with the other parties named, appear in the role of creditors of the new corporation as well as owners of it; they commonly come out of the transaction with large holdings of preferred stock or similar debentures at the same time that they hold the coommon stock. The preferr.ed stock, of course, is presently disposed of by the large holders to outside parties. The material equipment is then practically the same as it was before; the business capital has been augmented to comprise such proportion of the goodwill of the several concerns incorporated as had not previously been capitalized and hypothecated, together with the good-will imputed to the new corporation and such debentures as these items of wealth will float.

The effective capitalization resulting is, of course, indicated by the market quotations of the securities issued rather than by their face value. The value of the corporation's business capital so indicated need suffer no permanent shrinkage; it will suffer none if the monopoly advantage (good-will) of the new corporation is sufficient to keep its earning-capacity up to the rate on which the capitalization is based.

It appears, then, that in the affairs of latterday business, as shown by modern corporation finance, capital and credit extension are not always distinguishable in fact, nor does there appear to be a decisive business reason why they should be distinguished. "Capital" means "capitalized putative earning-capacity," expressed in terms of value, and this capitalization comprises the use of all feasible credit extension. The business capital of a modern corporation is a magnitude that fluctuates from day to day; and in the quotations of its debentures the magnitude of its credit extension also fluctuates from day to day with the course of the market. The precise pecuniary magn itude of the business community's invested wealth, as well as the aggregate amount of the community's indebtedness, depends from hour to hour on the quotations of the stock exchange; and it rarely happens that it remains nearly the same in the aggregate from one week's end to the next. Both capital and credit, therefore, vary from hour to hour. and, within narrow limits, from place to place. The magnitude and fluctuations of business capital, - "capital" in the sense in which that term is used in business affairs, - of course, stand in no hard and fast relation to the material magnitude of the industrial equipment; nor do variations in the magnitude of the business capital reflect variations in the magnitude or the efficiency of the industrial equipment in any but the loosest and most indecisive manner. So also, and for the same reason, the magnitude and the variations of the aggregate credit afloat at a given time bear, at the most, but a remote, indirect, and shifty relation to the aggregate of material wealth and the material changes to which this wealth is subject. All this applies with peculiar cogency wherever and in so far as industry and business are carried on hy modern expedients and in due contact with the market.

NOTES:

1. This, of course, has nothing to say to Bohm-Bawerk's theory of the enhancement of production through lengthening the processes of industry. His theory of the "roundabout method" applies to the technical, material efficiency of the mechanical process; whereas the point in question here is the interval occupied in the turning over of a given business capital. Bohm-Bawerk's position may be questionable, however, on other grounds.

2. Cf., e.g., Werner Sombart, "Der Stil des modernen Wirthschaftslebens." Achiv fur soz. Gestzg. u. Statistik, vol. XVII, pp. 1–20, especially pp. 4–15. Reprinted as ch. IV, vol. II of Der moderne Kapitalismus (Leipzig, 1902).

3. Cf., e.g., Marshall, Principles of Economics (3d ed.), bk VI, ch. VII, secs. 3 and 4.

4. Cf. Laughlin, Principles of Money, p. 86.

5. The turnover will count for more in gross earnings at current rates if instead of his own capital alone the business man also engages whatever funds he can borrow by using his capital as collateral. The turnover counted on capital (value of the industrial equipment) plus credit, at current rates, will be greater than that counted on the capital aaone used without credit extension. The turnover may be expressed as the product of the mass of values employed multiplied by the velocity. Hence, if credit be taken as an indeterminate fraction (capital/n) of the capital used as collateral, we may say that

Turnover = (1/time)(capital + capital/n), i.e.

$$T = (1/t)(c + c/n) = (c + c/n)/t;\ t = (c + c/n)/T$$

The algebraic statement serves to bring out the equivalence between an acceleration of the rate of turnover and an increase of the volume of business capital. Cf. Jevons, Theory of Political Economy, pp. 249–258.

Sombart is mistaken in saying (Kapitalismus, vol. II. ch. VI, p. 74) that the use of credit lengthens the time of turnover of capital. Credit shortens the time relatively to the magnitude of the turnover; i.e. a given initial capital by the help of credit turns over a larger pecuniary magnitude in a given time: $(c + c/n)/t > c/t$.

6. Marshall, as above.

7. Cf. Laughlin, Principles of Money, ch. IV.

8. Property convertible into cash at will.

9. The legally obligatory reserve for the National Banks, for instance, is 25 per cent of combined note circulation and deposits in central reserve banks, 15 per cent in others. -- Revised Statutes, 5191.

10. This takes accountof advance made by other lenders than the regular banking houses who exclude mortgages on real estate from their collateral; such, e.g., as the long time advances (investments in securities) made by saving banks, insurance companies, minor private and mortgage banks, private lenders, etc.

11. This truism is frequently overlooked in theoretical discussions; hence, as the present argument requires its recognition, it is here stated in this explicit way.

12. The cash loans made by depositors to savings banks in the form of deposits.

13. Cf. Twelfth Census of the United States, vol. VII, p. c.

14. Few, perhaps, would in set terms maintain an argument that the value of money does not vary, but still fewer would, in a credit transaction, proceed on a supposition at variance with that position. As the economists are accustomed to say, money is the standard of deferred payments. It is also, in the unreflecting apprehension of those who have practically to deal with wealth phenomena, felt to be the standard and inflexible measure of wealth. The fact that this converntional usage is embodied in law acts acts greatly to fortify the naive acceptance of money and price as the definitive terms of wealth. See pp. 82–86 above.

15. Cf. Knies, Geld and Credit, vol. II, ch. VI, sec. C, especially pp. 303 et seq.

16. The enhancement of the market value of the output does not, in fact, keep pace with the inflation of business capital during a period of speculative advance. In order that it should do so, and afford nominal earnings proportionate to the inflated capital, it would be necessary that incomes should increase proportionately to the inflation of capital; but, even if this happened, the expenses of production would thereby be so increased (through the advance of wages and the like) as to offset the entire of values for all consumptive goods and leave only the advance in the values of productive goods as a net margin from which to draw an increase of earnings. The discrepancy under discussion, however, is not due entirely to the presence of credit, and a fully detailed analysis of the causes out of which it arises can, therefore, not properly be presented in this place.

17. So long as the rating of the capitalized property remains undisturbed, the formual which expresses the creditors' claim maintain the form given above. It then signifies nothing more than that the creditors hold a claim on such a proportion of the aggregate capitalized property involved as their advances bear to the aggreage capitalization. But so soon as a rerating of the capitalized property enters the problem the formula becomes

$$\text{loans}/(\text{capitalization} + \Delta \text{capitalization})$$

or $\text{loans}/(\text{capitalization} - \Delta \text{capitalization})$,

according as the rerating of capitalization is in the direction of enhancement or depreciation: $1/(\text{cap} + \Delta \text{cap})$ or $1/(\text{cap} - \Delta \text{cap})$. During brisk times, when capitalization advances, the claim represented by a given loan covers a decreasing proportion of the aggregate capitalized property involved $1/(\text{cap} + \Delta \text{cap})$; the denominator increases and teh quotient consequently decreases. Whereas, in a period of liquidation the ratio of the creditors' claim to the aggregate capitalization increases by force of the lowered rating of the capitalized property $1/(\text{cap} - \Delta \text{cap})$.

18. All those who, at a period of liquidation, are holders of fluent funds or of claims to fixed sums of money are, for the present purpose, in the position of creditors.

19. This disregards the indirect effects of a speculative advance in the way of heightened intensity of application and fuller employment of the industrial plant.

20. See chapter VI.

21. The question of "stock watering" "overcapitalization" and the like is scarcely pertinent in the case of a large industrial corporation financed as the modern situation demands. Under modern circumstances the common stock can scarcely fail to be all "water", unless in a small concern or under incompetent

management. Nothing but "water" – under the name of good–will – belongs in the common stock; whereas the preferred stock, which represents material equipment, is a debenture. "Overcapitalization," on the other hand, if it means anything under modern business conditions, must mean overcapitalization as compared with earning–capacity, for there is nothing else pertinent to compare it with; and earning–capacity fluctuates, while the basis (interest rates) on which the earning–capacity is to be capitalized also fluctuates independently.

In effect, the adjustment of capitalization to earning–capacity is taken care of by the market quotations of stock and other securities; and no other method of adjustment is of any avail, because capitalization is a question of value, and market quotations are the last resort in questions of value. The value of any stock listed on the exchange, or otherwise subject to purchase and sale, fluctuates from time to time; which comes to the same thing as saying that the effectual capitalization of the concern, represented by the securities quoted, fluctuates from time to time. It fluctuates more or less, sometimes very slowly, but always at least so much as to compensate the long–period fluctuations of discount rates in the money market; which means that the purchase price of a given fractional interest in the corporation as a going concern fluctuates so as to equate it with the capitalized value of its putative earning–capacity, computed at current rates of discount and allowing for risks. Cf. Report of the Industrial Commission, vol. I. p. 587 (Testimony of Rogers); vol. XIII. pp. 106–107 (Testimony of E.R. Chapman). See also Chapter VI below.

22. See, e.g. Emery, Speculation on the Stock and Produce Exchanges of the United States, ch. IV; Hadley, Economics, ch. IV.

23. Report of the Industrial Commission, vol. I, (Testimony of W.H. Moore) pp. 960–963, (W.E. Reis) p. 949, (Gates) p. 1032; vol. IX. (T.L. Greene) p. 491; vol. XIII, p. viii, with corresponding testimony. See also Chapter VI below.

24. Report of the Industrial Commission, vol. I (Testimony of Dodd) pp. 1054–1055, 1057, 1058–1059, (Gates) pp. 1021–1022; vol. XIII, p. ix, with testimony.

25. Report of the Industrial Commission, vol. I (Testimony of Dos Passos) p. 1179; vol. XIII (C.R. Flint) p. 48. Testimony to the same effect recurs elsewhere in the Report. See p. 125, n. 1 above.

26. See Chapter VI below.

Chapter 6. Modern Business Capital

What has been said on the use of loan credit has anticipated much of what is peculiar in modern business capital. Such is necessarily the case, since it is in the extensive use of credit that the later phases of the management of capital contrast most strikingly with the corresponding features of earlier business traffic. To follow the terminological precedents set by German writers, the late–modern scheme of economic life is a "credit economy," as contrasted with the "money economy" that characterizes early–modern times. The nature of business capital and its relations to the industrial process under the later, more fully developed, credit economy is in some degree different from what it was before the full and free use of credit came to occupy its present central position in business traffic; and more particularly is it at variance with the theoretical expositions of the economists of the past generation.

It has been the habit of economists and others to speak of "capital" as a stock of the material means by which industry is carried on, – industrial equipment, raw materials, and means of subsistence. This view is carried over from the situation in which business and industry stood at the time of Adam Smith and of the generation before Adam Smith, from whose scheme of life and of thought he drew the commonplace materials and conceptions with which his speculations were occupied. It further carries over the point of view occupied by Adam Smith and the generation to whom he addressed his speculations. That is to say, the received theoretical formulations regarding business capital and its relations to industry proceed on the circumstances that prevailed in the days of the "money economy," before credit and the modern corporation methods became of first-class consequence in economic affairs. They canvass these matters from the point of view of the material welfare of the community at large, as seen from the standpoint of the utilitarian philosophy. In this system of social philosophy the welfare of the community at large is accepted as the central and tone-giving interest, about which a comprehensive, harmonious order of nature circles and gravitates. These early speculations on business traffic turn about the bearing of this traffic upon the wealth of nations, particularly as the wealth of nations would stand in a "natural" scheme of things, in which all things should work together for the welfare of mankind.

The theory, or what there is in the way of a theory, of business capital in the received body of doctrines is worked out from the point of view and for the theoretical purposes of the eighteenth century scheme of natural liberty, natural rights, and natural law; and the received theorems concerning the part played by capital and by the capitalist are substantially of the character of laws of nature, as that term was understood during the period to which these theorems owe their genesis. What these received theorems declare concerning the nature and normal function of capital and of the capitalist need not be recited here; their content is familiar enough to all readers, lay and learned. Also the merits of such a point of view for purposes of economic theory, and the adequacy of the received concept of capital for the purposes to which it was originally applied, need not detain the inquiry. Modern business management does not take that point of view, nor does "capital" carry such a meaning to the modern business man; because the guiding circumstances under which modern business is carried on are not those supposed to be given by a beneficent order of nature, nor do the controlling purposes of business traffic include that general well-being which constituted the final term of Adam Smith's social philosophy.

As a business proposition, "capital" means a fund of money values; and since the credit economy and corporation finance have come to be the ruling factors in industrial business, this fund of money values (taken as an aggregate) bears but a remote and fluctuating relation to the industrial equipment and the other items which may (perhaps properly) be included under the old-fashioned concept of industrial capital.(1*)

Capital has been spoken of as the capitalized (aggregated) cost of industrial equipment, etc.,(2*) a view which had its significance for economic theory a hundred years ago; but since corporation finance has come to pervade the management of business this view is no longer of particular use for a theoretical handling of the facts. To avoid the tedium of argument it may be conceded that under the old dispensation, of partnerships and individual management in business, the basis of capitalization was the cost of the material equipment owned by any given concern; and so far as the methods of partnership and private firms still prevails such may still be the current method of capitalization, especially de jure. But in so far as business procedure and business conceptions have been shaped in the image of the modem corporation (or limited liability company), the basis of capitalization has gradually shifted, until the basis is now no longer given by the cost of material equipment owned, but by the earning-capacity of the corporation as a going concern.(3*)

A given corporation's capital is, of course, de jure a magnitude fixed in the past by an act of legislature chartering the company, or by an issuance of stock by the company under the terms of its charter or of the acts which enable it. But this de jure capitalization is nominal only, and there are few, if any, cases in which the effective capital of a company coincides with its de jure capital. Such could be the case only so long as all the securities which go to make up the company's capital were quoted at par on the market. The effective capitalization of any modern company, that is to say, the capitalization which is effective for current business purposes as distinct from the formal requirements of the charter, is given by the quotations of the company's securities, or by some similar but less overt market valuation in case the company's capital is not quotable on the market. The effective (business) capitalization, as distinct from the de jure capitalization, is not fixed permanently and inflexibly by a past act of incorporation or stock issue. It is fixed for the time being only, by an ever recurring valuation of the company's properties, tangible and intangible, on the basis of their earning-capacity. (4*)

In this capitalization of earning-capacity the nucleus of the capitalization is. not the cost of the plant, but the concern's good-will, so called, as has appeared in the last preceding chapter.(5*) "Good-will" is a somewhat extensible term, and latterly it has a more comprehensive meaning than it once had. Its meaning has, in fact, been gradually extended to meet the requirements of modern business methods. Various items, of very diverse character, are to be included under the head of "good-will"; but the items included have this much in common that they are "immaterial wealth," "intangible assets"; which, it may parenthetically be remarked, signifies among other things that these assets are not serviceable to the community, but only to their owners. Good-will taken in its wider meaning comprises such things as established customary business relations, reputation for upright dealing, franchises and privileges, trade-marks, brands, patent rights, copyrights, exclusive use of special processes guarded by law or by secrecy, exclusive control of particular sources of materials. All these items give a differential advantage to their owners, but they are of no aggregate advantage to the community.(6*) They are wealth to the individuals concerned differential wealth; but they make no part of the wealth of nations.(7*)

It is in the industrial corporations that this capitalization of good-will is seen to the best advantage - including, under the term "industrial corporations," railway companies, iron and steel concerns, mines, etc., as well as what are known in the stock market specifically as "industrials." The corporation is, of course, not the only form of business concern in the industrial field, but it is the typical, characteristic form of business organization for the management of industry in modem times, and the peculiarities of modem capital are therefore best seen in these modern corporations. Many of these corporations have grown out of partnerships and firms previously existing, and such is still the genesis of many of the corporations that come forward from time to time. In such a case of conversion from partnership or firm to corporation the rule is that the new corporation takes over a body of good-will, under one form and name or another, previously pertaining to the partnership which it displaces. Conversely, when a flourishing partnership or similar private firm has gained an assured footing of good-will, in the way of any or all of the items enumerated under that term above, its lot, as prescribed by modern business exigencies, is to go up into a corporation, either by simple conversion into the corporate form or through coalition with other firms into a larger corporate whole. There is in this matter no hard and fast rule, of course. On the one hand, the approved methods of corporation finance may in some measure be resorted to by a private firm, Without formal conversion of the concern into the corporate form; and on the other hand, an incorporated company may continue to carry on its business after the manner usual with privately owned concerns. But taken by and large, it will be found that with the assumption of the corporate form is associated a more modern method of capitalization and a freer use of credit. The advantages which the corporate form offers in these respects are commonly not neglected. The more archaic forms of organization and business management, in which recourse is commonly not had to the characteristic methods of corporation finance, prevail chiefly in those "backward" lines of industry in which monopoly or other differential advantages of an intangible nature are not readily attainable; such, e.g., as farming, fishing, local merchandising, and the minor mechanical trades and occupations. In this range of industries large (corporate) organization has hitherto been virtually impracticable, and here at the same time differential advantages, of the nature of good-will (as indicated above), are relatively scant and precarious. Where extensive differential advantages of this kind come in, the corporate form of organization is also likely to come in.

The cases are also frequent where a corporation starts out full-fledged from the beginning, without derivation from a previously existing private firm. Where this happens, the start is commonly made with some substantial body of immaterial goods on which to build up the capitalization; it may be a franchise, as in the case of a railway, telegraph, telephone, street-car, gas, or water company; or it may be the control of peculiar sources of material, as in the case of an oil or natural gas company, or a salt, coal, iron, or lumber company; or it may be a special industrial process, patented or secret; or it may be several of these. When a corporation begins its life history without such a body of immaterial differential advantages, the endeavors of its management are early directed to working up a basis of good-will in the way of trade-marks, clientele, and trade connections which will place it in something of a monopoly position, locally or generally (8*) Should the management not succeed in these endeavors to gain an assured footing on some such "immaterial" ground, its chances of success among rival corporations are precarious, its standing is insecure, and its managers have not accomplished what is looked for at their hands. The substantial foundation of the industrial corporation is its immaterial assets.

The typical modern industrial corporation is a concern of sufficient magnitude to be of something more than barely local consequence, and extends its trade relations beyond the range of the personal contact of its directive officials. Its properties and its debts are also commonly owned, in part at least, by persons who stand in no direct personal relation to the board of managers. In an up-to-date corporation of this character the typical make-up of the corporate capital, or capitalization, is somewhat as follows: The common stock approximately covers the immaterial properties of the concern, unless these immaterial properties are disproportionately large and valuable; in case of a relatively small and local corporation the common stock will ordinarily somewhat more than cover the value of the immaterial property and comprise something of the plant; in case of the larger concerns the converse is likely to be true, so that here the immaterial property, intangible assets, is made to serve in some measure as a basis for other securities as well as for the common stock. The common stock, typically, represents intangible assets and is accounted for by valuable trade-marks, patents, processes, franchises, etc. Whatever material properties, tangible assets, are in hand or to be acquired are covered by preferred stock or other debentures. The various forms of debentures account for the material equipment and the working capital (the latter item corresponding roughly to the economists' categories of raw materials, wages fund, and the like). Of these debentures the preferred stock is the most characteristic modern development. It is, de jure, counted as a constituent of the concern's capital and the principal is not repayable; in this (legal) respect it is not an evidence of debt or a credit instrument.(9*) But it has little voice in the direction of the concern's business policy.(10*) In practice the management rests chiefly on the holdings of common stock. This is due in part to the fact that the preferred bears a stated rate of dividends and is therefore taken up by scattered purchasers as an investment security to a greater extent than the common. In this (practical) respect it amounts to a debenture. Its practical character as a debenture is shown by the stated rate of dividends, and where it is "cumulative" that feature adds a further step of assimilation to the ordinary class of debentures. Indeed, in point of practical effect preferred stock is in some respects commonly a more pronounced credit instrument than the ordinary mortgage; it alienates the control of the property which it represents more effectually than the ordinary bond or mortgage loan, in that it may practically be a debt which, by its own terms, cannot be collected, so that by its own terms it may convey a credit extension from the holder to the issuing corporation in perpetuity. Its effect is to convey the discretionary control of the material properties which it is held to represent into the hands of the holders of the common stock of the concern. The discretionary management of the corporate capital is, by this device, quite as effectually as by the use of ordinary credit instruments, vested in the common stock, which is held to represent the corporation's goodwill. The discretionary disposal of the entire capital vests in securities representing the intangible assets. In this sense, then, the nucleus of the modern corporate capitalization is the immaterial goods covered by the common stock.(11*)

This method of capitalization, therefore, effects a somewhat thoroughgoing separation between the management and the ownership of the industrial equipment. Roughly speaking, under corporate organization the owners of the industrial material have no voice in its management, and where preferred stock is a large constituent of the capital this alienation of control on the parts of the owners may be, by so much, irrevocable. Preferred stock is, practically, a device for placing the property it represents in perpetual trust with the holders of the common stock, and, with certain qualifications, these trustees are not answerable for the administration of the property to their trustors. The property relation of the owners to their property is at this point attenuated to an extreme degree. For most business purposes, it should be added, the capital covered by other forms of debentures is in much the same position as that covered by the preferred stock.(12*)

The various descriptions of securities which in this way represent corporate capital are quotable on the market and are subject to market fluctuations; whereby it comes about that the aggregate effective magnitude of the corporate capital varies with the tone of the market, with the manoeuvres of the business men to whom is delegated the management of the companies, and with the accidents of the seasons and the chances of peace and war. Accordingly, the amount of the business capital of a given concern, or of the business community as a whole, varies in magnitude in great measure independently of the mechanical facts of industry, as was noted above in speaking of loan credit.(13*) The market fluctuations in the amount of capital proceed on variations of confidence on the part of the investors, on current belief as to the probable policy or tactics of the business men in control, on forecasts as to the seasons and the tactics of the guild of politicians, and on the indeterminable, largely instinctive, shifting movements of public sentiment and apprehension. So that under modern conditions the magnitude of the business capital and its mutations from day to day are in great measure a question of folk psychology rather than of material fact.

But in this uncertain and shifting relation of the business capital to the material equipment there are one or two points which may be set down as fairly secure. Since the credit instruments involved in modern capitalization may be used as collateral for a further credit extension, as noted in the chapter on loan credit,(14*) the aggregate nominal capital in hand at a given time is, normally, larger by an appreciable amount than the aggregate value of the material properties involved;(15*) and at the same time the current value of these material properties is also greater than it would be in the absence of that credit financiering for which corporate capitalization affords a basis.(16*)

German writers have familiarized economic readers with the terms "credit economy," "money economy" (Geldwirtschaft), and "natural economy" (Naturalwirtschaft), the later–modern scheme of economic life being characterized as a "credit economy." What characterizes the early–modern scheme, the "money economy," and sets it off in contrast with the natural economy (distribution in kind) that went before it in West–European culture, is the ubiquitous resort to the market as a vent for products and a source of supply of goods. The characteristic feature of this money economy is the goods market. About the goods market business and industrial interests turn in early modern times; and to this early–modern system of industrial life the current doctrines of political economy are adapted, as indicated above.

The credit economy – the scheme of economic life of the immediate past and the present – has made an advance over the money economy in the respect which chiefly distinguishes the latter. The goods market, of course, in absolute terms is still as powerful an economic factor as ever, but it is no longer the dominant factor in business and industrial traffic, as it once was. The capital market has taken the first place in this respect. The capital market is the modern economic feature which makes and identifies the higher "credit economy" as such. In this credit economy resort is habitually had to the market as a vent for accumulated money values and a source of supply of capital.(17*)

Trading under the old regime was a traffic in goods; under the new regime there is added, as the dominant and characteristic trait, trading in capital. Both in the capital and in the goods market there are professional traders, as well as buyers and sellers who resort to the market to dispose of their holdings and to supply their needs of what the market affords. In either class of trading the ends sought by those engaged in the business are generically the same. The endeavors of those who are in the business of trading, who buy in order to sell and sell in order to buy, are directed to the pecuniary gain that is to be got through an advantageous discrepancy between the price paid and the price obtained; but on the part of those who resort to the market to supply their needs the end sought is not the same in the two cases. The last buyer of goods buys for consumption, but the last negotiator of capital buys for the sake of the ulterior profit; in substance he buys in order to sell again at an advance. The advance which he has in view is to come out of the prospective earnings of the capital for which he negotiates. What he has in view as his ulterior end in the transaction is the conversion of the values for which he negotiates into a larger outcome of money values, – whatever process of production and the like may intervene between the inception and the goal of his traffic.(18*)

The value of any given block of capital, therefore, turns on its earning-capacity; or, as the mathematical expression has it, the value of capital is a function of its earning-capacity, (19*) not of its prime cost or of its mechanical efficiency. It is only more remotely, and through the mediation of the earning-capacity, that these last-named factors sensibly affect the value of the capital. This earning-capacity of capital depends in its turn, not so much on the mechanical efficiency of the valuable items bought and sold in the capital market, as on the tension of the market for goods. To recur to an expression already employed in a similar connection, the question of earning-capacity of capital relates primarily to its effectiveness for purposes of vendibility, and only at the second remove to its effectiveness in the way of material serviceability. But the earning-capacity which in this way affords ground for the valuation of marketable capital (or for the market capitalization of the securities bought and sold) is not its past or actual earning-capacity, but its presumptive future earning-capacity; so that the fluctuations in the capital market – the varying market capitalization of securities – turn about imagined future events. The forecast in the case may be more or less sagacious, but, however sagacious, it retains the character of a forecast based on other grounds besides the computation of past results.

All capital which is put on the market is in this way subjected to an interminable process of valuation and revaluation – i.e. a capitalization and recapitalization – on the basis of its presumptive earning-capacity, whereby it all assumes more or less of a character of intangibility. But the most elusive and intangible items of this marketable capital are, of course, those items which consist of capitalized good-will, since these are intangible goods from start to finish. It is upon this factor of good-will in capital that a change in presumptive earning-capacity falls most immediately, and this factor shows the widest and freest market fluctuations. The variations in the capitalized value of merchantable good-will are relatively wide and unstable, as is shown by the quotations of common stock.

In the capital market the commodity in which trading is done, then, is the capitalized putative earning-capacity of the property covered by the securities bought and sold. This property is in part tangible, in part intangible, the two categories being seldom clearly distinguishable. The items bought and sold are put into merchantable form by being standardized in terms of money and subdivided into convenient imaginary shares, which greatly facilitates the traffic. The earning-capacity on which the market capitalization runs and about which the traffic in merchantable capital turns is a putative earning-capacity. It follows that this putative earning-capacity of a given block of capital, as it takes shape in the surmises of outside investors, may differ appreciably from the actual earning-capacity of the capital as known to its managers; and it may readily be to the latter's interest that such a discrepancy between actual and imputed earning-capacity should arise.(20*) When, e.g., the putative earning-capacity of the capital covered by a given line of securities, as shown by the market quotations, rises appreciably above what is known to its managers to be its actual earning-capacity, the latter may find their advantage in selling out, or even in selling short; while in the converse case they will be inclined to buy. Moreover, putative earning-capacity is the outcome of many surmises with respect to prospective earnings and the like; and these surmises will vary from one man to the next, since they proceed on an imperfect, largely conjectural, knowledge of present earning-capacity and on the still more imperfectly known future course of the goods market and of corporate policy. Hence sales of securities are frequent, both because outsiders vary in their estimates and forecasts, and because the information of the outsiders does not coincide with that of the insiders. The consequence is that a given block of capital, representing, e.g., a controlling interest in a given industrial enterprise, may, and in practice it commonly will, change owners much more frequently than a given industrial plant was wont to change owners under the old regime, before the fully developed corporation finance came to occupy the field of industrial business.(21*)

It follows, further, that under these circumstances the men who have the management of such an industrial enterprise, capitalized and quotable on the market, will be able to induce a discrepancy between the putative and the actual earning-capacity, by expedients well known and approved for the purpose. Partial information, as well as misinformation, sagaciously given out at a critical juncture, will go far toward producing a favorable temporary discrepancy of this kind, and so enabling the managers to buy or sell the securities of the concern with advantage to themselves. If they are shrewd business men, as they commonly are, they will aim to manage the affairs of the concern with a view to an advantageous purchase and sale of its capital rather than with a view to the future prosperity of the concern, or to the continued advantageous sale of the output of goods or services produced by the industrial use of this capital.

That is to say, the interest of the managers of a modern corporation need not coincide with the permanent interest of the corporation as a going concern; neither does it coincide with the interest which the community at large has in the efficient management of the concern as an industrial enterprise. It is to the interest of the community at large that the enterprise should be so managed as to give the best and largest possible output of goods or services; whereas the interest of the corporation as a going concern is that it be managed with a view to maintaining its efficiency and selling as large an output as may be at the best prices obtainable in the long run; but the interest of the managers, and of the owners for the time being, is to so manage the enterprise as to enable them to buy it up or to sell out as expeditiously and as advantageously as may be. The interest of the community at large demands industrial efficiency and serviceability of the product; while the business interest of the concern as such demands vendibility of the product; and the interest of those men who have the final discretion in the management of these corporate enterprises demands vendibility of the corporate capital. The community's interest demands that there should be a favorable difference between the material cost and the material serviceability of the output; the corporation's interest demands a favorable pecuniary difference between expenses and receipts, cost and sale price of the output; the corporation directorate's interest is that there should be a discrepancy, favorable for purchase or for sale as the case may be, between the actual and the putative earning-capacity of the corporation's capital.

It has been noted in an earlier chapter that there unavoidably results a discrepancy, not uncommonly a divergence, between the industrial needs of the community and the business needs of the corporations. Under the regime of the old-fashioned "money economy," with partnership methods and private ownership of industrial enterprises, the discretionary control of the industrial processes is in the hands of men whose interest in the industry is removed by one degree from the interests of the community at large. But under the regime of the more adequately developed "credit economy," with vendible corporate capital,(22*) the interest of the men who hold the discretion in industrial affairs is removed by one degree from that of the concerns under their management, and by two degrees from the interests of the community at large.

The business interest of the managers demands, not serviceability of the output, nor even vendibility of the output, but an advantageous discrepancy in the price of the capital which they manage. The ready vendibility of corporate capital has in great measure dissociated the business interest of the directorate from that of the corporation whose affairs they direct and whose business policy they dictate, and has led them to centre their endeavors upon the discrepancy between the actual and the putative earning-capacity rather than upon the permanent efficiency of the concern. Their connection with the concern is essentially transient; it can be terminated speedily and silently whenever their private fortune demands its severance. Instances are abundant, more particularly in railway management, where this discrepancy between the business interest of the concern and the private business interest of the managers for the time being has led to very picturesque developments, such as could not occur if the interests of the management were bound up with those of the corporation in the manner and degree that once prevailed. The fact is significant that the more frequent and striking instances of such management of corporate affairs for private ends have hitherto occurred in railroading, at the same time that the methods and expedients of modern corporation finance have also first and most widely reached a fair degree of maturity in railroading. It holds out a suggestion as to what may fairly be looked for when corporation finance shall have made itself more thoroughly at home in the "industrials" proper. Indeed, the field of the "industrials" is by no means barren of instances comparable with the maturer and more sagacious railroad financiering.(23*)

The stock market interest of those men who have the management of industrial corporations is a wide and multifarious one. It is not confined to the profitable purchase and sale of properties whose management they may have in hand. They are also interested in making or marring various movements of coalition or reorganization, and to this ulterior end it is incumbent on them to "manipulate" securities with a view to buying and selling in such a manner as to gain control of certain lines of securities.(24*) Hence it is a rule of this class of business traffic to cultivate appearance, − to avoid, or sometimes to court, the appearance of sin. So that under this leadership the course of industrial affairs is, in great measure, if not altogether, guided with a view to a plausible appearance of prosperity or of adversity, as the case may be. Under given circumstances it may as well become the aim of men in control to make an adverse showing as a favorable one. The higher exigencies of the captain of industry's personal fortunes, as distinct from those of the corporation controlled by him, may from time to time be best sewed by an apparent, if not an actual, mismanagement of industrial affairs. A convincing appearance of decline or disaster will lower the putative earning−capacity of the concern below its real earning−capacity and so will afford an advantageous opportunity for buying with a view to future advance or with a view to strategic control. Various other expedients looking to the like outcome are well known to the craft, besides bona fide mismanagement. A given line of securities may be temporarily depressed by less heroic tactics; but the point in question here is the fact that under this system of corporation finance the affairs of the corporation are in good part managed for tactical ends which are of interest to the manager rather than to the corporation as a going concern.

What was said in speaking of credit extension without a determinate time interval (25*) applies to this class of business, with a slight change of phrase. In this higher development of corporation finance, in the manipulations of vendible capital, the interval of the turnover spoken of above becomes an indeterminate factor. The gains of the business come to have but an uncertain and shifty relation to the lapse of time and cannot well be calculated per cent. per time−unit. There is, therefore, on these higher levels of business management, properly speaking no ascertainable ordinary rate of earnings. The capital which may be distinctively regarded as operative in the business of manipulation, the valuable items specifically employed in the traffic in vendible corporate capital, is made up of the operator's good−will and his financial solvency. Solvency on a large scale is requisite to carrying on traffic of this class, but the collateral on which this extensive solvency constructively rests is to but a partial extent drawn into the business as a basis for an actual credit extension. What counts in the case is the solvency of the operator rather than an outright resort to the credit extension which this solvency might afford. The working capital involved in these transactions is accordingly of a peculiarly elusive character, and the time element in the use of this capital is hard to determine, if such a time element can properly be said to enter into the case at all.

More in detail, the business man in pursuit of gain along this line must, in the ordinary case, be possessed of large holdings of property, this being the basis of the solvency necessary to the business. These holdings are commonly in the form of securities in the concern whose vendible capital is the subject of his traffic, as well as in other corporations. These securities represent capital, tangible and intangible, which is already employed in the ordinary business of the concern by which they have been issued; the capital, therefore, is already in use to the full extent and is presumably yielding the ordinary rate of earnings. But the solvency for which the ownership of this capital affords a basis may further be useful in enabling the owner to carry on a traffic in vendible corporate capital without withdrawing any appreciable portion of his holdings from the lucrative investments in which they have been placed. In other words, he is able, under modern circumstances, to make a secondary use of his investments for the purpose of trading in vendible corporate capital; but this secondary use of investments bears no hard and fast quantitative relation to the investments in question, nor does it in any determinate way interfere with the ordinary employment of this invested capital in the commonplace conduct of the corporations' business traffic. The capital employed, as well as the potential credit extension which it affords for the purposes of this higher business traffic, is therefore in a peculiar degree intangible, and, in respect of its amount, highly elusive.

Much the same is true of the good-will employed in this traffic. It is also in good part good-will which already serves the purposes of the commonplace business traffic of the corporations on whose securities the business man in question rests his solvency. So that in this higher business traffic the good-will engaged is also here turned to a secondary use. The business economies which are in this way made practicable by a reduplication of uses and made to inure to the greater business men's profit are of great magnitude; but the magnificent additions which are in this way made to the business community's capitalizable forces need scarcely be dwelt on here.

The elusive and flexuous character of the elements of wealth engaged, as well as the absence of an ascertainable ordinary rate of earnings in this line of business, has led economists to speak of this traffic in vendible capital as a "speculative" business.(26*) The mere buying and selling of stocks by outsiders for a rise or a decline is of course a speculative business; it is a typical form of speculative business. But in so far as such buying and selling is carried on by the managers of the corporations whose securities are the subject of the traffic, and especially where the securities are bought and sold with a view to the control of the corporations in question and their management for private, tactical ends, a characterization of the business as "speculative" is inadequate and beside the point. This higher reach of corporation financiering has little if any more of a speculative character than what belongs to the commonplace business management of any industrial enterprise. In all business enterprise that stands in relations with the market and depends on vendibility of its output there is more or less uncertainty as to the outcome.(27*) In this sense all industrial business, as well as commercial business, has something of a speculative character. But it is little to the purpose on that account to lump industrial enterprises and corporation financiering together as "speculative business" and deal with them as if this were their most salient and consequential bearing. What speculative risk there is in these lines of business is incidental, and it neither affords the incentive to engaging in these pursuits nor does it bound the scope of their bearing upon economic affairs. The speculative risk involved is no greater, relatively to the magnitude of the interests involved, in this larger traffic that deals in vendible capital than it is in the ordinary lines of business traffic that deal in vendible products. In both cases there may be speculation, but in both cases it is a side issue. Indeed, as near as one may confidently hold an opinion on so dark a question, the certainty of gain, though perhaps not the relative amount of it, seems rather more assured in the large-scale manipulation of vendible capital than in business management with a view to a vendible product.

What may obscure the question is the fact that the manipulations involved in this traffic in vendible capital commonly impose increased risks upon the business concerns engaged in industry – the corporations whose capital is involved, as well as other firms. The everyday business of the corporations whose securities are involved, as well as of other business concerns engaged in rival or related lines of industry, is rendered more hazardous than it might be in the absence of this financiering traffic in vendible capital. The manipulations carry risk, not so much to the manipulators as such, as to the corporations whose properties are the subject of manipulation; but since the manipulators commonly own but a relatively small proportion of the properties involved or touched by their manipulations, the risks which arise do not fall chiefly on them. To this is to be added, as of prime importance for the whole question, that the manipulators have the advantage of being able, in great part, to foresee the nature, magnitude, and incidence of the risks which they create. Rightly seen, this, of course, goes to say that the increased speculative risk due to the traffic in vendible capital does not fall on that traffic, but on the business enterprise engaged about the output of vendible goods. The traffic in vendible capital is not without its speculative risks, but the risks which it creates fall with relatively greater weight upon the business men who are not immediately concerned in this traffic. Indeed, so secure and lucrative is this class of business, that it is chiefly out of gains accruing, directly and indirectly, from such traffic in vendible capital that the great modern fortunes are being accumulated; and both the rate and the magnitude of these accumulations, whether taken absolutely or relatively to the total increase of wealth, surpass all recorded phenomena of their kind. Nothing so effective for the accumulation of private wealth is known to the history of human culture.

The aim and substantial significance of the "manipulations" of vendible capital here spoken of is an ever recurring recapitalization of the properties involved, whereby the effective capitalization of the corporations whose securities are the subject of the traffic is increased and decreased from time to time. The fluctuations, or pulsations, of this effective capitalization are shown by the market quotations of the securities, as noted above.(28*) It is out of these variations in capitalization that the gains of the traffic arise, and it is also through the means of these variations of capitalization that the business men engaged in this higher finance are enabled to control the fortunes of the corporations and to effect their strategic work of coalition and reorganization of business enterprises. Hence this traffic in vendible capital is the pivotal and dominant factor in the modern situation of business and industry.(29*) It has been noted above that what may be called the working capital on which this higher corporation finance proceeds is made up, chiefly, of two elements: the solvency (and consequent potential credit) of the men engaged, and the "good-will" of these men. Both of these elements are of a somewhat intangible and elusive character, resting, as they do, somewhat indirectly and shiftily on elements already elsewhere engaged in business enterprise. The solvency in question rests in large part on the capital of the corporations whose capitalization is subject to the fluctuations induced by the traffic in vendible capital. It is therefore necessarily a somewhat indeterminate and unstable magnitude. To this is to be added the "floating capital" and banking capital at the disposal of these men. If a common-sense view be taken of the business, the good-will engaged must also be added to the assets. There is involved a very considerable and very valuable body of good-will, appertaining to the financiers engaged and to the financing firms associated with them.(30*) This goodwill and this solvency is capital, for the purpose in hand, as effectually as the good-will and securities incorporated in the capitalization of any corporation engaged in industrial business.

But hitherto this particular category of goodwill has not been formally capitalized. There may be peculiar difficulties in the way of reducing this good-will to the form of a fund, expressing it in terms of a standard unit, and so converting it into quotable common stock, as has been done with the corresponding good-will of incorporated industrial enterprises. So also as regards the body of solvency engaged, – the potential credit, or credit capacity, of the promoters and financiers. Perhaps this latter had best also be treated as an element of good-will; it is difficult to handle under any other, more tangible, conception. It may be difficult to standardize, fund, and capitalize these unstable but highly efficient factors of business enterprise; but the successful capitalization of good-will and credit extensions in the case of the modern industrial corporations argues that this difficulty should not be insurmountable in case an urgent need, – that is to say, the prospect of a profitably vendible result, – should press for a formal capitalization of these peculiar elements of business wealth. There can be no question, e.g., but that the good-will and large solvency belonging to such a firm as J.P. Morgan and Company for the purposes of this class of business enterprise are an extremely valuable and substantial asset, as is also, and more unequivocally, the good-will of the head of that firm. These intangible assets, immaterial goods, should, in all consistency, be reduced to standard units, funded, issued as common stock, and so added to the statistical aggregate of the country's capitalized wealth.

It is safe to affirm that this good-will of the great reorganizer has in some measure entered in capitalized form into the common stock of the United States Steel Corporation, as also into that of some of the other great combinations that have latterly been effected. The "good-will" of Mr Carnegie and his lieutenants, as well as of many other large business men connected with the steel industry, has also no doubt gone to swell the capitalization of the great corporation. But good-will on this higher level of business enterprise has a certain character of inexhaustibility, so that its use and capitalization in one corporation need not, and indeed does not, hinder or diminish the extent to which it may be used and capitalized in any other corporation.(31*) The case is analogous, though scarcely similar, to that of the workmanlike or artistic skill of a handicraftsman, or an artist, which may be embodied in a given product without abating the degree of skill possessed by the workman. Like other good-will, though perhaps in a higher degree of sublimation, it is of a spiritual nature, such that, by virtue of the ubiquity proper to spiritual bodies, the whole of it may undividedly be present in every part of the various structures which it has created. Indeed, the fact of such good-will having been incorporated in capitalized form in the stock of any given corporation seems rather to augment than to diminish the amount at which it may advantageously be capitalized in the stock of the next corporation into which it enters. It has also the correlative spiritual attribute that it may imperceptibly and inscrutably withdraw its animating force from any one of its creatures without thereby altering the material circumstances of the corporation which suffers such an intangible shrinkage of its forces.

There can be no question but that the good-will of the various great organizers and their financiering houses has repeatedly been capitalized, probably to its full amount, in the common stock of the various corporations which they have created; but taken in the sense of an asset belonging to the financing house as a corporation, it is not known that this item of immaterial wealth has yet been formally capitalized and offered in quotable shares on the market or included in the schedules of personal property.(32*)

The sublimation of business capital that has been going forward in recent times has grave consequences for the owners of property as well as for the conduct of industry. In so far as invested property is managed by the methods of modem corporation finance, it is evident that the management is separated from the ownership of the property, more and more widely as the scope of corporation finance widens. The discretion, the management, lies in the hands of the holders of the intangible forms of property; and with the extension of corporation methods it is increasingly true that this management, again, centres in the hands of those greater business men who hold large blocks of these intangible assets. The reach of a business man's discretionary control, under corporation methods, is not proportioned simply to the amount of his holdings. If his holdings are relatively small, they give him virtually no discretion. Whereas if they are relatively large, they may give him a business discretion of much more than a proportionate reach. The effective reach of a business man's discretion might be said to increase as the square of his holdings; although this is to be taken as a suggestive characterization rather than as an exact formula.

Among the holdings of industrial property that count in this way toward control of the business situation, the intangible assets (represented by common stock, good-will, and the like) are chiefly of consequence. Hence follow these two results: the fortunes of property owners are in large measure dependent on the discretion of others the owners of intangible property; and the management of the industrial equipment tends strongly to centre in the hands of men who do not own the industrial equipment, and who have only a remote interest in the efficient working of this equipment. The property of those who own less, or who own only material goods, is administered by those who own more, especially of immaterial goods; and the material processes of industry are under the control of men whose interest centres on an increased value of the immaterial assets.(33*)

NOTES:

1. The distinction between business capital and "industrial capital" or "capital goods" has been shown by Knies, Geld und Credit, vol. I. ch. II. pp. 40-60. Distinctions having a very similar erect in some bearings are to be found in Rodbertus ("private capital" and "national capital"), in Bohm-Bawerk ("acquisitive capital" and "productive capital," or "private capital" and "social capital"), in Clark ("capital" and "capital goods"). Similar distinctions are made by various writers to help out the incompetency of the received definition of the term. The merit of these distinctions does not concern the present inquiry, since they are made for other purposes than that here aimed at. The distinction made above is not an attempt to recast the terminology of economic theory, but is simply an expedient for present use. It amounts to an unqualified acceptance of the concept (more or less well defined) which business men habitually attach to the term "capital." Mr F.A. Fetter has lately spoken for the restriction of "capital," as a technical term, practically to what is here called "business capital." Mr Fetter's "capital concept," however, should probably not be taken to cover intangible assets. The practical distinction is visible in the testimony of various

witnesses before the Industrial Commission, as also in the special report on "Securities," Report, vol. XIII.

2. Even so late and competent a student of corporate capital as J. von Korosi is bound by this antique preconception, and his work has suffered in consequence. See Finanzielle Ergebnisse der Actiengesellschaften, p. 3.

3. This state of the case is brought out, in a veiled manner, by the well-known proposition, expounded in varying form by various writers, that the cost of equipment on which capitalization must, in theory, take place is the cost of reproduction of all valuable items included, tangible and intangible.

4. "Nothing is more illusive and delusive than the idea that if a corporation's stock be only paid in in money at the outset it is therefore better off than one that has issued its stock for property that could not be converted for one cent on the dollar. The question is what assets the corporation has got at the time of the particular transaction, and that can be ascertained only by present inquiry." – Testimony of F.L. Stetson, Report of the Industrial Commission, vol. I. p. 976. Cf. Meade, Trust Finance, ch. XVI and XVIII.

5. Earning-capacity is practically accepted as the effective basis of capitalization for corporate business concerns, particularly for those whose securities are quoted on the market. It is in the stock market that this effective capitalization takes place. But the law does not recognize such a basis of capitalization; nor are business men generally ready to adopt it in set form, although they constantly have recourse to it, in effect, in operations of investment and of credit extension. Cf. Report of the Industrial Commission, vol. I. pp. 6, 17, 21 (Test. F.B. Thurber); p. 967 (Test. F.L. Stetson); pp. 585-587 (Test. H.H. Rogers); pp. 110-111, 124 (Test. H.O. Havemeyer); pp. 1021, 1032 (Test. J.W. Gates); pp. 1054-1055 (Test S. Dodd); vol. XIII. pp. 287-288 (Test. H. Burn); p. 388 (Test. J. Morris); pp. 107-108 (Test. E.R. Chapman). See Quarterly Journal of Economics, February 1903, pp. 344-345, "The Holyoke Water Case," for an illustrative decision.

6. The advantages afforded their owners by these intangible assets have latterly been discussed by economists under such headings as "Rent" or "Quasi-Rent." These discussions, it is believed, are of great theoretical weight. In business practice, however, the items in question are treated as capital, which must avail as an excuse for including them here in business Capital.

7. Compare Bohm-Bawerk's and Clark's distinctions between "private" and "social" capital, and between "capital" and "capital goods."

8. See Chapter III above.

9. On the books of the corporation it is, of course, carried as an item of liability; as is the common stock; but that is a technical expedient of accountancy, and does not touch the substantial question.

10. See testimony of various witnesses on "Capitalization" before the Industrial Commission, vols. I, IX, XIII.

11. As one of many illustrative cases, the Rubber Goods Manufacturing Company may be taken as a typical instance of a corporation organized in a conservative but up-to-date manner for permanent success and stable value. Its authorized issue of stock is $25,000,000 7 per cent cumulative preferred, and $25,000,000 common. The actual issue in 1901 was about $8,000,000 preferred and $17,000,000 common, of which the preferred was presumed to cover the value of the tangible assets. Another coalition organized by the same promoter (Mr C.R. Flint), the American Chicle Company, illustrates the same general feature. The preferred stock of this company ($3,000,000) "in round numbers was three times the amount of tangible assets," while the common stock ($6,000,000) represents no tangible assets. The aggregate capitalization is about nine times the tangible assets. The witness says that this corporation has been proved by events to be

"on a conservative basis from the fact that the company has paid 8 per cent on its common stock," which has been selling at 80. – Report of the Industrial Commission, vol. XIII. pp. 47, 50.

12. It may be argued that this identification of the common stock with the intangible assets holds true in theory only, in the sense that this is the view held by the business men who occupy themselves with such matters; while in point of fact no distinction of this nature between common and preferred stock is or can practically be maintained after the stock has once found its way into the market. It might seem, in other words, that when the stock has once passed the stage of organization and gone into the hands of the purchasers, each share represents nothing but an undivided interest in the aggregate capitalization of the concern, so that the particular item of wealth represented by a given share or given form of security can no longer be identified.

On the face of the situation such appears to be the case, but there are facts which argue for the view set out above. It is, e.g., well known that whenever circumstances arise which immediately affect the value of the good-will of a corporation, it is the quotations of the common stock that first and most decidedly are affected. If the goodwill of the concern makes a great and rapid gain, e.g. through manoeuvres which put it in a position of monopoly or through changes in the goods market which greatly increase the demand for the concern's product, and the like, it is the quotation of the common stock that measures and registers the advantage which thereby accrues to the concern, and the market fluctuation of the common stock is likewise the instrument by means of which manipulations are carried through that affect these intangible assets. At the same time this rule does not hold hard and fast, as is seen in case of a liquidation when the capital of the concern may have shrunk to such dimensions that the entire capital, including the intangible assets, will no more than satisfy the claims represented by the debentures. Still, in point of practical fact, the (theoretical) preconception of businessmen that the common stock in some intelligible sense covers the intangible assets is fairly borne out by everyday experience, taken by and large.

A curious parallel might be traced between the current endeavors of the business community to organize and manage the industrial equipment on the basis of immaterial assets and the medieval business perplexities and actions relative to loans on interest. In both cases the business community has had to face untried exigencies together with a popular, traditional prejudice that discountenances the expedients by which these exigencies are to be met. The medieval presumption was that the management of productive goods and the profits accruing from their use must go to their users. (Cf. Ashley, Economic History, vol. I. ch. III, vol. II ch. VI; Endemann, Die nationalokonomische Grundsatze der kanonistischen Lehre.) The modern presumption is that the management of the equipment and the gains from such management must vest in the owner. The modern exigencies decide that the equipment must be managed by others than the owners and that profits must largely accrue to those who financially manage the concern. The expedient by which this result is sought to be reached is the fiction of intangible assets and the impersonal, irrevocable credit extension covered by the preferred stock. The effect is to dissociate ownership from management. This is the necessary outcome of a "credit economy" consistently and fully carried through. The management of the material equipment of industry is thrown into the hands of those who own the immaterial wealth; that is to say, those who own the claim to manage the equipment. The current prejudice which insists on management by the owners is set aside by feigning that this claim has an industrial value, and so capitalizing it on the basis of the differential advantage which accrues to its holders.

13. See also a discussion by E.S. Meade, Quarterly Journal of Economics, February 1902, pp. 217 et seq., of how "good-will" may vary in magnitude, or even disappear, when a concern eaters a larger coalition; also, on the same general head, W.F. Willoughby," Integration of Industry in the United States," ibid., November 1902.

14. p. 113 above.

15. cap' = cap + cap/n > cap, in which cap' is the nominal capital, as increased by the credit element cap/n.

16. mat' = mat + (1/n)(cap/n) > mat, in which mat' is the current value of the material equipment, as increased (over mat) by the competitive demand for equipment due to the credit element cap/n. One of the substantial secondary benefits to be noted as flowing from these modem business expedients is the effect of corporation finance upon the aggregate nominal wealth of the community. A given community, possessed of a given complement of material wealth, is richer in capital if a large proportion of its industrial equipment is capitalized and managed by corporation methods, quite apart from any increase in the material items of which the community is possessed. (Cf. Twelfth Census of the United States, "Manufactures," pt. I. p. xcvi) Wealth may in this way be increased (about twofold on an average), inexpensively, by the simple expedient of incorporating the community's business concerns in the form of joint-stock companies. The more highly involved and the more widely extended the corporation financiering is, the richer, in statistical terms of capital, is the community, other things equal. Among these other things are the material facts of the case.

17. The commodities bought and sold in the goods market are the outcome of a process of production and are useful for a material purpose; those bought and sold in the capital market are the outcome of a process of valuation and are useful for purposes of pecuniary gain.

18. Cf. Marx, Kapital (4th ed.) bk. I, ch. IV.

19. Effective capital = current market value of nominal capital = presumptive earning capacity x purchase period, neglecting fortuitous and incalculable items which may affect any given case.

If nominal capital = cap, effective capital = cap', presumed annual earnings = ea', and the purchase period of capitalized property (years' purchase) = yp = 1/interest rate per annum, we have cap cap' = ea' x yp = ea'/int.

This equation between cap' and ea' is disturbed by the presence in any given case of variable factors which cannot be included in the equation, but it remains true after all qualification has been made that cap' = f(ea'/int).

20. Something of this kind is the usual ground of the obstinate resistance which most business men oppose to publicity of accounts. In lines of business, as, e.g. railroading, in which accounts are readily and effectually sophisticated ("doctored"), the objections to publicity are commonly less strenuous.

21. Cf., e.g., Eberstadt, Deutsche Kapitalismarkt.

22. The capital of any industrial concern under the "money economy" is, of course, also vendible, but with relative difficulty; while the readier vendibility of modern corporate capital is so characteristic and consequential a factor in business and contrasts so broadly with the old-fashioned business methods that it may fairly be spoken of as vendibility par excellence. The "holding company" is the mature development of this traffic in vendible capital in industrial business.

23, It may be noted, by the way, that the question of the turnover (spoken of on p. 95 above) becomes, under the circumstances of the modern corporation finance, in great part a question of the interval between the purchase and sale of the capital engaged in industry on the one hand, and of the magnitude of the discrepancy between actual and putative earning-capacity on the other hand, rather than a question of the period of the industrial process and the magnitude of the output and its price. The formula there shown becomes: —

turnover = capital/time (actual earning capacity/n = putative earning capacity − actual earning capacity) in which capital is the amount of the operator's investment in the concern's securities, the time is the interval between purchase and sale of the securities, and the putative earning capacity is taken to exceed the actual earning capacity by an indeterminate fraction of the latter.

24. Cf. Chapter III above.

25, Cf. Chapter V above.

26. Cf. Emery, "Place of the Speculator in the Theory of Distribution." Proceedings of the twelfth annual meeting of the American Economic Association; also "Discussion" following Mr Emery's paper.

27. Well shown in Mr Emery's paper cited above.

28. p. 154.

29. As is true of good−will and credit extensions generally, so with respect to the good−will and credit strength of these greater business men ; it affords a differential advantage and gives a differential gain. In the traffic of corporation finance this differential gain is thrown immediately into the form of capital and so is added to the nominal capitalized wealth of the community. What it gives to its holders in this capitalized form is a claim to a proportionate share in the existing wealth. If other things are supposed to remain the same (which may not be the case), the claim so enforced by the great financiers on the basis of good−will and credit extension deducts that much from the wealth held by the rest, the previous holders, as counted in terms of material wealth; as counted in term of money value, of course, the holdings of previous holders do (or need) not suffer, since the new claim take the form of an edition to the number of capitalized value units, although the increased aggregate number of value units constitutes a claim on the same aggregate mass of wealth as before. The pro rata reduction of the material magnitude of the several shares of wealth is not felt as an impoverishment, because it does not take the form of a reduction of the nominal value of the shares.

This capitalization of the gains arising from a differential advantage results in a large "saving" and increase of capital. The wealth so drawn in by the financiers (entrepreneurs) is nearly all held as capital, very little of it being consumed in current expenses of living. It has been cogently argued that the profits of the undertakers is the chief and normal source of capitalized savings in the modern situation, and the method here indicated seem to be the method by which such saving is chiefly effected. An extremely suggestive discussion of the undertaker's gains in this connection occurs in a paper by L.V. Birck ("Driftsherrens Geviust"), read before the Danish Economic Association, December 1901. More immediately to the point still is V. Schou's discussion of Mr Birck's paper. (See Nationalokonomisk Tidsskrift, January−February 1902, pp. 76, 78−80) J.B. Clark, in lectures hitherto unprinted, follows a line of analysis somewhat closely parallel with Schou, though not carried to quite the same length.

This process of combined recapitalization and saving may be stated formally as follows: The initial value of the properties submitted for coalition and recapitalization, cap, is in the normal case augmented by the increment delta, making the effective value of the properties = cap + delta, in effective units, Uc. This augmented effective value of the properties = Uc(cap + delta) is capitalized at a nominal value of cap' = Un(cap + delta), in nominal units, Un, nominally equivalent to Uc. In the recapitalization the number of units of capitalization is increased by an element of intangible assets assigned the owners on account of a presumed increase of earning−capacity due to the coalition. This element of good−will due to coalition may be called co. Further there is added the bonus of the promoter, taken as a block of stock in the new capitalization, pro. Hence Un(cap') = Un(cap + delta) = Un(cap + co + pro). Un (pro) = Un (cap' − cap − co) = Un (delta − co) is evidently a secure gain to the promoter of Uc(delta − co) , which is a fraction of the effective value Uc(cap + delta). This is saved by him in the capitalized form. The account of the former owners of the properties will then stand as follows: Uc(cap + delta − pro) Uc(cap) according as Uc delta Uc(pro). The nominal gain of the owners, co, may or may not be a real gain according as the event may prove that the promoter's bonus has not or has absorbed the entire effective augmentation of value, delta, due to the coalition ; it is therefore a problematical gain, which may or may not, in the event, prove to be an effective element of capitalized savings.

The constitution of delta will decide what is the ultimate source of the savings effected by this transaction. If delta consists entirely of economies of production, the capitalized savings held by the promoter and former owners as a result of the transaction represent new values added to, or saved to, the aggregate wealth of the community. If delta consists entirely of good-will in the shape of monopoly advantage, the saving is effected at the cost of the community and for the benefit of the promoter and owners; it is then an involuntary or subconscious saving on the part of the community, whereby a part of the community's wealth at large passes into the hands of the recapitalized corporation. Where delta is made up of these two constituents together, the result, as regards the present point, should be plain without discussion. If, on the other hand, delta = 0, so that cap' = cap, then the promoter's savings; pro, are secured at the cost of the former owners; Uc(cap' − pro) = Uc(cap + (delta = 0) − pro) = Uc(cap − pro). Whereas if Uc(pro) = Uc(delta), Uc(co) = 0, leaving the owners without effective profit or loss in spite of any nominal increase of the capitalization.

30. "Good-will" in this field of enterprise most frequently takes the form of a large ability to help or hinder other financiers and financing houses in any similar manoeuvres in which they may be engaged, or an ability to put them in the way of lucrative financing transactions. The guild of financiers is commonly split up into more or less well-defined factions, each comprising an extensive ramification of financing houses and financiers furthering one another's endeavors under more or less settled working arrangements. These working arrangements are a large part of the financiers' "good-will."

31. This category of good-will stands in a relation to the creation of vendible capital similar to that which the corporate good-will of an industrial business concern bears to the creation of vendible products.

32. Parenthetically it may be remarked that the failure to capitalize such items of good-will is likely to involve a virtual evasion of the tax on personal property, and may, therefore, be questionable on moral grounds.

The case of J.P. Morgan and Company is, of course, not here cited as being a unique or peculiar instance, but simply as a typical and striking illustration of what happens and of what might be accomplished in a number of large and very consequential cases of the same class.

33. This dissociation of the business control from workmanlike efficiency and from immediate contact with or ownership of the industrial plant gives the existing situation a superficial resemblance to the feudal system, in so far as touches the immateriality of the captain's connections with the everyday life and interests of the community of whose affairs he is master. It gives a certain plausibility to the attempted interpretation of latter-day economic developments in feudalistic terms. − See Ghent, Our Benevolent Feudalism.

Chapter 7. The Theory of Modern Welfare

Before business principles came to dominate everyday life the common welfare, when it was not a question of peace and war, turned on the ease and certainty with which enough of the means of life could be supplied. Since business has become the central and controlling interest, the question of welfare has become a question of price. Under the old regime of handicraft and petty trade, dearth (high prices) meant privation and might mean famine and pestilence; under the new regime low prices commonly mean privation and may on occasion mean famine. Under the old regime the question was whether the community's work was adequate to supply the community's needs; under the new regime that question is not seriously entertained.

But the common welfare is in no less precarious a case. The productive efficiency of modern industry has not done away with the recurrence of hard times, or of privation for those classes whose assured pecuniary position does not place them above the chances of hard times. Distress may not be so extreme in modern industrial communities, it does not readily reach the famine mark; but such a degree of privation as is implied in the term "hard times" recurs quite as freely in modern civilized countries as among the industrially less efficient peoples on a lower level of culture. The oscillation between good times and bad is as wide and as frequent as ever, although the average level of material well-being runs at a higher mark than was the case before the machine industry came in.

This visible difference between the old order and the new is closely dependent on the difference between the purposes that guide the older scheme of economic life and those of the new. Under the old order, industry, and even such trade as there was, was a quest of livelihood; under the new order industry is directed by the quest of profits. Formerly, therefore, times were good or bad according as the industrial processes yielded a sufficient or an insufficient output of the means of life. Latterly times are good or bad according as the process of business yields an adequate or inadequate rate of profits. The controlling end is different in the present, and the question of welfare turns on the degree of success with which this different ulterior end is achieved. Prosperity now means, primarily, business prosperity; whereas it used to mean industrial sufficiency.

A theory of welfare which shall account for the phenomena of prosperity and adversity under the modern economic order must, accordingly, proceed on the circumstances which condition the modern situation, and need not greatly concern itself with the range of circumstances that made or marred the common welfare under the older regime, before the age of machine industry and business enterprise.(1*) Under the old order, when those in whose hands lay the discretion in economic affairs looked to a livelihood as the end of their endeavors, the welfare of the community was regulated "by the skill, dexterity, and judgment with which its labor was generally applied."(2*) What would mar this common welfare was the occasionally disastrous act of God in the way of unpropitious seasons and the like, or the act of man in the way of war and untoward governmental exactions. Price variations, except as conditioned by these untoward intrusive agencies, had commonly neither a wide nor a profound effect upon the even course of the community's welfare. This holds true, in a general way, even after resort to the market had come to be a fact of great importance in the life of large classes, both as an outlet for their products and as a base of supplies of consumable goods or of raw materials, – as in the better days of the handicraft system.

Until the machine industry came forward, commerce (with its handmaiden, banking) was the only branch of economic activity that was in any sensible degree organized in a close and comprehensive system of business relations. "Business" would then mean "commerce," and little else. This was the only field in which men habitually took account of their own economic circumstances in terms of price rather than in terms of livelihood. Price disturbances, even when they were of considerable magnitude, seem to have had grave consequences only in commerce, and to have passed over without being transmitted much beyond the commercial houses and the fringe of occupations immediately subsidiary to commercial business.

Crises, depressions, hard times, dull times, brisk times, periods of speculative advance, "eras of prosperity," are primarily phenomena of business; they are, in their origin and primary incidence, phenomena of price disturbance, either of decline or advance. It is only secondarily, through the mediation of business traffic, that these matters involve the industrial process or the livelihood of the community. They affect industry because industry is managed on a business footing, in terms of price and for the sake of profits. So long as business enterprise habitually ran its course within commercial traffic proper, apart from the industrial process as such, so long these recurring periods of depression and exaltation began and ended within the domain of commerce.(3*) The greatest field for business profits is now afforded, not by commercial traffic in the stricter sense, but by the industries engaged in producing goods and services for the market. And the close-knit, far-reaching articulation of the industrial processes in a balanced system, in which the interstitial adjustments are made and kept in terms of price, enables price disturbances to be transmitted throughout the industrial community with such celerity and effect that a wave of depression or exaltation passes over the whole community and touches every class employed in industry within a few weeks. And somewhat in the same measure as the several modern industrial peoples are bound together by the business ties of the world market, do these peoples also share in common any wave of prosperity or depression which may initially fall upon any one member of this business community of nations. Exceptions from this rule, of course, are such periods of prosperity or depression as result from local (material) accidents of the seasons and the like, − accidents that may inflict upon one community hardships which through the mediation of prices are transmuted into gain for the other communities that are not touched by the calamitous act of God to which the disturbance is due.

The true, or what may be called the normal, crises, depressions, and exaltations in the business world are not the result of accidents, such as the failure of a crop. They come in the regular course of business. The depression and the exaltation are in a measure bound together. In the recent past, since depression and exaltation have been normal features of the situation, every strongly marked period of exaltation (prosperity) has had its attendant period of depression; although it does not seem to follow in the nature of things that a wave of depression necessarily has its attendant reaction in the way of a period of business exaltation. In the recent past − the last twenty years or so − it has been by no means anomalous to have a period of hard times, or even a fairly pronounced crisis, without a wave of marked exaltation either preceding or following it in such close sequence as conveniently to connect the two as action and reaction. But it would be a matter of some perplexity to a student of this class of phenomena to come upon a wave of marked business exaltation (prosperity) that was not promptly followed by a crisis or by a period of depression more or less pronounced and prolonged. Indeed, as the organization of business has approached more and more nearly to the relatively consummate situation of to-day, − say during the last twenty years of the nineteenth century, − periods of exaltation have, on the whole, grown less pronounced and less frequent, whereas periods of depression or "hard times" have grown more frequent and prolonged, if not more pronounced. It might even be a tenable generalization, though perhaps unnecessarily broad, to say that for a couple of decades past the normal condition of industrial business has been a mild but chronic state of depression, and that any marked departure from commonplace dull times has attracted attention as a particular case calling for a particular explanation. The causes which have given rise to any one of the more pronounced intervals of prosperity during the past two decades are commonly not very difficult to trace, but it would be a bootless quest to go out in search of special causes to which to trace back each of the several periods of dull times that account for the greater portion of the past quarter of a century. Under the more fully developed business system as it has stood during the close of the century dull times are, in a way, the course of nature; whereas brisk times are an exceptional invention of man or a rare bounty of Providence.

What current economic theory has to say on the common welfare is more frequently found under the caption of crisis and depression than in any other one connection. And the theory of crisis and depression has, as is well known, been one of the less happy passages in the economists' repertory of doctrines. It has been customary to approach the problem from the side of the industrial phenomena involved − the mechanical facts of production and consumption; rather than from the side of business enterprise − the phenomena of price, earnings, and capitalization. This untoward accident of a false start is probably accountable for the fact that no tenable theory of these phenomena has yet been offered. The solutions attempted have commonly proceeded by an analysis of industrial life apart from business enterprise; that is to say, they have sought to explain the occurrence of crises under that old-fashioned "natural economy" or "money economy" under which crises did not normally occur.(4*)

Taking as a point of departure the patent fact that crises, depressions, and brisk times are in their first incidence phenomena of business, of prices and capitalization, an explanation of their appearance and disappearance, and of their bearing upon the common welfare, may be sought by harking back to those business principles that underlie modern capitalistic enterprise. An analysis of the current, common-sense business views of price and investment should indicate the genesis and manner of growth of these mass movements of the business community, as well as the character of those circumstances which may further or inhibit such movements. Business depression and exaltation are, at least in their first incidence, of the nature of psychological fact, just as price movements are a psychological phenomenon.

The everyday circumstances which condition the modern business management of industry are sufficiently well known, and they have already been reviewed in some detail in earlier chapters; but they may perhaps advantageously be outlined again in so far as they bear immediately on the question in hand.

(1) Industry is carried on by means of investment, which is made with a view to pecuniary gain (the earnings). The business man's endeavors in managing the affairs of the concern in which investment has been made look to the same end. The gains are kept account of as a percentage on the investment, and both they and the industrial plant or process through the management of which they are procured are counted in terms of money, and, indeed, in no other terms. The plant or process (or the investment, whatever form it takes) is capitalized on the basis of the gains which accrue from it, and this capitalization proceeds on the ground afforded by the current rate of interest, weighted by consideration of any prospective change in the earning-capacity of the concern. The management of the concern is effected by a more or less intricate and multifarious sequence of bargains. The decisive consideration at every point in this traffic of investment and administration is the consideration of price in one relation or another.

(2) The industry to which the business men in this way resort as the ways and means of gain is of the nature of a mechanical process, or it is some employment (as commerce or banking) that is closely bound up with the mechanical industries. Broadly, it is such industry as lies under the dominion of the machine, in that it is involved in that comprehensive quasi-mechanical process of modern industrial life that has been discussed in an earlier chapter. This implication of each industry in a comprehensive system, or this articulation with other branches of industry, is of such a nature as to place each industrial concern in dependence on one or more other branches of industry, from which it draws its materials, appliances, etc., and to which it disposes of its output; and these relations of dependence and articulation form an endless sequence. That is to say, the interindustrial relations into which any branch of industry necessarily enters do not run to a final term in any direction; within the process of industry at large there is no member that stands in the relation of an initial term to any sequence of processes. The ramification of industrial dependence is without limits. The method of these relations of one concern to another, or of one branch of industry to another, is that of bargaining, contracts of purchase and sale. It is a pecuniary relation, in the last resort a price relation, and the balance of this system of interstitial relations is a price balance.

(3) These interstitial pecuniary relations, between the several concerns or branches of industry that make up the comprehensive industrial system at large, involve credit relations of greater or less duration. The bargaining, by means of which industry is managed and the interstitial relations adjusted, takes the form of contracts for future performance. All industrial concerns of appreciable size are constantly involved in such contracts, which are, on an average, of considerable magnitude and duration, and commonly extend in several directions. These contracts may be of the nature of loans, advances, outstanding accounts, engagements for future delivery or future acceptance, but in the nature of the case they involve credit obligations. Credit, whether under that name or under the name of orders, contracts, accounts, and the like, is inseparable from the management of modern industry in all that concerns the working relations between businesses that are not under one ownership, or between which the relations resting on separate ownership have not been placed in abeyance by some such expedient as lease, pool, syndicate, trust agreement, and the like. Credit relations of one kind and another are also found expedient and profitable at many points where their employment is not

precisely unavoidable. These extended credit relations are requisite to the most expeditious and profitable conduct of business, and so to the highest degree of success of the business. Under the regime of the machine industry and modern business methods it is probably fair to say that the use of credit, apart from loan capital and leases, unavoidably goes to the extent required to cover all goods in process of elaboration, from the raw material to the finished goods, in so far as the goods change hands (in point of ownership) during the process.

(4) The conduct of industry by competing business concerns involves an extensive use of loan credit, as spoken of in Chapter V above.

The four conditions recited are characteristic features of that recent past during which brisk times, crises, and depressions followed one another with some regularity as incidents of the normal course of business.(5*) Certain qualifications of this characterization are necessary to fit the immediate present. These will be indicated presently.

In brisk times the use of credit is large; it may be as a cause or an effect of the acceleration of business; most commonly it seems to be both a cause and an effect. No appreciable business acceleration takes place without an extension of credit, at least in the form of contracts of purchase and sale for future performance, if not also in the form of loans. In times of protracted depression the use of credit seems on the whole to be somewhat restricted, at least such is the current apprehension of the case among business men. Still, it cannot confidently be said that seasons of protracted depression are due solely to an absence of credit relations or to an unwillingness to enter into credit relations. A comparison of the course of interest rates, e.g., does not warrant the generalization that the readiness with which loans can be negotiated need be appreciably different in brisk and in dull times.(6*) The readiness with which contracts of purchase and sale are negotiated is appreciably greater in brisk times than in times of depression; that, indeed, is the obvious difference between the two.

Of the three phases of business activity, depression, exaltation, and crisis, the last named has claimed the larger and livelier attention from students, as it is also the more picturesque phenomenon. An industrial crisis is a period of liquidation, cancelment of credits, high discount rates, falling prices and "forced sales," and shrinkage of values. It has as a sequel, both severe and lasting, a shrinkage of capitalization throughout the field affected by it. It leaves the business men collectively poorer, in terms of money value; but the property which they hold between them may not be appreciably smaller in point of physical magnitude or of mechanical efficiency than it was before the liquidation set in. It commonly also involves an appreciable curtailment of industry, more severe than lasting; but the effects which a crisis has in industry proper are commonly not commensurate with its consequences in business or with the importance attached to a crisis by the business community. It does not commonly involve an appreciable destruction of property or a large waste of the material articles of wealth. It leaves the community at large poorer in point of market values, but not necessarily in terms of the material means of life. The shrinkage incident to a crisis is chiefly a pecuniary, not a material, shrinkage; it takes place primarily in the intangible items of wealth, secondarily in the price rating of the tangible items. Apart from such rerating of wealth, the most substantial immediate effect of a crisis is an extensive redistribution of the ownership of the industrial equipment, as noted in speaking of the use of credit.

The play of business exigencies which lead to such a period of liquidation seems to run somewhat as follows: Many firms have large bills payable falling due at near dates, at the same time that they hold bills receivable also in large amounts. To meet the demand of their creditors they call upon their debtors, who may in their turn have bills receivable or may hold loans on collateral. The initial move in the sequence of liquidation may be the calling in of a call loan, or a call for additional collateral on a call loan. At some point, earlier or later, in the sequence of liabilities the demand falls upon the holder of a loan on collateral which is, in the apprehension of his creditor, insufficient to secure ready liquidation, either by a shifting of the loan or by a sale of the collateral. The collateral is commonly a block of securities representing capitalized wealth, and the apprehension of the creator may be formulated as a doubt of the conservative character of the effective capitalization on which it rests. In other words, there is an apprehension that the property represented by the collateral is over-capitalized, as tested by the current quotations, or by the apprehended future quotations, of the securities in question. The market capitalization of the collateral has taken place on the basis of high prices and brisk trade which prevail in such a period of business exaltation as always precedes an acute crisis. When such a call comes upon a given debtor, the call is passed along to the debtors farther along in the sequence of liabilities, and the sequence of liquidations thereby gets under way, with the effect, notorious through unbroken experience, that the collateral all along the line declines in the market. The crisis is thereby in action, and the further consequences follow as a wellknown matter of course. All this is familiar matter, known to business men and students by common notoriety.

The immediate occasion of such a crisis, then, is that there arises a practical discrepancy between the earlier effective capitalization on which the collateral has been accepted by the creditors, and the subsequent effective capitalization of the same collateral shown by quotations and sales of the securities on the market. But since the earlier capitalization commonly, in the normal case, comes out of a period of business prosperity, the point of inquiry is as to the ground and method of this effective capitalization of collateral during the period of prosperity that goes before a crisis, and this, in turn, involves the question of the nature and causes of a period of prosperity.

The manner in which the capitalization of collateral, and thereby the discrepancy between the putative and actual earning-capacity of capital, is increased by loan credit during an era of prosperity has been indicated in some detail in Chapter V above. But it may serve to enforce the view there taken, if it can be shown on similar lines that a period of prosperity will bring on a like discrepancy between putative and actual earning-capacity, and therefore between putative and eventual capitalization of collateral, even independently of the expansion effected by loan credit.

A period of prosperity is no more a matter of course than a crisis. It has its beginning in some specific combination of circumstances. It takes its rise from some traceable favorable disturbance of the course of business. In such a period the potent fact which serves as incentive to the acceleration of business is a rise of prices. This rise of prices presently becomes general as prosperity progresses and becomes an habitual fact, but it takes its start from some specific initial disturbance of prices. That is to say, prices rise first in some one industry or line of industries.(7*)

By new investments, as well as by extending the operations of the plants already employed, business men forthwith endeavor to take advantage of such a rise. The endeavor to market an increased supply of the things for which there is an enlarged demand, brings on an increased demand and an advance of prices in those lines of industry from which the concerns that had the initial advantage draw their supplies. In part by actual increase of demand and in part through a lively anticipation of an advanced demand, aggressive business enterprise extends its ventures and pushes up prices in remoter lines of industry. This transmission of the favorable disturbance of business (substantially a psychological phenomenon) follows very promptly under modern conditions, so that any differential advantage that accrues at the outset to the particular line of industry upon which the initial disturbance falls is presently lost or greatly lessened. In the meantime extensive contracts for future performance are entered into in all directions, and this extensive implication of the various lines of industry serves, of itself, to maintain the prosperity for the time being. If the original favorable disturbance of demand and prices, to which the prosperity owes its rise, falls off to the earlier level of demand, the era of prosperity has thereby a term set to its run; although the date of its termination is always at some distance in the future, beyond the time when the original demand has ceased to act. The reason for this retardation, whereby the close of an era of prosperity is always delayed, other things equal, beyond the lapse of the cause from which it has arisen, is (1) the habit of buoyancy, or speculative recklessness, which grows up in any business community under such circumstances, (2) the continued life of a considerable body of contracts for future performance, which acts to keep up the demand for such things as are required in order to fill these contracts and thereby keeps up prices in so far. In general it may be said that after the failure of the favorable price disturbance to which it is due, an era of prosperity will continue for that (indefinite) further period during which the fringe of outstanding contracts continues to dominate the business situation. Some further, new contracts will always continue to be made during this period, and some unfilled contracts will always be left standing over when the liquidation sets in; but, broadly speaking, the wind-up comes, not when this body of outstanding contracts have run out or been filled, but when the business of filling them and of filling the orders to which they give rise no longer occupies the attention of the business community in greater measure than the rest of current business.

The run of business exigencies on which an era of prosperity goes forward may be sketched in its general features somewhat as follows: Increased demand and enhanced prices, with the large contracts which follow from such a state of the market, increase the prospective earnings of the several concerns engaged. These prospective earnings may eventually be realized in full measure, or they may turn out to have been putative earnings, only. that is largely a question of how far in the future the liquidation lies. The business effect of increased prospective earnings, however, is much the same whether the event proves the expectation of increased earnings to have been well grounded or not. The expectation in either case leads the business men to bid high for equipment and supplies. Thereby the effective (market) capitalization is increased to answer to the increased prospective earnings. This recapitalization of industrial property, on the basis of heightened expectation, increases the value of this property as collateral. The inflated property becomes, in effect, collateral even without a formal extension of credit in the way of loans; because, in effect, the contracts entered into are a credit extension, and because the property of the contracting parties is liable to be drawn into liquidation in case of non-fulfilment of the contracts. But during the free swing of that buoyant enterprise that characterizes an era of prosperity contracts are entered into with a somewhat easy scrutiny of the property values available to secure a contract. So that as regards this point not only is the capitalization of the industrial property inflated on the basis of expectation, but in the making of contracts the margin of security is less closely looked after than it is in the making of loans on collateral. There results a discrepancy between the effective capitalization during prosperity and the capitalization as it stood before the prosperity set in, and the heightened capitalization becomes the basis of an extensive ramification of credit in the way of contracts (orders); at the same time the volume of loan credit, in set form, is also greatly increased during an era of prosperity.(8*)

An era of prosperity is an era of rising prices. When prices cease to rise prosperity is on the wane, although it may not promptly terminate at that juncture. This follows from the fact that the putative increase of earnings on which prosperity rests is in substance an apprehended differential gain in increased selling price of the output over the expenses of production of the output. Only so long as the selling price of the output realizes such a differential gain over the expenses of production, is the putative increased rate of earnings realized; and so soon as such a differential advantage ceases, the era of prosperity enters on its closing phase.

Such a differential advantage arises mainly from two causes: (1) The lines of industry which are remote, industrially speaking, from the point of initial disturbance, – from which, that is to say, the lines of industry first and chiefly affected by the rise draw supplies of one kind or another, – these remote lines of industry are less promptly and less acutely affected by the favorable disturbance of the price level; this retardation of the disturbance affords the industries nearer the seat of disturbance a differential advantage, which grows less the farther removed the given enterprise is from the point of initial disturbance.(9*) (2) The chief and most secure differential advantage in the case is that due to the relatively slow advance in the cost of labor during an era of prosperity. Wages ordinarily are not advanced at all for a considerable period after such an era of prosperity has set in; and so long as the eventual advance of wages does not overtake the advance in prices (which in the common run of cases it never does in full measure), so long, of course, a differential gain in the selling price accrues, other things equal, to virtually all business enterprises engaged in the industries affected by the prosperity.

There are, further, certain (outlying) lines of industry, as, e.g., farming, which may not be drawn into the movement in any appreciable degree, and the price of supplies drawn from these outlying industries need not rise; particularly they need not advance in a degree proportionate to the advance in the prices of the goods into which they enter as an element of their expenses of production. To an uncertain but commonly appreciable extent there is also a progressive cheapening of the processes of production during such an era, and this cheapening, particularly in so far as it affects the production of the goods contracted for, as contrasted with the appliances of production, serves also to maintain the differential advantage between the contracted sale price and the expenses of production of the goods contracted for.

In the ordinary course, however, the necessary expenses of production presently overtake or nearly overtake the prospective selling price of the output. The differential advantage, on which business prosperity rests, then fails; the rate of earnings falls off. the enhanced capitalization based on enhanced putative earnings proves greater than the earnings realized or in prospect on the basis of an enhanced scale of expenses of production; the collateral consequently shrinks to a point where it will not support the credit extension resting on it in the way of outstanding contracts and loans; and liquidation ensues, after the manner frequently set forth by those who have written on these subjects.(10*)

At some point in the system of investment and business extension will be found some branches of industry which have gradually lost what differential advantage they started out with when they entered on the era of prosperity; and if these are involved in large contracts and undertakings which are carried over into the phase of the movement at which this particular branch of industry has ceased to have a differential advantage in the price of its output over the cost of its supplies of material or labor, then what may have been a conservative capitalization of their holdings at an early phase, while their earning-capacity rested on a large differential advantage, will become an excessive capitalization after their earning-capacity has declined through loss of their differential advantage. Some branch or branches and some firms or class of firms necessarily fall into this position in the course of a period of phenomenally brisk times. A business concern so placed necessarily becomes a debtor, and its liabilities necessarily become, in some degree, bad debts. It is forced by circumstances to deliver its output at prices which preclude its obtaining such a margin as its extension of business presupposed. That is to say, its capitalization becomes excessive through shrinkage of its earning-capacity (as counted in terms of price). A concern of this class which is a debtor is precluded from meeting its obligations out of its current earnings; and if, as commonly happens in an appreciable proportion of cases, its obligations have already been augmented to the extent which its recent earning-capacity would warrant, then the concern is insolvent for the time being. If the claims against it are pressed, it has no recourse hut liquidation through forced sales or bankruptcy. Either expedient, if the case is one of considerable magnitude, is disastrous to the balanced sequence of credit relations in which the business community is involved. The system of credit relations prevailing at such a time has grown up on the basis of an earning-capacity transiently enhanced by a wave of differential price advantage; and when this wave has passed, even if it leaves prices higher all around, the differential advantage of at least most concerns is past. The differential price advantage has come to the several branches or firms in succession, and has, in the typical case, successively left each with an excessive capitalization, and has left many with a body of liabilities out of proportion to their subsequent earning-capacity. This situation may, evidently, come about in this manner, even without lowering the aggregate (pecuniary) earning-capacity of the business community to the level at which it stood before the wave of prosperity set in.(11*)

But when such a situation has come, all that is required to bring on the general catastrophe is that some considerable creditor find out that the present earning-capacity of his debtor will probably not warrant the capitalization on which his collateral is appraised, In self-defence he must decline the extension of a loan, and forced liquidation must follow. Such a liquidation involves cutting under the ruling prices of products, which lessens the profits of competing firms and throws them into the class of insolvents, and so extends the readjustment of capitalization.

The point of departure for the ensuing sequence of liquidation is not infrequently the failure of some banking house, but when this is the case it is pretty sure to be a bank whose funds have been "tied up" in "unwise" loans to industrial enterprises of the class spoken of above.(12*)

The abruptness of the recapitalization and of the redistribution of ownership involved in a period of liquidation may be greatly mitigated, and the incidence of the shrinkage of values may be more equably distributed, by a judicious leniency on the part of the creditors or by a well-advised and discreetly weighted extension of credit by the government to certain sections of the business community. Such measures of alleviation were had, with happy effect, in the case of a recent stringency which is sometimes spoken of as an averted crisis. But where the situation answers the specifications recited above, in respect of a large and widely prevalent discrepancy between earning-capacity and capitalization, a drastic readjustment of values is apparently unavoidable.

The point has already been adverted to once or twice that the most substantial immediate outcome of such a liquidation as is involved in a crisis is a redistribution of the ownership of the property concerned in the liquidation, whereby creditors and similar claimants gain at the expense of the solvent debtors. Such being the case, it would logically follow that the large creditors should see and follow up their advantage by concertedly pushing the body of debtors to an abrupt liquidation, and so realizing as large a gain as possible with the least practicable delay, whenever the situation offers.

Such may be the logic of the circumstances, but such is not the course practically taken by the large creditors under the circumstances. For this there is more than one reason. It is not, apparently, that human kindness overrules the creditors' impulse to gain at the expense of the debtors. The ever recurring object-lessons afforded by operations in the stock and money market enforce the belief that when one business man gets the advantage of another he will commonly use the advantage without humanitarian reserve, if only the advantage is offered hIm in terms which he can comprehend. But short-sightedness and lack of insight beyond the conventional routine seem to be fairly universal traits of the class of men who engage in the larger business activities. So that, while it would be to the unequivocal advantage of the large creditor, in point of material gain, to draw in his debtor's property at such a reduced valuation as comes in a period of abrupt liquidation, yet he does not ordinarily see the matter in that light; because the liquidation involves a shrinkage of the money value of the property concerned, and the business man, creditor or debtor, is not in the habit of looking beyond the money rating of the property in question or beyond the most immediate future. The conventional base line of business traffic, of course, is the money value, and a recognition of the patent fact that this base line wavers incontinently, and that it may on occasion shift very abruptly, apparently exceeds the business man's practical powers of comprehension. Money value is his habitual bench-mark, and he holds to the conviction that this bench-mark is stable, in spite of the facts.(13*)

It is true, cases occur, from time to time, of transactions of some appreciable magnitude in which some degree of recognition of this fact is met with. Some large business man may yet rise to the requisite level of intelligence, and may comprehend and unreservedly act upon the fact that the money base line of business traffic at large is thoroughly unstable and may readily be manipulated, and it will be worth going out of one's way to see the phenomenal gains and the picturesque accompaniments of such a man's work. Parenthetically it may be remarked that if such a degree of insight should become the common property of the business community, business traffic as now carried on might conceivably collapse through loss of its base line. What is yet lacking in order to such a consummation is perhaps nothing more serious than that business capital be reduced to a somewhat more thorough state of intangibility than it has yet attained, and that does not seem a remote contingency.(14*)

There is, however, another and more constraining circumstance which hinders the large creditors from wilfully pushing the debtors to a reckoning when things are ripe for liquidation. As was indicated above, the sequence of credit relations in an era of prosperity is endlessly ramified through the business community;

whereby it happens that very few creditors are not also debtors, or stand in such relation to debtors as would involve them in some loss, even if this loss should not be commensurate with their eventual gain at the cost of other debtors. This circumstance by itself has a strong deterrent effect, and when taken in connection with what was said above of the habitual inability of the men in business to appreciate the instability of money values, it is probably sufficient to explain the apparently shortsighted conduct of those large creditors to seek to mitigate the severity of liquidation when the liquidation has come due.

The account here offered of the "method" of crises and eras of prosperity does not differ greatly from accounts usually met with, except in explaining these phenomena as primarily phenomena of business rather than of industry. The disturbances of the mechanical processes of industry, which are a conspicuous feature of any period of crisis, follow from the disturbance set up in the pecuniary traffic instead of leading up to the latter. While industry and business stand in a relation of mutual cause and effect, in this as in other cases, the initiative in such a movement belongs with the business traffic rather than with the industrial processes.

Industry is controlled by business exigencies and is carried on for business ends. The effects of a wide disturbance in business, therefore, reach the industrial processes pretty directly, and the consequences, in the way of an expansion or curtailment of industrial activity and an enlarged or shortened output of product, are, of course, both immediate and important. As a primary effect, on the industrial side, of an era of prosperity, the community gains greatly in aggregate material wealth. The gain in material wealth, of course, is not equally distributed; most of it goes to the larger business men, eventually in great part to those who come out of the subsequent liquidation on the credit side. To some extent this aggregate material gain is offset by the unavoidable waste incident to the stagnation that attends upon an era of prosperity. It is further offset by the fact that good times carry with them an exceptionally wasteful expenditure in current consumption. Also, the usual and more effectual impetus to an era of prosperity, when it is not an inflation of the currency, is some form of wasteful expenditure, as, e.g., a sustained war demand or the demand due to the increase of armaments, naval and military, or again, such an interference with the course of business as is wrought by a differentially protective tariff. The later history of America and Germany illustrates both these methods of procuring an era of prosperity. These methods, it will be noticed, are, in their primary incidence, of the nature of a waste of industrial output or energy; but the prosperity achieved is, none the less, to be recognized as a beneficial outcome in point of heightened industrial activity as well as in point of increased comfort for the industrial classes.

To the workmen engaged in industry, particularly, substantial benefits accrue from an era of prosperity. These benefits come, not in the way of larger returns for a given amount of work, but more work, fuller employment, at about the earlier rate of pay. To the workmen it often means a very substantial gain if they can get a fuller livelihood by working harder or longer, and an era of prosperity gives them a chance of this kind. Gradually, however, as prosperity – that is to say, the advancing price level rises and spreads, the increased cost of living neutralizes the gain due to fuller employment, and after the era of prosperity has been under way for some time the gain in the amount of work obtainable is likely to be fairly offset by the increased cost of living. As noted above, much of the business advantage gained in an era of prosperity is due to the fact that wages advance more tardily than the prices of goods. An era of prosperity does not commonly bring an increase of wages until the era is about to close. The advance of wages in such a case is not only a symptom indicating. that the season of prosperity is passing, but it is a business factor which must by its own proper effect close the season of prosperity as soon as the advance in wages becomes somewhat general. Increasing wages cut away the securest ground of that differential price advantage on which an era of prosperity runs.

Periods of crisis or of prosperity are, after all, relatively simple phenomena with strongly marked features, and a passable explanation of them is correspondingly easy. They have also the ad vantage of having received much attention at the hands of the students of economic history. On the other hand, protracted depression, not traceable to widespread hardship or calamity arising from circumstances outside the range of business transactions, is a relatively new and untried subject for economic theory. Newer, more obscure. with less pronounced features and less definite limits than movements of speculative advance or speculative crises, this phenomenon has to a less extent engaged the steady attention of students. An inquiry into the life history and the causes and effects of depression, from the point of view of a theory of business, may therefore scarcely be expected to yield concise or secure conclusions.

Since industry waits upon business, it is a matter of course that industrial depression is primarily a depression in business. It is in business that depression is felt, since it is on the business side of economic activity that the seat of economic sensibility may be said to lie; it is also in business (pecuniary) terms that the depression is measured whenever a measure or estimate of the matter is attempted. In so far as there is an attendant derangement of the mechanical processes and of the mechanical articulation of processes in industry, the derangement follows from the pecuniary exigencies of business. Depression and industrial stagnation follow only in case the pecuniary exigencies of the situation are of such a character as to affect the traffic of the business community in an inhibitory way. But business is the quest of profits, and an inhibition of this quest must touch the seat of its vital motives. Industrial depression means that the business men engaged do not see their way to derive a satisfactory gain from letting the industrial process go forward on the lines and in the volume for which the material equipment of industry is designed. It is not worth their while, and it might even work them pecuniary harm. Commonly their apprehension of the discrepancy which forbids an aggressive pursuit of industrial business is expressed by the phrase "overproduction." An alternative phrase, intended to cover the same concept, but less frequently employed, is "underconsumption."(15*)

The controversial question as to the tenability of any given "overproduction" doctrine may, for the present purpose, be left on one side; it lies outside the theory of business and it has no merits or demerits for the purposes of a theory of business. The point of interest here is rather the ground of its acceptance among business men and the meaning which this notion has for them; that is to say, it is chiefly of interest here to inquire into the habits of thought which give cogency and effect to the dogma of "overproduction" as practically held by the body of business men, – what it practically means, why the dogma is held, and what is its effect on the course of business enterprise.

"Overproduction," or "underconsumption," as it is met with in the views of business men, is neither a vacant dogma nor a shifty apology wherewith to cover their own delinquencies, but a very concretely real state of affairs. It is a state of affairs that prevails when business is persistently dull; and the concept covered by the term comprises the sufficient cause of the dulness, in the apprehension of the business community, even though they may not always speak of the difficulty by that name. It may be worth while, even at the risk of tedium, to point out that this concept of "overproduction" applies, not to the material, mechanical bearing of the situation, but to its pecuniary bearing. The notion is never seriously entertained that there is or may be an embarrassing excess of goods, or of the appliances for their production, above what would be of some human use if the business situation permitted them to be turned to use.

(1) The supply of consumable goods is, practically, never greater than the community's capacity for consuming them. An embarrassing excess in any line is practically a remote contingency at the most (16*) There are many eloquent passages in the economic manuals which may be called in witness of this truism, where much pains is taken to show that human wants are, in the nature of the case, indefinitely extensible. Nothing stands in the way, we are told, but "difficulty of attainment" of the goods with which to satisfy these wants. (2) In times of depression, or "hard times," there is, under the modern industrial system at least, no overproduction in the sense of a production so large as to overtax the working capacity of the industrial appliances and processes employed, nor so large, even, as to overtax the normal powers of the force of workmen or require them to work overtime and holidays. Quite the contrary. That sort of thing happens only in brisk times, when there is no overproduction. Seriously to recite such platitudes as these may seem like a

trifling with the patience of the printer, or it may be taken for a light-headed excess of "wissenschaftlicher Methode"; but these two formulations appear to cover all the conceivable ways in which overproduction may occur, so long as the term is construed from the point of view of the mechanical facts of the case. Seen from this side a period of depression is a period of underproduction; mills run on half time or none, and the supply of goods that finds its way into the hands of consumers is sensibly scant for the demands of comfort.

The difficulty is, of course, a pecuniary one, and the phrase is used by business men in that pecuniary sense in which it has an immediate bearing on business. "Excessive competition" is an alternative phrase. There is an excess of goods, or of the means of producing them, above what is expedient on pecuniary grounds, - above what there is an effective demand for at prices that will repay the cost of production of the goods and leave something appreciable over as a profit. It is a question of prices and earnings. The difficulty is that not enough of a product can be disposed of at fair prices to warrant the running of the mills at their full capacity, or running them at a rate near enough to their capacity to yield a fair profit. Or, to turn the proposition about, as business men are in the habit of doing, there is more of an output offered than will be carried off at a fair price, such a price as will afford fair or ordinary profits on the investment and the running expenses. There is too large a productive capacity; there are, too many competitive producers and too much industrial apparatus to supply the market at reasonable prices. The matter reduces itself to a question of fair prices and ordinary profits.(17*)

If there is a large volume of outstanding credit obligations, that will complicate the situation. There is always a considerable amount of interest bearing securities outstanding, and the claims of these securities have to be satisfied before dividends can be paid on stock, or before profits accrue to industrial ventures which have issued the Securities. These fixed charges, together with others of a like kind, narrow the margin from which profits are derived and increase the handicap which a season of dull times brings to the business men in charge of industry. At the same time fixed charges preclude shutting down, except at a sure and considerable loss. The business men involved are constrained to go on, and in the absence of wide combinations in industry they are constrained to go on at such competitive prices as to preclude reasonable profits.

The question of fair prices and reasonable profits has some reference to current rates of interest. A "fair" rate of profits is such a rate as bears a reasonable relation to the current rate of interest, although this relation of profits to interest rates does not appear to be a strict one. Still, there undoubtedly is some reference to the current rate of interest as a sort of zero line to which profits should not decline. New investments are made on the basis of current rates of interest and with a view to securing the differential gain promised by the excess of prospective profits over interest rates.

In a period of depression the aggregate industrial equipment is, notoriously, not running at its full capacity; there are many idle and half-idle plants and many idle workmen. The concerns in question find themselves unable to do a full run of business at reasonable profits. Still, unless the depression is of exceptionally short duration, there is always some new investment going on. More or less of new capital continues to find its way into industrial business in competition with the concerns that are already in the field.(18*) In case of a protracted depression the aggregate of new investments so made may, in the course of years, amount to a very considerable addition to the industrial outfit, and the production of the new establishments may very appreciably increase the aggregate output. Indeed, the output of the new establishments is a notable factor in swelling the supply and keeping down prices. But the new investments made during the depression are profitable, at least at the start. Or even if this should be questioned when stated in this broad way, it will at least hold true that they are commonly entered upon with a well-advised expectation of their being profitable if the situation does not materially change between the time when the new venture was entered upon and the time when the new equipment has got under way. If the interval between the inception of the new enterprise and its completion is a long one, the situation may so change in the meantime as to leave it unprofitable even if it has been conservatively planned. There are also, of course, fraudulent enterprises which are not expected by their promoters to pay a profit on the investment; and there are probably, also, always some ventures entered upon during dull times with a view to being beforehand in preparation for better times. But after all has been said in qualification of the main proposition, it remains true that some new investment is going on with a well-advised expectation of reasonable profits on the basis of current costs, prices, and rates of interest.(19*) The rate of interest in times of depression may be unsatisfactory to lenders; it may be discouraging by comparison with the customary range of interest rates during better times. Still, the obstacle to business is not to be sought in an effectual discouragement of lenders, for in point of fact money is readily to be had on good security during any protracted depression.(20*)

There is also the fact that investment is continually going on, which argues that the difficulty is neither that capital cannot be found for investment, nor that investment has no prospect of reasonable profits. Practically, no exceptional amount of fluent funds is withheld from the market, − except in time of panic, which is another matter. It may be added that the rate of interest need not be notably low in time of depression, just as, on the other hand, a period of business exaltation is not uniformly accompanied by a notably high rate of interest.

But a low or declining rate of interest is effective in the way of depressing the business situation, even though a depression may go on without it. The line of its bearing upon business depression, or at least one line, is as follows: Established business concerns (particularly corporations) engaged in industry have some appreciable fixed (interest) charges to meet − on leases, mortgages, and interest-bearing securities (preferred stock and bonds). These outstanding obligations and securities may have been negotiated, "floated," at an earlier period of higher interest rates and higher profits, or they may have been carried over through a period of higher interest rates. In the former case these interest charges are excessively high as compared with the present capitalized value of the property on which they rest, computing the capitalization on the basis of the present cost of replacing this property and the present interest charge which this cost of replacement would bear. In the latter case the original capitalization of the corresponding items of property will have undergone a practical (effective) recapitalization at a lower figure to correspond with the higher rate of interest prevalent during the interval in question; and in the subsequent period of low interest, the fixed charge on this recapitalization is excessively high as compared with the current effective capitalization of the property. The liabilities are excessive, in respect of their interest charges, as compared with the present earning-capacity of the property represented by them.(21*)

What gives effect to this drawback for the business enterprises which have such fixed interest charges to meet is the fact that the new investments, and those concerns that have gone into bankruptcy or receivers' hands, come into competition with the old. These new or rejuvenated concerns are not committed to a scale of fixed charges carried over from a higher interest level; and these are therefore carrying only such interest charges as the current effective capitalization of their property will warrant, whether effective capitalization be taken to mean cost of production of the equipment, earning-capacity of the concern, or market quotation of its securities. These unincumbered competitors are presumed to be making reasonable profits at current prices, and their presence in the competitive market therefore precludes an advance of prices to such a scale as would afford a reasonable profit to the other establishments after paying their interest charges on what is, in effect, over-capitalized property.

This tentative explanation of depression applies only so far as the period of depression is a time of relatively low rates of interest. But depression does not uniformly coincide with low interest rates; besides which, there are other facts in the case which limit the applicability of the explanation formulated above. To explain protracted depression, e.g., this line of argument would be convincing only on the supposition of a progressively falling rate of interest, − a condition not commonly met with in a protracted period of depression.

But this explanation, applicable within a limited range of the phenomena that make up a period of depression, points the way to another class of considerations that go far toward explaining the rest. It appears that the phase of the difficulty covered by this explanation is traceable to a discrepancy between the accepted capitalization, the interest charges, and the earning-capacity. And it appears equally plain that the only remedy applicable to the case (barring a speculative exaltation of business) is a recapitalization of the concerns affected on a lower basis, to fit the lowered cost of production of the equipment and its lowered earning-capacity. But under existing conditions of law such a remedy cannot be applied to the interest bearing securities, – except by process of insolvency, – and it is very reluctantly applied to other capitalized wealth; besides which it is, practically, very difficult to effect such an avowed recapitalization as applied to the stock of incorporated companies, particularly in the case of those whose stock is ostensibly the capitalized value of their plant.

Such a readjustment of nominal value to actual value as shown by the facts of earning-capacity is continually going on, in some measure; but it does not cover the entire range of facts involved, and it is nearly always of the nature of a reluctant concession, following only after the need of it has become somewhat pressing. It can, therefore, in the common run of cases, not catch up with the progressive difficulty which it is designed to meet, in so far as the difficulty is of a progressive character.

A discrepancy between accepted capitalization and current earning-capacity, similar to the discrepancy discussed above but of a progressive character, arises under modern conditions apart from a fall in the rate of interest. The discrepancy pointed out and provisionally disposed of above, due to a fall in interest rates, is a discrepancy between the nominal value (accepted capitalization) of the older establishments, computed on their earlier earning-capacity or on the original cost of their equipment, on the one hand, and their present actual value on the other hand, computed on their current earning-capacity in competition with rivals that have the advantage of a lower cost of equipment, or, in other words, a lower interest charge per unit of earning-capacity. Under the regime of the later, more fully developed machine production, a discrepancy having a similar effect arises out of a persistent divergence between the past cost of production of a given equipment and the current cost of a like or equivalent equipment at any subsequent date, – supposing that there intervenes no inflation of prices and no extraneous cause making for a speculative advance.(22*)

Suppose prices of finished goods to be stable or to vary by inconsequential fluctuations, negligible for purposes of the argument, and suppose the rate of interest to be in a similarly negligible position. In other words, suppose such a condition as the business community would recognize as ordinary, normal, sound, without ground for pronounced hopes or fears. Under modern circumstances, dominated as the modern situation is by the machine industry, such a state of affairs is unstable, even apart from any disturbance of an extraneous kind. It is unstable by virtue of the forces at work in its own process, and these forces, on the whole, make for a progressive change in. the direction of depression.

It has appeared above that the depressing effect which a relatively low (declining) rate of interest has upon industrial business is due to its setting up a discrepancy between the accepted capitalization of older establishments and the cost of new establishments of an equivalent earning-capacity. Now, under the circumstances of the more fully developed machine industry, such as it has stood for a couple of decades past, a similar discrepancy results from the gradual but uninterrupted progressive improvements of industrial processes. "The state of the industrial arts," as the older economists are in the habit of calling it, is no longer to be conceived as stationary, even for the time being. No "statical" theory of the industrial arts or of business prosperity is tenable, even for the purposes of a "statical" theory of the industrial situation. Progressively increasing efficiency of the processes in use is a pervading trait of the industrial situation. No two successive years are now on the same, or virtually the same, plane in respect of the efficiency of the industrial arts; indeed, the "period of production" can no longer safely be construed to begin and end on the same level in this respect. At the same time the progressively wider and more close-knit articulation of the several industries in a comprehensive process is also going forward, and this also affects all branches of industrial business in some degree and in the same direction, as will appear presently.

The items of the equipment (plant, materials, and in a measure even good-will) in which any industrial enterprise invests, and by the use of which the business men in industry turn out their output of vendible goods, are themselves products of the machine industry. Machine processes, ever increasing in efficiency, turn out the mechanical appliances and materials with which the processes are carried on, at an ever decreasing cost; so that at each successive step the result is a process having a higher efficiency at a lower cost.(23*) This is now no longer a sporadic effect of ingenious contrivances having a local and limited application, to be handled as trade secrets and exploited as an enduring differential advantage.

The cost of production of "capital goods" is steadily and progressively lowered, as counted in terms of the processes involved in their production. In a competitive market this is reflected, with greater or less promptitude, in the prices of such capital goods to all buyers. But the buyers whose purposes this lower scale of prices particularly subserves are chiefly the new investors who go into business in the way of new industrial establishments or extensions of the old. Each new venture or extension goes into the competitive traffic of producing and selling any line of staple goods with a differential advantage, as against those that have gone before it, in the way of a lower scale of costs. A successively smaller aggregate value of new equipment will turn out a given volume of vendible product. In so far as there is no collusive control of the output or the prices, this means that the newcomers will cut under the scale of prices at which their predecessors have been content to supply the goods. The run of competitive prices is lowered; which means that at the new competitive prices, and with their output remaining on its old footing as regards expenses of production, the older establishments and processes will no longer yield returns commensurate with the old accepted capitalization.(24*) From the inherent character of the machine industry itself, therefore, it follows that the earning-capacity of any industrial enterprise enters on a decline from the outset, and that its capitalization, based on its initial putative earning-capacity, grows progressively antiquated from the start. The efficiency of the machine process in the "instrumental industries" sets up a discrepancy between cost and capitalization. So that a progressive readjustment of capitalization to correspond with the lowered earning-capacity is required by the nature of the case It is also, in the nature of the case, impracticable.

In so far as the process of investment and business management involves the use of credit, in the way of interest-bearing securities or loans equivalent to such securities, this element of credit retards the readjustment by force of the fixed charges which it involves. This retardation (aided as it is by the reluctance of business men to lower their capitalization) is of sufficient effect to hinder recapitalization, on the whole, from overtaking the progressive need of it, with the result that a fair or "ordinary" rate of profits on industrial investments is not permanently attainable in the field of open competition. In order that the rate of interest should effectually further business depression in this way, therefore, it is not necessary that the rate should rise or fall, or that it should be relatively high or low, or that it should be uniform over the field, but only that there should be a rate of interest in each case, and that there should be some appreciable volume of credit involved in industrial investments. Credit is, in fact, a ubiquitous factor in modern industrial business, and its effects in the way indicated are therefore to be counted in as a constant force in the situation.

However, even apart from the presence of this ubiquitous credit element, a similar effect would probably result from the progressive enhancement of industrial efficiency when this enhancement proceeds at such a rate as has been the case for some time past. As has been shown in an earlier chapter, business men keep account of their wealth, their outgo and their income, in terms of money value, not in terms of mechanical serviceability or of consumptive effect. Business traffic and business outcome are standardized in terms of the money unit, while the industrial process and its output are standardized in terms of physical measurements (mechanical efficiency). In the current habits and conventions of the business community, the unit of money is accepted and dealt with as a standard measure. The stability of the standard unit cannot be effectually questioned within the scope of business traffic. According to the practical metaphysics of the business community, the money unit is an invariable magnitude, whatever may be true of it in fact. A man imbued with these business metaphysics and not given to fine-spun reflection, as business men commonly are not, is richer or poorer in his own apprehension, according as his balance sheet shows a greater or less number of these standard units of value. Investment, expenses, vendible output, earnings, fixed charges, and capitalization run in terms of this value unit. A reduction of earnings or of capitalization, as rated in terms of the value unit, is felt as an impoverishment. The reduction of capitalization in these terms is, therefore, a hardship, which is only reluctantly and tardily submitted to, even if it carries no hardship in the way of a reduced command over the material means of production, of life, or of comfort. A business man's rating in the business community likewise rests on the pecuniary magnitude of his holdings and his transactions, not on the mechanical serviceability of his establishment or his output; and this business rating is a large part of the business man's everyday ambition. An enhancement of it is a source of secure gratification and self-respect, and a reduction of it has a very substantial contrary effect.(25*) A reduction of the pecuniary showing is submitted to only reluctantly and tardily, after it has become unavoidable, and only to the least feasible extent. But under conditions, such as now prevail, which involve the requirement of a progressive rerating of this kind, this reluctant concession never overtakes the need of readjustment, – and the discrepancy between capitalization and earning-capacity is therefore chronic so long as no extraneous circumstances come in temporarily to set aside the trend of business affairs in this respect. It may, therefore, be said, on the basis of this view, that chronic depression, more or less pronounced, is normal to business under the fully developed regime of the machine industry.(26*)

This deplorable trend given to business by the excessive prevalence and efficiency of the machine industry can, however, be set aside by several factors more or less extraneous to the industrial system proper. Even within the mechanical system of industry there is at least one factor of some consequence that consistently acts to mitigate the trend indicated, and that may even put it in abeyance from time to time. As has been pointed out above, questions of business are fundamentally questions of price. A decline of prices which widely touches business interests brings depression. Conversely, an appreciable advance in prices, from whatever cause, means improvement in business. Such an advance in prices may come of a speculative movement; which in turn may arise from a variety of circumstances, for the most part circumstances extraneous to the industrial process. For the present, however, the question of a speculative movement is best left on one side. Another factor touches the case more intimately. As has more than once been the case, prices may be advanced through a freer supply of the precious metals, or by an inflation of the currency, or a more facile use of credit instruments as a subsidiary currency mechanism. Now, the growing efficiency of industry has an effect in lowering the (material) cost of production of the precious metals and so increasing the ease with which they are supplied, after the same manner as it affects the supply of goods for industrial or consumptive use. But the increased supply of the precious metals has, of course, an effect upon prices contrary to that exerted by the increasing supply of goods. In so far as this effect is had, it acts to correct or mitigate the trend of business toward chronic depression.(27*)

But certain circumstances come in to qualify the salutary effect of a lowered cost of the precious metals. Improvements in the industrial processes affect the (industrial) cost of production of the precious metals in a less degree than the cost of other goods; at least, such seems to have been the case recently. But beyond this, and of graver consequence, is a peculiarity affecting the value of the money metals. The annual product of the money metals is not annually consumed, nor nearly. The use of them as money does not consume them except incidentally and very slowly. The mass of these metals in hand at any given time is very considerable and is relatively imperishable, so that the annual accretion is but a small fraction of the aggregate supply. The lowered cost of the annual supply has therefore but a relatively slight effect upon the aggregate value of the available supply.

The case is different as regards the annual output of vendible products, whether for industrial or consumptive use. In this case, and particularly as regards this matter of new Investments and extensions of Industrial equipment, the annual output counts for by far the greater factor in making the current value of the available supply, if indeed it is not to be regarded as substantially the only factor that comes in question here. Accordingly, it is only under very exceptional circumstances, at times when the precious metals are supplied with extraordinary freedom, that the in creased output of these metals can offset the trend of business toward depression. Ordinarily this factor can count for no more than a mitigation of the "tendency of profits to a minimum." And even this mitigating effect, it may be remarked, appears to be of less radical consequence for the general situation of business now than it was during the earlier phases of the machine industry's regime. The most telling effect of an increased supply of the precious metals seems to be the incitement which it gives to speculative inflation.(28*)

It will be noted that the explanation here offered of depression makes it a malady of the affections. The discrepancy which discourages business men is a discrepancy between that nominal capitalization which they have set their hearts upon through habituation in the immediate past and that actual capitalizable value of their property which its current earning-capacity will warrant. But where the preconceptions of the business men engaged have, as commonly happens, in great part been fixed and legalized in the form of interest-bearing securities, this malady of the affections becomes extremely difficult to remedy, even though it be true that these legalized affections, preconceptions, or what not, centre upon the metaphysical stability of the money unit.

But while it is true that depression is primarily a business difficulty and rests on emotional grounds, that does not hinder its having grave consequences for industry and for the material welfare of the community outside the range of business interests. Business enterprise, it is true, proceeds on metaphysical grounds and is swayed by considerations of nominal wealth rather than by considerations of material serviceability; but, none the less, business enterprise and business metaphysics control the course of industry.

Dull times in business means dull times in industry, of course. But a caution is necessary on this head. The yearly output does not usually vary extremely between brisk and dull times, except as measured in price. As measured in material terms the discrepancy in the volume of output between brisk and dull times is much less. The gross output as measured by weight and tale is less in dull than in brisk times, other things equal; but the deficiency as measured in these terms is much less than the price returns would indicate. Indeed, the output as measured by weight and tale need not average very appreciably less during a protracted depression than during a preceding period of good times.(29*) The volume of business as well as the volume of output (by weight and tale) of industry may increase during a few years of depression at nearly if not quite as high a rate as during a corresponding period of good times. A transition from dull to brisk times, however, commonly if not invariably involves a rapid increase in values, while a converse transition involves a corresponding shrinkage of values, though commonly a slower shrinkage, – except where a crisis intervenes.

The primary hardship of a period of depression is a persistent lesion of the affections of the business men; the greatest secondary hardship is what falls upon the workmen, in the way of partial unemployment and a decline in wages, with consequent precariousness and reduction of their livelihood.(30*) For those workmen who continue to find fairly steady employment during the depression, however, even at reduced wages, the loss is more apparent than real; since the cheapening of goods offsets the decline in wages. Indeed, the cheapening of the means of living is apt to offset the fall in wages fully, for such workmen as have steady work. So that in the case of the workmen also, as well as in that of the business men, the distress which dull times brings is in some part a spiritual, emotional matter.

To the rest of the community, those classes that are outside of business enterprise and outside of the industrial occupations proper, that is to say, those (non-industrial) classes who live on a fixed salary or similar fixed income, dull times are a thinly disguised blessing. They suffer in their affections from the reflected emotional detriment of the business community, but they gain in their ease of livelihood and in their savings by all the difference between the price scale of brisk and of dull times. To these classes an era of prosperity brings substantially nothing but detriment.(31*)

Depression is primarily a malady of the affections of the business men. That is the seat of the difficulty. The stagnation of industry and the hardships suffered by the workmen and other classes are of the nature of symptoms and secondary effects. Any proposed remedy, therefore, must be of such a nature as to reach this emotional seat of the trouble and restore the balance between the nominal value of the business capital engaged and the earnings of the business; that is to say, a remedy, to be efficacious, must restore profits to a "reasonable" rate; which means, practically, that prices must be brought to the level on which the accepted capitalization has been made. Such a remedy, to offset the disastrous cheapening of products through mechanical improvements, has been found in business coalitions and working arrangements of one kind and another, looking to the "regulation" of prices and output. Latterly this remedy is becoming familiar to the business community as well as to students of the business situation, and its tangible, direct, and unequivocal efficiency in correcting this main infirmity of modern business is well recognized. So much so, indeed, that its urgent advisability has been formulated in the maxim that "Where combination is possible competition is impossible." What is required is a business coalition on such a scale as to regulate the output and eliminate competitive sales and competitive investment within a field large enough to make up a self-balanced, passably independent industrial system, – such a coalition of business enterprises as is loosely called a "trust."

Such a business coalition, if it is comprehensive and closely controlled, can adjust the output of goods and services to the market with some nicety, and can maintaIn the balance of the ruling prices, or the price scale agreed upon, with such effect that the received capitalization need not become obsolete even in the face of very radical improvements in the processes of industry. Its effect, in the case of ideal success, is to neutralize the cheapening of goods and services effected by current industrial progress. It offsets industrial improvements in so far as these improvements affect the cost of goods more than they affect the value of the money metals. It might seem at first sight that by thIs inhibitory effect of the trust the entire advantage derivable from industrial improvements within the scope of the trust should inure to the gaIn of the business men in the combination, but such does not appear to be the practical outcome. The practical outcome appears more nearly to be that material advantage inures to no one from industrial improvements under the control of the trust, in so far as the trust successfully carries its point. This feature of trust management will be taken up again in a different connection.

In addition to its prime purpose of checking the decline of earnings on past investments, such a business coalition is also enabled to distribute any unavoidable effect of the progressively reduced cost of production of the productive goods employed, somewhat equally over the entire field of industry comprised in the coalition, and so obviate the pressure of this untoward industrial progress falling with exceptional severity at any given point. Economies effected are at the same time made to accrue to the collective business organization, showing themselves in the way of increased dividends and increased effective (market) capitalization of the coalition's property, instead of being dissipated in competitive selling, and so going to the body of consumers or to the industrial system at large.

To return to a point temporarily set aside above. By supposition, in what has just been said, anything like a speculative inflation has been excluded from the discussion of business depression; and necessarily so, since the two do not come at the same time. But at one point the two show a feature in common. Under both of these two widely different conditions of the business situation there is a discrepancy between the accepted capitalization and the actual earning-capacity.(32*) But the two differ even at this point in that, in the case of inflation, the discrepancy is not felt until the climax, when a widespread realization of the discrepancy brings on an abrupt readjustment, in the crisis which follows inflation; whereas in a period of depression the sense of this discrepancy and the protest against it is the most striking circumstance of the case. The discrepancy between capitalization and earning-capacity in a period of speculative movement comes of an inflation of capitalization; whereas in time of depression the discrepancy is due to a shrinkage of earning-capacity, – both capitalization and earning-capacity being, of course, counted in terms of money values. A speculative movement offsets or checks the trend to depression whenever it occurs; and for some appreciable time past, such speculative movements appear to have been the only force which has from time to time broken the otherwise uninterrupted course of business depression. Under the regime of a perfected machine industry and a perfect business organization, with active competition throughout, it is at least probable that depression would not be seriously interrupted by any other cause.

But it has been a point of economic dogma in modern times – not to call it a point of theory, since it is not held on reasoned grounds – that depression and inflation, followed by crisis, succeed one another with a rough periodicity, interminably and in the nature of the case. The periodicity (with an interval of some ten to twelve years from phase to phase) has not been established with any cogent show of evidence, except for the period from 1816 to 1873; and even within that period the evidence has not been convincing to all students of these phenomena. A tentative explanation of the periodicity, such as there may have been within that period, as well as of its absence before and after the period in question, may be offered on the basis of the views here set forth. keeping in mind the point that the disturbance, both in the case of inflation and in that of depression, is a discrepancy between capitalization and earning-capacity, and also the manner in which this discrepancy arises, it may be said that prior to the earlier date mentioned the modern industrial system was not such a comprehensive and articulate process that a disturbance in one part or one member of the system need be transmitted forthwith through the channels of business to all the rest. A speculative movement need not spread forthwith throughout the industrial system. The great episodes of speculation and collapse that occurred during earlier modem times were not of the nature of speculative inflation affecting the entire business community occupied with industry. They are rather of the nature of commercial speculation verging on gambling.(34*) So also, the crises of that earlier time, when they were not collapses of gambling ventures, were commonly produced by some great disaster which brought an absolute material loss upon the community, such as crop failures, invasions, or heavy war expenditures. On the other hand, as regards periods of depression prior to the early years of the nineteenth century, they were also rare if not unknown, except when due to failure of resources or the burdens of government. The conditions out of which depression could come, as a persistent disturbance of business through a divergence between the capitalization and the earning-capacity of investments, were not had. The developed machine system was absent, and without this the cost of production of productive goods could not be progressively lowered at a rate large enough to set up and maintain a persistent divergence between capitalization and earning-capacity in industrial enterprises.

At some uncertain point in the first half of the nineteenth century the system of machine industry and the business system based upon it, attained such a breadth and consistency that business disturbances of appreciable magnitude in any part would affect values throughout the system. It had then grown so large and was so closely articulated a structure that the relations of its members to one another and to the system as a whole were of greater moment for the fortunes of these members and for the orderly process of the whole than were the relations of the members to industrial factors lying outside the system of the machine industry and the business community. Hence industrial crises in the proper sense of the word seem well at home in this period. They spread with great force and facility whenever they came; and they had the true character of business crises, in that they ran with great severity without involving an appreciable aggregate loss of material wealth, except in terms of price. They commonly meant a cancelment of values, without appreciable aggregate loss of goods. They seem also to have been true to the staple definition of crises in that they followed upon a period of speculative inflation in industrial investments.

Chronic depression, however, does not seem to belong, as a consistent feature of the course of things, in this nineteenth-century period, prior to the eighties or the middle of the seventies. The usual course, it is commonly held, was rather: inflation, crisis, transient depression, gradual advance to inflation, and so on over again.(35*)

On the view of these phenomena here spoken for, an attempt at explaining this circuit may be made as follows: A crisis, under this early nineteenth-century situation, was an abrupt collapse of capitalized values, in which the capitalization was not only brought to the level of the earning-capacity which the investments would have shown in quiet times, but appreciably below that level. The efficiency and the reach of the machine industry in the production of productive goods was not then so great as to lower the cost of their production rapidly enough to overtake the shrinkage in capitalization and so prevent the latter from rising again in response to the stimulus of a relatively high earning-capacity. The shock-effect of the liquidation passed off before the cheapening of the means of production had time to catch up with the shrinkage of capitalization due to the crisis, so that after the shock-effect had passed there still remained an appreciable under-capitalization as a sequel of the period of liquidation. Therefore there did not result a persistent unfavorable discrepancy between capitalization and earning-capacity, with a consequent chronic depression. On the other hand, the earning-capacity of investments was high relatively to their reduced capitalization after the crisis. Actual earning-capacity exceeded the nominal earning-capacity of industrial plants by so appreciable a margin as to encourage a bold competitive advance and a sanguine financiering on the part of the various business men, so soon as the shock of the liquidation had passed and business had again fallen into settled channels. But such a bold competitive advance means the beginning of an extension of credit and a speculative movement in industry, such as has been discussed some pages back in connection with crises. This movement has a cumulative character, after the manner there indicated, and its outcome is an inflation of capitalization and a large extension of credit, which normally ends in a period of liquidation.

Within the period spoken of (1816-1873) this liquidation is apparently always brought on by some extraneous disturbance. But it seems that the theory would require us to say that the extraneous disturbance requisite to bring such a speculative movement to a head will be slighter the farther the movement has gone; so that in the earlier stages of a given period of inflation a liquidation could be brought on only by some relatively violent disturbance, whereas at a higher phase of speculative inflation a relatively slight disturbance would suffice.

Now, it takes some time for such a speculative movement to bring on so large a discrepancy between capitalization and earning-capacity as may not be adjusted by other means than a widespread and severe liquidation.(36*) Hence a rough periodicity in the recurrence of these seasons of buoyancy and of collapse in capitalized values. Other factors, and varying ones, have, no doubt, been present in each of the historic crises of the nineteenth century, and these other factors would have to be taken due account of in any history of crises, and even in any theory of crises, which aimed at anything like an exhaustive treatment; but the factors here pointed out seem to be the characteristic and constant ones in the sequence of crises within this period, at the same time that they are the factors which are in a peculiar degree connected with that process of business management in modern industry which is the objective point of the present inquiry.

Since the seventies, as an approximate date and as applying particularly to America and in a less degree to Great Britain, the course of affairs in business has apparently taken a permanent change as regards crises and depression. During this recent period, and with increasing persistency, chronic depression has been the rule rather than the exception in business. Seasons of easy times, "ordinary prosperity," during this period are pretty uniformly traceable to specific causes extraneous to the process of industrial business proper. In one case, the early nineties, it seems to have been a peculiar crop situation, and in the most notable case of a speculative inflation, the one now (1904) apparently drawing to a close, it was the Spanish-American War, coupled with the expenditures for stores, munitions, and services incident to placing the country on a war footing, that lifted the depression and brought prosperity to the business community. If the outside stimulus from which the present prosperity takes its impulse be continued at an adequate pitch, the season of prosperity may be prolonged; otherwise there seems little reason to expect any other outcome than a more or less abrupt and searching liquidation.

What would be an adequate pitch of the stimulus making for prosperity is, of course, not easy to say, but it is probably safe to say that in order to keep up the season of prosperity for a considerable number of years the stimulus would have to be gradually increased. That is to say in other words, the absorption of goods and services by extra-industrial expenditures, expenditures which as seen from the standpoint of industry are pure waste, would have to go on in an increasing volume. If the wasteful expenditure slackens, the logical outcome should be a considerable perturbation of business and industry, followed by depression; if the waste on war, colonization, provincial investment, and the like, comes to an abrupt stop, the logical consequence, in the absence of other counteracting factors, should be a crisis of some severity. (37*)

It was said above that since the seventies the ordinary course of affairs in business, when undisturbed by transient circumstances extraneous to the industrial system proper, has been chronic depression. The fact of such prevalent depression will probably not be denied by any student of the situation during this period, so far as regards America and, in a degree, England.(38*) For the Continent of Europe this characterization would have to be materially qualified. But the reply is ready to hand that governmental interferences with trade have been so ubiquitous on the Continent, particularly in the German-speaking communities, that their case is fairly to be thrown out of any general theory. It may also be questioned whether the industrial system of Germany, e.g., throughout this period conforms to the requirements of the theory in respect of the degree of development of the machine industry which such a state of affairs supposes.(39*)

The explanation of this persistent business depression, in those countries where it has prevailed, is, on the view here spoken for, quite simple. By an uncertain date toward the close of the seventies the advancing efficiency and articulation of the processes of the machine industry reached such a pitch that the cost of production of productive goods has since then persistently outstripped such readjustment of capitalization as has from time to time been made. The persistent decline of profits, due to this relative overproduction of industrial apparatus, has not permitted a consistent speculative expansion, of the kind which abounds in the earlier half of the nineteenth century, to get under way. When a speculative movement has been set up by extraneous stimuli, during this late period, the inherent and relatively rapid decline of earning-capacity on the part of older investments has brought the speculative inflation to book before it has reached such dimensions as would bring on a violent crisis. And when a crisis of some appreciable severity has come and has lowered the capitalization, the persistent efficiency and facile balance of processes in the modern machine industry has overtaken the decline in capitalization without allowing time for recovery and consequent boom. The cheapening of capital goods has overtaken the lowered capitalization of investments before the shock-effect of the liquidation has worn off. Hence depression is normal to the industrial situation under the consummate regime of the machine, so long as competition is unchecked and no deus ex machina interposes.(40*)

The persistent defection of reasonable profits calls for a remedy. The remedy may be sought in one or the other of two directions: (1) in an increased unproductive consumption of goods; or (2) in an elimination of that "cutthroat" competition that keeps profits below the "reasonable" level. If enough of the work or of the output is turned to wasteful expenditures, so as to admit of but a relatively slight aggregate saving, as counted by weight and tale, profitable prices can be maintained on the old basis of capitalization. If the waste is sufficiently large, the current investment in additional industrial equipment will not be sufficient to lower prices appreciably through competition.(41*)

Wasteful expenditure on a scale adequate to offset the surplus productivity of modern industry is nearly out of the question. Private initiative cannot carry the waste of goods and services to nearly the point required by the business situation. Private waste is no doubt large, but business principles, leading to saving and shrewd investment, are too ingrained in the habits of modern men to admit an effective retardation of the rate of saving.(42*) Something more to the point can be done, and indeed is being done, by the civilized governments in the way of effectual waste. Armaments, public edifices, courtly and diplomatic establishments, and the like, are almost altogether wasteful, so far as bears on the present question. They have the additional advantage that the public securities which represent this waste serve as attractive investment securities for private savings, at the same time that, taken in the aggregate, the savings so invested are purely fictitious savings and therefore do not act to lower profits or prices. Expenditures met by taxation are less expedient for this purpose; although indirect taxes have the peculiar advantage of keeping up the prices of the goods on which they are imposed, and thereby act directly toward the desired end. The waste of time and effort that goes into military service, as well as the employment of the courtly, diplomatic, and ecclesiastical personnel, counts effectually in the same direction. But however extraordinary this public waste of substance latterly has been, it is apparently altogether inadequate to offset the surplus productivity of the machine industry, particularly when this productivity is seconded by the great facility which the modern business organization affords for the accumulation of savings in relatively few hands. There is also the drawback that the waste of time involved in military service reduces the purchasing pow er of the classes that are drawn into the service, and so reduces the amount of wasteful consumption which these classes might otherwise accomplish.(43*)

So long as industry remains at its present level of efficiency, and especially so long as incomes continue to be distributed somewhat after the present scheme, waste cannot be expected to overtake production, and can therefore not check the untoward tendency to depression. But if the balance cannot be maintained by accelerating wasteful consumption, it may be maintained by curtailing and regulating the output of goods.

"Cutthroat" competition, that is to say, free competitive selling, can be done away by "pooling the interests" of the competitors, so soon as all or an effective majority of the business concerns which are rivals in the market combine and place their business management under one directive head. When this is done, by whatever method, selling of goods or services at competitively varying prices is replaced by collective selling ("collective bargaining") at prices fixed on the basis of "what the traffic will bear." That is to say, prices are fixed by consideration of what scale of prices will bring the largest aggregate net earnings, due regard being had to the effect of a lower price in increasing sales as well as to the reduction of cost through the increase of output. The outcome, as regards the scale of prices, may easily be a reduction of the price to consumers; but it may also, and equally readily, be an increase of the average price. But the prices of the output which is in this way brought to a monopoly basis are nearly certain to run more even than prices of the like output while sold competitively by rival concerns.

What has been said in the last paragraph supposes that the combination of business enterprises is so comprehensive as to place the resulting coalition in a position of practical monopoly. Such a result is not always attained, however, especially not in the earlier attempts at coalition in any particular branch of industry; although the endeavor is commonly related until at last a virtual monopoly is achieved. But even where no effective monopoly is achieved, a coalition of this kind has a salutary effect, at least temporarily. In almost all cases a consolidation of this kind is able to effect considerable economies in the cost of production, as pointed out in an earlier chapter, and such economies bring relief through enabling the combined industrial ventures to earn a reasonable profit at a lower price for their product than before. They are therefore able to go on on a scale of prices which was not remunerative while they stood on their old footing of severalty. But the relief which comes of such measures, so long as competitive selling goes on in rivalry with concerns standing outside the coalition, is only transient. The declining cost of production, and the consequent competitive investment and extension in the industry, presently catches up with the gain in economy; the margin of advantage in the competition is lost, and depression again overtakes the consolidated enterprises on their new footing. The remedy again is a wider coalition, making possible farther economies, and making some approach to a position of secure monopoly.

It is only on a footing of monopoly that this grinding depression can be definitively set aside. But the monopoly need not be absolute in order to afford a somewhat enduring relief. What is necessary is that the monopoly should comprehend all but a negligible fraction of the business concerns and the equipment engaged in the field within which competition has kept profits below a reasonable level. What is a negligible quantity in such a case is not to be determined on general considerations, since it depends in each case on circumstances affecting the particular industry. But, in a general way, the more nearly complete the monopoly, the more effectually is it likely to serve its purpose,(44*)

Such business coalitions have the effect of bringing profits to a reasonable level, not only by making it possible to regulate output and prices, but also by the economies which are made practicable on this footing. Coalitions of a less comprehensive character, as spoken of above, also effect economies in the cost of production. But the larger coalitions which bring the business to a monopoly basis have not only the advantage which comes of the large-scale organization of the industrial process, but they also enjoy peculiar advantages in the matter of cost, due to their monopoly position. These added advantages are more particularly advantages in buying or bargaining for all goods, materials, and services required, as well as in selling the output. So long as the coalitions are not comprehensive enough effectually to eliminate competition, they are constrained to both buy and sell in competition with others. But when the coalition comes effectually to cover its special field of operation, it is able, not only to fix the prices which it will accept (on the basis of what the traffic will bear), but also in a considerable measure to fix the prices or rates which it will pay for materials, labor, and other services (such as transportation) on a similar basis, – unless it should necessarily have to do with another coalition that is in a similar position of monopoly.

The rule which governs the fixing of rates on this side of the business dealings of a monopolistic coalition is similar to that which guides its transactions in the matter of sales. Prices and rates, as, e.g., for materials and labor, are not depressed to the lowest possible point, but to the lowest practicable point, – to the point compatible with the largest net profits. This may or may not be a point below the rates necessary under a regime of competitive buying. It may be added that only in rare cases does a coalition attain so strong a position in respect of its purchases (of materials or services) as to lift this side of its business entirely above the reach of competition.(45*)

Wherever this expedient of coalition has been found practicable, the chronic depression of recent times and the confusion and uncertainty which goes with a depressed competitive business situation have been obviated. The great coalitions do not suffer acutely from the ills of depression, except in cases where their industrial processes are to a peculiar degree in the position of intermediaries within the range of the competitive industries, as is the case, e.g., with most railroads. But even in such a case the coalition which has a monopoly is more fortunate as regards the stability of its balance sheet than the same traffic would be without the advantage of monopoly.

Barring providential intervention, then, the only refuge from chronic depression, according to the view here set forth, is thoroughgoing coalition in those lines of business in which coalition is practicable. But since this would include the greater part of those lines of industry which are dominated by the machine process, it seems reasonable to expect that the remedy should be efficacious. The higher development of the machine process makes competitive business impracticable, but it carries a remedy for its own evils in that it makes coalition practicable. The ulterior effects of thoroughgoing monopoly, as regards the efficiency of industry, the constancy of employment, the rates of wages, the prices of goods to consumers, and the like, are, of course, largely matter of surmise, and cannot be taken up in this inquiry, the present purpose being merely to give in outline an economic theory of current business enterprise.

A further consideration bearing on the later phases of the business situation may be added. The great coalitions and the business manoeuvres connected with them have the effect of adding to the large fortunes of the greater business men; which adds to the large incomes that cannot be spent in consumptive expenditures; which accelerates the increase of investments; which brings competition if there is a chance for it; which tends to bring on depression, in the manner already indicated. The great coalitions, therefore, seem to carry the seed of this malady of competition, and this evil consequence can accordingly be avoided only on the basis of so comprehensive and rigorous a coalition of business concerns as shall wholly exclude competition, even in the face of any conceivable amount of new capital seeking investment.

What has made chronic depression the normal course of things in modern industrial business is the higher development of the machine process, given, of course, the traits of human nature as it manifests itself in business traffic. The machine process works this effect by virtue, chiefly if not altogether, of these two characteristics: (1) a relatively rapid rate of increasing efficiency; and (2) the close interdependence of the several lines of industrial activity in a comprehensive system, which is growing more comprehensive and closeknit as improvement and specialization of industrial processes go on. The last-named factor counts for more in proportion as the interdependence grows closer and more comprehensive. Disturbances are progressively transmitted with greater facility and effect throughout the system, and each line of industrial business comes to stand in relatively intimate relations to an ever increasing range of other lines with which it carries on a traffic of purchase or sale. A consequence of this state of things is that any business coalition, in order effectually to serve its purpose of maintaining earnings and capitalization, is required to be of larger scope and closer texture. As the exigencies which enforce the resort to coalition uninterruptedly gain in scope and urgency, the "trust" must take the same course of growth to meet these exigencies; until, with some slight further advance along the accustomed lines, the trust which shall serve the modern business situation must comprehend in one close business coalition virtually the whole field of industry within which the machine process is the dominant industrial factor.(46*)

To this there is a broad exception, given by the circumstances of the industrial organization. This organization rests on the distinction between business management and ownership. The workmen do not and cannot own or direct the industrial equipment and processes, so long as ownership prevails and industry is to be managed on business principles. The labor supply, or the working population, can therefore not be included in the ideally complete business coalition suggested above, however consummate the machine system and the business organization built upon it may become. So that when the last step in business coalition has been taken, there remains the competitive friction between the combined business capital and the combined workmen.

From the considerations recited above it appears that the competitive management of industry becomes incompatible with continued prosperity so soon as the machine process has been developed to its fuller efficiency. Further technological advance must act to heighten the impracticability of competitive business. As it is sometimes expressed, the tendency to consolidation is irresistible. Modern circumstances do not permit the competitive management of property invested in industrial enterprise, much less its management in detail by the individual owners. In short, the exercise of free contract, and the other powers inhering in the natural right of ownership, are incompatible with the modern machine technology. Business discretion necessary centres in other hands than those of the general body of owners. In the ideal case, so far as the machine technology and its business concomitants are consistently carried through, the general body of owners are necessary reduced to the practical status of pensioners dependent on the discretion of the great holders of immaterial wealth; the general body of business men are similarly, in the ideal outcome, disfranchised in point of business initiative and reduced to a bureaucratic hierarchy under the same guidance; and the rest, the populace, is very difficult to bring into the schedule except as raw material of industry. What may take place to accentuate or mitigate this tendency is a question of the drift of sentiment on the matter of property rights, business obligations, and economic policy. So far as the economic factors at play in the modern situation shape this drift of sentiment they do so in large part indirectly, through the disciplinary effect of new and untried circumstances of politics and legal relation to which their working gives rise.

NOTES:

1. Such a discussion as Patten's Theory of Prosperity applies to the regime of "natural economy", and passably also to that of handicraft and petty trade, but does not seriously touch the modern situation. The like is true generality for current discussions of this topic.

2. Wealth of Nations, Introduction.

3. This means, in concrete terms, prior to the regime of the machine industry. Since the coming in of the machine, modern business enterprise has taken over the management of industry; that is to say, industry has come to be managed by the method of investment for a profit by what is in aim and animus essentially the commercial method. As has been remarked above, capital has become vendible in a decisive degree. The material factors engaged in industry, particularly in the machine industry proper, are vendible in about the same (perhaps on an average in a higher) degree as the material items handled by commercial traffic are vendible. This is true of raw materials, labor power, and industrial equipment, but it is peculiarly true of the industrial equipment – the mechanical factors in the stricter sense. It is in these mechanical appliances primarily, but in the other factors of the machine industry in only a slightly lower degree, that the traffic of investment, and of purchase and sale connected with investment, is particularly active. Within these wider limits a further limitation may be made. "Vendibility" of all items involved is, as a broadly general rule, carried to the highest pitch in those branches of industry that have to do with the production of "producer's goods." These branches are at the same time, and partly in consequence of this fact, more widely and intimately related to other branches of industry than are any other group of industrial processes that might be named. It seems to be this extreme prevalence of vendibility, together with this more far-reaching and more exacting articulation with the industrial process at large, that chiefly gives substantial significance to a classification of these lines of industry as "Produktivmittel-Industrien" by late German writers. There is, for business purposes, a difference of degree, in both of the respects named, between this (ill-defined) group of industrial processes on the one hand, and the contrasted group occupied with the production of consumption goods on the other hand. The "productive-goods industries" show the modern industrial and business traits in an accentuated form and force, and they are, by consequence, in a strategically primary position in the business situation.

4. Cf., e.g., A. Spiethoff, Jahrbuch f. Gesetzgebung Verwaltung u. Volkswirtschaft, vol. XXVI. Heft 2 . "Vorbemerkungen zu einer Theorie der Uberproducktion." and vol. XXVII, pp. 348-353; Turgan-Baranowsky, Theorie und Geschicte der Handelskrisen in England, pp. 16-28; L. Pohle, Periodische Wirschaftskrisen, especially sec. II, with subjoined notes.

5. This is well exemplified in Tugan-Baranowsky (Handelskrise), who declares at the outset (p. 17) that money and price are negligible factors for the purpose in hand. He thereby commits himself to the position that these crises are phenomena of the material processes of economic life (production and consumption), not of business traffic. Hence the ultimate failure of this acute observer and theoretician to reach a tenable solution to the question. Substantially the is true of Marx, whom Tugan follows, though with large reservations. (Cf. Marx, Capital, vol. III, ch. XV)

6. The "cycle" of exaltation, crisis, and depression has frequently been describe. Perhaps as effective a description and analysis as any is that of Tugan-Baranowsky, Handelskrisen, chap. VIII.

7. Cf., however, Cassel, "Om Kriser och Daliga Tider," Ekonomisk Tidskrift, vol. vi, no. 2, pp. 69-78.

8. As, e.g., the era of prosperity 1897-1902 took its start from the demand for supplies caused by the Spanish-American War, though other favorable circumstances acted to give it volume. Mr Carver, possibly following suggestions given by Spiethoff's discussion, has suggested that the lines of business in which the favorable initial disturbance arises are necessarily those engaged in the production of "producer's goods"; the reason for this being that, in the nature of the case, "the value of producer's goods tends to fluctuate more violently than the value of consumer's goods," inasmuch as the value of producer's goods varies somewhat as the magnitude of the margin of profits, while that of the consumer's goods varies somewhat as the magnitude of the entire demand on which this margin of profits rests as an increment. (The value of producer's goods = $f(\delta)$, that of consumer's goods = $f(\text{demand} + \delta)$.) From the like line of argument it should follow that the initial break in time of crisis must come in some line of business occupied

with producer's goods. Cf. Quarterly Journal of Economics, May 1903, pp. 497–500. See also foot-note on p. 181 above.

9. Cf. Sombart, Kapitalismus, vol II, ch. I, on the motive forces at work in advancing business enterprise.

10. The "intitial disturbance" here spoken of may of course be of a progressive or recurring character, and so may keep the differential advantage going in a progressive manner, as, e.g., in the case of a progressive demand for supplies due to a protracted war or to a period of continued preparation for war, such as has occurred in America during the last few years.

11. There is a point or two of further detail in what may be called the method of prosperity and crisis, which are best discussed in connection with the phenomena of depression. These will, therefore, be taken up presently. The above characterization of an era of prosperity and the manner of its exhausting itself will serve as a description of the course which such an era takes under the regime of the more highly developed business methods of the high tide of the nineteenth century. For the earlier, less fully developed, business situation of the early nineteenth century the corresponding course of events runs somewhat different, owing, chiefly at least, (1) to a slower rate of transmission of any price disturbance, and (2) to the greater range and value of "outlying" industries which are very tardily if at all drawn into the exuberant movement of prosperity. In this connection it is worth noting that during this earlier period of the nineteenth century the production of specifically productive goods had not been carried to the point afterward attained, either in the differentiation and specialization of industries occupied with this class of goods or in the relative volume of this class of industries.

12. The several phases of this sequence of exaltation and depression for any given business concern, may be stated as follows: –

Let ea = earnings; pr = sale price of output; exp = expenses of production of output; mar = margin of gain on output = $pr - exp$; cap = intitial effective capitalization; yp = year's purchase at (current rates = int) = $1/int$, disregarding risk; cr = normal credit extension on given cap = cap/n = $f(cap/int)$.

Then at the initial phase,

$$ea = (mar = pr - exp)outp,$$

$$cap = ea \times yp = ea/int,$$

$$cr = cap/n,$$

At the subsequent phase, of exaltation,

$$ea' = ea + \Delta ea = mar' \times outp$$

$$= [(pr' = pr + \Delta pr) - exp]\, outp$$

$$= (mar + \Delta mar)\, outp > ea,$$

$$cap' = ea'/int = (ea + \Delta ea)/int > cap,$$

$$cr' = cap'/n = (cap + \Delta cap)/n > cr.$$

At the concluding phase, of depression,

$$ea'' = ea' - \Delta ea' = mar'' \times outp$$

$$= [pr' - (exp' = exp + \Delta exp)]\, outp\, ea'$$

$$cap'' = ca''/int = (ea' - \Delta ea')/int\, cap',$$

$$cr'' = cap''/n = (cap' - \Delta cap')/n\, cr'.$$

For simplicity of statement, in all this no account is taken of the element of risk, nor of the fluctuations of discount rates or the variations of volume of output. If these be included in the calculation as variables, the result is much the same. They are functions of the variables already included, and their inclusion would, on the whole, accentuate the oscillations shown by the computation as it stands.

13. A crisis may take its rise from credit extension in other than properly industrial business. Such, e.g., was in great measure the American crisis in 1837, when the most obvious and disastrous inflation was in speculative land values and the credits based on them. But it is no stretch of the concept to say that in that case the situation out of which the crisis arose was an overcapitalization of the land values in question. Capitalized land is, of course, "capital" for business purposes as truly as any other body of values that are capitalized and drawn into the money market.

14. It is, in great part, through or by force of fluctuations of this base line of money values that large accumulations of wealth are made. One might almost say that this is the "normal" method by which saving are made and capitalized in later modern times. Fluctuations in the stock market, of course, are of this character, as are commonly also large variations of the course of prices outside the stock market, as well as fluctuations of the money market. The great gains of successful promoters of corporations and the like come in this manner usually. They are due to enlargement of the money value of a given block of industrial equipment independently of any change in the physical character of the equipment which comes near saying that the large fortunes originate in such changes of the base line, − from which it follows that the larger accretions to the volume of capital are of this origin. The large profits are made in the form of capital, which is acquired by virtue of a price variation. See foot−note, pp. 168−170.

15. A substantial move in this direction would be that advocated by Mr F.S. Stetson before the New York Bar Association, and reiterated before the United States Industrial Commission: "To permit the formation of a distinct class of business stock corporations whose capital stock may be issued as representing proportional parts of the whole capital without any nominal or money value." The market value of such shares would be the only value assigned them, and little of a base line in the way of a legally imputed value would remain. The de jure value would no longer hinder a free recognition of the facts. − Report of the Industrial Commission, vol. I. p. 976.

16. Cf. Hobson, Problem of the Unemployed, ch. V., Vialles, La consommation et les crises economiques, especially "Introduction" and ch. III.

17. Something that might bear such a construction occurs, e.g., locally, when a run of fish exceeds the ability of the workmen to take care of them. The fatuity of appealing to such an example is plain.

18. Cf. Smart, Studies in Economics, ch. VII.

19. For the present purpose a concern which passes through a liquidation and reappears with a rerated and reorganized capitalization and body of liabilities also has much of the character of a new investment.

20. Cf. L. Pohle, Bevolkerungsbewegung, Kapitalbildung und periodische Wirtschaftskrisen, who concludes that depression is due to a scarcity of capital as compared with population; the rate of increase of capital is conceived to fall short of the rate of increase of population, hence periodical depression.

Cf., on the other hand, Macrosty, Trusts and the State, p. 133, who finds, by recourse to the testimony before the Royal Commission on the Depression of Trade and Industry, that there is at such times capital constantly seeking investment and entering into competition with what is already invested. Cf. Final Report of the Royal Commission on Depression of Trade and Industry (1886). "The replies received from Chambers of Commerce to the inquiries we addressed to them confirm the statements made by the witnesses who appeared before us. Those replies testify to the general maintenance or increase of the volume of trade, accompanied in many cases by a shrinkage in its value, and in all cases by a serious diminution of profit. They also show how general is the belief in commercial circles that overproduction, the fall of prices, and more effective foreign competition, assisted by high tariffs, go far to account for the existing position of trade and industry in this country." (pp. ix−x). Cf. also pp. xi−xv of the Report.

21. Cf., e.g., Burton, Crises and Depressions, ch. IV, especially pp 113−115.

22. More in detail, what happens in connection with interest−bearing securities carried over an interval of high interest rates and business activity may be formulated as follows: When current interest rates advance, securities bearing a fixed rate (of dividends or interest) decline on the market. That is to say, the

effective capitalized value of the claim to these fixed rates of income, as shown by the market quotations, shrinks. At the same time, since the period during which this readjustment occurs is a period of acceleration in business, the earning-capacity (actual or putative) of the property on which these securities rest has increased over what it was at the time the securities were floated. Hence this property (industrial equipment) is also recapitalized, in the market quotations, at a higher value than it had when the securities were floated. The effective recapitalization carried out by the market quotations acts, for the present purpose, to the same effect upon the value of both of the items considered, this effect being to leave a margin of the property previously covered by the securities uncovered and available as collateral on which to float a new extension of credit, in the form of mortgage loan or interest-bearing security. In the common run of business procedure this available margin, between the current (higher) capitalized value of the property (collateral) and the current (lower) capitalized value of the securities resting upon it is promptly covered by a fresh credit extension ; whether this extension takes the set form of loan, bonds, preferred stock, and the like, or the less patent form of a larger volume of obligations in the way of contracts and the like, – the result, as touches the securities and their basis, being that the same nominal volume of securities with the same aggregate interest charge rests on a (materially) smaller block of the industrial equipment after this readjustment of capitalization is had than it did when the securities were placed. When depression ensues, and the rate of earnings and interest declines, the effective capitalization of the securities with a fixed rate of income is increased (if the securities are felt to be secure) to correspond with the lower rate of interest; whereas the capitalized value of the block of industrial equipment on which these securities (plus whatever may have been added in the interval) rest shrinks to correspond with the same facts. A discrepancy, such as was adjusted by a recapitalization during the interval of high rates, reappears, but in the inverse sense. And this discrepancy cannot be corrected, since the margin on which the previous adjustment was made has disappeared, and no corresponding margin on the other side emerges. Business accounts do not deal in negative quantities, except under stress of a necessity that violates the premises on which business accountancy proceeds.

Recurring to the notation employed on page 153, and letting l = par value of securities with fixed charges, r = rate per annum of fixed charges, l' = market value (effective capitalization) of these securities,

$$cap' = ea(yp = 1/int), \quad l' = lr/int,$$

but if int becomes int' (= int + delta int), l' becomes

$$l'' = lr/(int + delta\ int = int')\ l',$$

cap' at the same time becomes $cap'' = (ea + delta\ ea)/(int + delta\ int) = ea'/int'$; whereas in a period of falling interest,

$$int' = int - delta\ int, \text{ and } i'' = lr/(int' = (int - delta\ int) > l'.$$

23. Compare Hobson, Problem of the Unemployed, ch. V, and Tugan–Baranowsky, Handelskrisen, ch. I and VI. In his criticism (pp. 191–193) Tugan has quite missed the point of Hobson's theory as well as of his illustration, having apparently not understood Hobson's exposition, which is, in effect, very similar to his own. See also Hobson, Modern Capitalism, ch. VII, especially secs. 8 and 16.

24. The typical form taken by this acceleration in the machine production of machinery, but in fact it involves the production of other material factors as well as the mechanical apparatus, notably the materials used in industry.

25. The established concerns having been capitalized on the basis of past cost, we can say that in the older establishments, $cap - f(cost)$, but in the new establishments with an equal earning capacity, $cap1 = f(cost1 = cost - \text{delta cost})$; hence the rate of earnings $[= f(ea/cost)]$ will be progressively higher as cost decreases:

$$f(ea/cost)\ f(ea/(cost - \text{delta cost}))\ f(ea/(cost - 2\ \text{delta cost})), \text{etc.}$$

26. Recurring to the notation employed in note 2, page 168, and letting Um = unit of material efficiency, then a given established concern, A, with a given equipment $Um(cap)a = Ue(cap) = Um(cap) = Ue(ea/int)$, presently finds itself in competition with a younger concern, B, having an equivalent material equipment = $Um(cap)b$ procured at a lower cost and requiring lower earnings (=ea') and lower fixed charges.

$$Um(cap)b = Uc(ea'/int = (ea - \text{delta ea})/int) = Ue(cap' = cap - \text{delta cap}).$$

But $Um(cap)a = Um(cap)b$ as competitors in the market. Hence, with the competitive lowering of earnings, and therefore of effective capitalization, A's account comes to stand:

$$Um(cap)a = Uc(cap') - Uc(cap - \text{delta cap})\ Un(cap).$$

In effect A is overcapitalized by $Uc(cap - cap')$. A's nominal capital, $Un(cap)a = Uc(cap' + \text{delta cap})$, while A's effective capitalization

$$Uc(cap')a = Uc(cap - \text{delta cap}).$$

The business man's sensibilities in the case, therefore, suffer a lesion

$$= f[Un(ea/int) - Uc((ea - \text{delta ea})/int)],$$

which is a monotonic function. The discrepancy between $Un(cap)z$ and $Uc(cap')$ is, in large part, embodied in securities with fixed charges; which makes a readjustment very difficult even apart from A's reluctance.

27. With the above analysis may be contrasted Marx's discussion of the declining rate of profits and the manner in which he conceives overproduction, speculation, and crises to arise out of the tendency of profits to a minimum. (Kapital, vol. III, ch. XV) In the same connection, see Tugan–Baranowsky's criticism of Marx, Handelskrisen, ch. VII.

28. In point of direct material serviceability, no doubt, a fresh supply of the precious metals is one of the least useful forms of wealth to the production of which industrial effort can be directed, but for the purposes of business prosperity at large it is probably the most serviceable solution that can be made to the aggregate wealth. Rapidly increasing efficiency in the production of other forms of wealth is detrimental to the business interests, in that it brings depression; but a rapid increase of the precious metals is the most fortunate material circumstances for the business interests that industrial activity can bring, because it puts off depression by keeping up prices.

29. Cf. Smart, Studies in Economics, Essay VI, "Must Prices Fall?" Distribution of Incomes, bk. II, ch. III.

30. Work goes on during dull times, though at a slackened pace, and extensions and improvements are continually being made. The volume of output consequently increases, so that, even if there has been a setback to production at the beginning of the depression, the aggregate output presently again reaches the volume which it had when the dull times set in. It may be added that the rate of consumption is also appreciably lower during dull times, particularly in the more wasteful forms of consumption. This lowered aggregate consumption offsets the lowered intensity of production during dull times to such an extent that it is probably safe to say that the net surplus product, measured by weight and tale, is at least not appreciably smaller during depression than during prosperity. Cf. Carroll D. Wright, Testimony in Report of the Industrial Commission, vol. VII. p. 25.

31. The reduced scale of living of the working population is the chief factor that counts as an offset against the reduction of the gross production during dull times, as indicated above.

32. Cf. articles by G. Cassel, "Om Kriser och Daliga Tider," now running in Ekonomisk Tidskrift (1904, Nos. 1 and 2), for a parallel discussion of the topics here dealt with. Mr Cassel's exposition connects more closely with the received notions of Capital, Production, etc. and goes more into detail at certain points, particularly on Saving, Investment (Kapitalbildning), and Pecuniary Expectancy (Vantandet). His exposition is not yet completed, but so far as may be gathered from what has come to hand he should reach substantially the same outcome as that given above.

33. In the case of a speculative inflation,

$$cap = ea/cost \times 1/int \quad cap' = (ea + \Delta ea)/cost \times 1/int;$$

in the case of depression,

$$cap' = ea/(cost \times int) > cap'' = (ea - \Delta ea)/(cost \times int)$$

In the former case the current capitalization during inflation, being cap', exceeds the bona fide capital value as proved by events, cap; while in the same of depression the nominal capital, being cap', exceed the capitalization warranted by current earning capacity, cap".

34. So impressive a fact has the gambling character of early periods of inflation and crises been that it has led economists to look for gambling as a matter of course in later phenomena that have been classed as inflation and crises, even when no gambling element has been obviously present. It has been felt that gambling must presumptively be present whenever there is inflation or crises, because the showing of earlier history runs that way.

35. Cf., e.g., Burton, Crises and Depressions, ch. VIII, for a succinct account of depressions and crises in the United States during this period.

36. The speculative movement requires time, because the inflation is a cumulative one and is carried out unintentionally and in a sense unconsciously.

37. These extra-industrial expenditures that have brought prosperity are here spoken of as wasteful, not thereby implying that they may not be beneficial to the community even in respect to their effect upon the aggregate income or the aggregate accumulation of wealth in the community. They are called wasteful simply because these expenditures directly, in their first incidence, merely withdraw and dissipate wealth and work from the industrial process, and unproductively consume the products of industry. Indirectly they have a beneficial aggregate effect upon industry by inducing an employment of the fill productive efficiency of the industrial apparatus; so that in a very short time, it is at least conceivable, the aggregate net output of the industrial process may be as large and serviceable as before the wasteful expenditures were entered upon, even with the destruction of that portion of the product which goes to maintain the wasteful expenditures. At the same time, the effect upon business must be held to be patently favorable. The wasteful expenditures enhance demand and so increase the vendibility of the output, – they increase profits and raise capitalization. They therefore act unequivocally to advance the values of the business men's holdings and increase their gains, as counted in business terms. The wasteful expenditure is good for trade. It is only in the eventual liquidation that a disadvantageous business consequence comes in view.

It will be seen that on this view of the effect of wasteful expenditure the position occupied by some early economists, as Malthus, Lauderdale, Chalmers, and others, as well as by some later ones, as Robertson, Hobson, is substantially well taken, although the defence of waste which these economists offer may be incomplete. Waste seems necessary to keep trade brisk, and therefore to keep the industrial processes working at their full capacity. The ulterior reason for this state of the case being the fact that the decisive ground which determines the margin of activity in business, and therefore in industry, is the business men's reluctance to accept a reduction of profits as measured in terms of price. The opponents of the Malthusian view failed to appreciate the decisive importance of price, as contrasted with serviceability, among the motives on which business proceeds.

38. The objection would not come unexpected that this state of the case is not to be taken as normal, – a point of opinion not readily to be decided, since it rests on a difference in the point of view.

39. Cf. Sombart, Kapitalismuc, vol. I, ch. XVIII–XX.

40. Cf. Hobson, Problem of the Unemployed, Appendix to ch. V.

41. Cf. Hobson, Problem of the Unemployed, ch. VI. Mr Hobson does not use the term "waste" in this connection. Also Vialles, Consommation, final chapter.

42. "Saving" at the same time takes place automatically in the current operations of coalition and incorporation, as indicated above, pp. 166–176.

43. Hobson (Problem of the Unemployed), whose analysis of overproduction and its relation to depression goes farther than any other, reviews and criticises (ch. VIII) the palliative measures that have been advocated. He finds them, all and several, inadequate and inconsequent, in that they do not touch the root of the evil – oversaving or "underconsumption." They do not touch this because they do not mitigate the automatic saving and investment process that necessarily goes with the possession of large private incomes. But in point of practical efficiency his own proposed remedies must also be scheduled under the head of 'palliatives." These proposed remedies are measures looking to a "Reformed Distribution of Consuming Power" (ch. VI), such as taxation of "unearned" incomes, higher wages, shorter working day. The aim is "to increase the proportion of the total wealth of the community, which falling to them as wages shall be spent in raising the general standard of working–class consumption." The contemplated move is manifestly chimerical in any community, such as the modem industrial communities, where public policy is with growing singleness of purpose guided by business interests with a naive view to an increase of profits.

Cf. also Smart, Studies in Economics, Essay VIII, On "Overproduction"; also Essay IX, "The Socializing of Consumption," particularly sec. 8, on "The Limits of Consumption," pp. 293–298.

44. The obvious remark may be added, for completeness of statement, that the various branches of industry lend themselves to management by monopoly in extremely varying degrees, some, e.g., farming, as an extreme instance, not being amenable to this method of management under existing circumstances; others, again, as, e.g., retail merchandising, can be managed by this method only to a very restricted extent; while at the other end of the scale, in such industries as railroading, monopoly management, more or less unqualified, is fairly unavoidable.

45. Hitherto probably none of the American coalitions have succeeded in freeing themselves from the inconveniences of competitive bidding for labor, and very few have achieved a purely monopolistic buying, either of materials or of any of the various kinds of services which they require. With regard to raw materials alone have some, as, e.g., the Standard Oil Company, been able to compass an effectual monopoly. Something approaching this position has been accomplished by a very few other coalitions, as, e.g., the Sugar Refineries, the Cotton Seed Oil Company, the United States Steel Corporation, and in a local way certain coal, railway, lumber, and warehouse companies.

46. It is, e.g., already apparent that the general railway system of America must presently come under one management, and it must fall into a coalition with the group of industries that are occupied with the supply and elaboration of iron, coal, and lumber.

Chapter 8. Business Principles in Law and Politics

Popular welfare is bound up with the conduct of business; because industry is managed for business ends, and also because there prevails throughout modern communities a settled habit of rating the means of livelihood and the amenities of life in pecuniary terms. But apart from their effect in controlling the terms of livelihood from day to day, these principles are also in great measure decisive in the larger affairs of life, both for the individual in his civil relations and for the community at large in its political concerns. Modern (civilized) institutions rest, in great part, on business principles. This is the meaning, as applied to the modern situation, of the current phrases about the Economic Interpretation of History, or the Materialistic Theory of History.

Because of this settled habit of seeing all the conjunctures of life from the business point of view, in terms of profit and loss, the management of the affairs of the community at large falls by common consent into the hands of business men and is guided by business considerations. Hence modern politics is business politics, even apart from the sinister application of the phrase to what is invidiously called corrupt politics. This is true both of foreign and domestic policy. Legislation, police surveillance, the administration of justice, the military and diplomatic service, all are chiefly concerned with business relations, pecuniary interests, and they have little more than an incidental bearing on other human interests. All this apparatus is also charged with the protection of life and personal liberty, but its work in this bearing has much of a pecuniary color.

Legislation and legal decisions are based on the dogma of Natural Liberty. This is peculiarly true as regards the English-speaking peoples, the foundation of whose jurisprudence is the common law, and it holds true in an especial degree of America. In other European communities the sway of natural rights preconceptions is not so unmitigated, but even with them there is a visibly growing predilection for the natural-rights standpoint in all matters touching business relations. The dogma of natural liberty is peculiarly conducive to an expeditious business traffic and peculiarly consonant with the habits of thought which necessarily prevail in any business community.

The current body of natural-rights preconceptions antedates the modern business situation. The scheme of natural rights grew up and found secure lodgement in the common sense of the community, as well as with its lawgivers and courts, under the discipline of the small industry and petty trade ("domestic industry") whose development culminated in the eighteenth century.(1*) In industrial matters the efficient and autonomous factor in the days of the small industry was the individual workman, his personal force, dexterity, and diligence; similarly in the petty trade of the precapitalistic English situation the decisive factor was the discretion and sagacity of the small merchant and petty employer, who stood in the direct personal relations with their customers and their employees. In so far as trade and industry was not restrained by conventional regulations, statutory or customary, both trade and industry was in effect an open field of free competition, in which man met man on a somewhat equable footing. While the competitors were not on a footing of material equality, the industrial system was sufficiently loose-jointed, of a sufficiently diffuse growth, to make competition effective in the absence of mandatory restrictions. The like will hold of the business organization associated with the small industry. Both trade and industry were matters of personal efficiency rather than comprehensively organized processes of an impersonal character.(2*)

Natural rights, as they found their way into the conceptions of law and equity, were in effect the assumed equal rights of men so situated on a plane of at least constructive equality that the individuals concerned would be left in a position of effectively free choice if conventional restrictions were done away. The organization was not, mechanically, a close-knit one, in the sense that the concatenation of industrial processes or of business transactions was not rigorous either in point of time relations or of the quantity and character of the output or the work. Neither were the place, pace, circumstances, means, or hours of work closely determined for the workman or his employer by mechanical circumstances of the industrial process or of the market. The standardization of life under the old regime was of a conventional character, not of a mechanical kind such as is visible in the more recent development. And this conventional standardization was gradually losing force.

The movement of opinion on natural-rights ground converged to an insistence on the system of natural liberty, so called. But this insistence on natural liberty did not contemplate the abrogation of all conventional prescription. "The simple and obvious system of natural liberty" meant freedom from restraint on any other prescriptive ground than that afforded by the rights of ownership. In its economic bearing the system of natural liberty meant a system of free pecuniary contract. "Liberty does not mean license;" which in economic terms would be transcribed. "The natural freedom of the individual must not traverse the prescriptive rights of property." Property rights being included among natural rights, they had the indefeasibility which attaches to natural rights. Natural liberty prescribes freedom to buy and sell, limited only by the equal freedom of others to buy and sell; with the obvious corollary that there must be no interference with others' buying and selling, except by means of buying and selling.

This principle of natural (pecuniary) liberty has found its most unmitigated acceptance in America, and has here taken the firmest hold on the legal mind. Nowhere else has the sacredness of pecuniary obligations so permeated the common sense of the community, and nowhere does pecuniary obligation come so near being the only form of obligation that has the unqualified sanction of current common sense. Here, as nowhere else, do obligations and claims of the most diverse kinds, domestic, social, and civil, tend to take the pecuniary form and admit of being fully discharged on a monetary valuation. To a greater extent than elsewhere public esteem is awarded to artists, actors, preachers, writers, scientists, officials, in some rough proportion to the sums paid for their work.

American civil rights have taken an extreme form, with relatively great stress on the inviolability of pecuniary relations, due to the peculiar circumstances under which the American community has grown up. The pioneers, especially in that North-Atlantic seaboard community that has been chiefly effective in shaping American traditions, brought with them a somewhat high-wrought variant of the English preconception in favor of individual discretion, and this tradition they put in practice under circumstances peculiarly favorable to a bold development. They brought little of the remnants of that prescriptive code that once bound the handicraft system, and the conditions of life in the colonies did not foster a new growth of conventional regulations circumscribing private initiative. America is the native habitat of the self-made man, and the self-made man is a pecuniary organism.(3*)

Presently, when occasion arose, the metaphysics of natural liberty, pecuniary and other, was embodied in set form in constitutional enactments. It is therefore involved in a more authentic form and with more incisive force in the legal structure of this community than in that of any other. Freedom of contract is the fundamental tenet of the legal creed, so to speak, inviolable and inalienable; and within the province of law and equity no one has competence to penetrate behind this first premise or to question the merits of the natural rights metaphysics on which it rests. The only principle (attested habit of thought) which may contest its primacy in civil matters is a vague "general welfare" clause; and even this can effectively contest its claims only under exceptional circumstances. Under the application of any general welfare clause the presumption is and always must be that the principle of free contract be left intact so far as the circumstances of the case permit. The citizen may not be deprived of life, liberty, or property without due process of law, and the due process proceeds on the premise that property rights are inviolable. In its bearing upon the economic relations between individuals this comes to mean, in effect, not only that one individual or group of individuals may not legally bring any other than pecuniary pressure to bear upon another individual or group, but also that pecuniary pressure cannot be barred.

Now, through gradual change of the economic situation, this conventional principle of unmitigated and inalienable freedom of contract began to grow obsolete from about the time when it was fairly installed; obsolescent, of course, not in point of law, but in point of fact. Since about the time when this new conventional standardization of the scheme of economic life in terms of free contract reached its mature development, in the eighteenth century,(4*) a new standardizing force, that of the machine process, has invaded the field.(5*) The standardization and the constraint of the system of machine industry differs from what went before it in that it has had no conventional recognition, no metaphysical authentication. It has not become a legal fact. Therefore it neither need nor can be taken account of by the legal mind. It is a new fact which fits into the framework neither of the ancient system of prescriptive usage nor of the later system of free personal initiative. It does not exist de jure, but only de facto. Belonging neither to the defunct system nor to the current legal system, since it neither institutes nor traverses a "natural right," it is, as within the cognizance of the law, non-existent. It is, perhaps, actual, with a gross, material actuality; but it is not real, with a legal, metaphysically competent reality. Such coercion as it may exert, or as may be exercised through its means, therefore, is, in point of legal reality, no coercion.

Where physical impossibility to fulfil the terms of a contract arises out of the concatenation of industrial processes, this physical impossibility may be pleaded as invalidating the terms of the contract. But the pecuniary pressure of price or subsistence which the sequence and interdependence of industrial processes may bring to bear has no standing as such in law or equity; it can reach the cognizance of the law only indirectly, through gross defection of one of the contracting parties, in those cases where the pressure is severe enough to result in insolvency, sickness, or death. The material necessities of a group of workmen or consumers, enforced by the specialization and concatenation of industrial processes, is, therefore, not competent to set aside, or indeed to qualify, the natural freedom of the owners of these processes to let work go on or not, as the outlook for profits may decide. Profits is a business proposition, livelihood is not.(6*)

Under the current de facto standardization of economic life enforced by the machine industry, it may frequently happen that an individual or a group, e.g., of workmen, has not a de facto power of free contract. A given workman's livelihood can perhaps, practically, be found only on acceptance of one specific contract offered, perhaps not at all. But the coercion which in this way bears upon his choice through the standardization of industrial procedure is neither assault and battery nor breach of contract, and it is, therefore, not repugnant to the principles of natural liberty. Through controlling the processes of industry in which alone, practically, given workmen can find their livelihood, the owners of these processes may bring pecuniary pressure to bear upon the choice of the workmen; but since the rights of property which enforce such pressure are not repugnant to the principles of natural liberty, neither is such pecuniary pressure repugnant to the law, the case is therefore outside the scope of the law. The converse case, where the workmen take similar advantage of their employers to bring them to terms, is similarly outside the scope of the common law, − supposing, of course, that there has in neither case been a surrender of individual liberty, a breach of contract, theft, a resort to violence, or threats of violence. So long as there is no overt attempt on life, liberty of the person, or the liberty to buy and sell, the law cannot intervene, unless it be in a precautionary way to prevent prospective violation of personal or property rights.

The "natural," conventional freedom of contract is sacred and inalienable. De facto freedom of choice is a matter about which the law and the courts are not competent to inquire. By force of the concatenation of industrial processes and the dependence of men's comfort or subsistence upon the orderly working of these processes, the exercise of the rights of ownership in the interests of business may traverse the de facto necessities of a group or class; it may even traverse the needs of the community at large, as, e.g., in the conceivable case of an advisedly instituted coal famine; but since these necessities, of comfort or of livelihood, cannot be formulated in terms of the natural freedom of contract, they can, in the nature of the case, give rise to no cognizable grievance and find no legal remedy.

The discrepancy between law and fact in the matter of industrial freedom has had repeated illustration in the court decisions on disputes between bodies of workmen and their employers or owners. These decisions commonly fall out in favor of the employers or owners; that is to say, they go to uphold property rights and the rights of free contract. The courts have been somewhat broadly taken to task by a certain class of observers for alleged partiality to the owners' side in this class of litigation. It has also been pointed out by faultfinders that the higher courts decide, on the whole, more uniformly in favor of the employer−owner than the lower ones, and especially more so than the juries in those cases where juries have found occasion to pass on the law of the case. The like is true as regards suits for damages arising out of injuries sustained by workmen, and so involving the question of the employer's liability. Even a casual scrutiny of the decisions, however, will show that in most cases the decision of the court, whether on the merits of the case or on the constitutionality of the legal provisions involved,(7*) is well grounded on the metaphysical basis of natural liberty. That is to say in other words, the decisions will be found on the side of the maintenance of fundamental law and order, "law and order" having, of course, reference to the inalienable rights of ownership and contract. As should fairly be expected, the higher courts, who are presumably in more intimate touch with the principles of jurisprudence, being more arduously trained and more thoroughly grounded in the law at the same time that they have also presumably a larger endowment of legal acumen, – these higher courts speak more unequivocally for the metaphysical principles and apply them with a surer and firmer touch. In the view of these higher adepts of the law, free contract is so inalienable a natural right of man that not even a statutory enactment will enable a workman to forego its exercise and its responsibility. By metaphysical necessity its exercise attaches to the individual so indefeasibly that it cannot constitutionally be delegated to collective action, whether legislative or corporate.(8*) This extreme consequence of the principle of natural liberty has at times aroused indignation in the vulgar; but their grasp of legal principles is at fault. The more closely the logical sequence is followed up, the more convincingly does the legitimacy of such a decision stand out.

In comparing the decisions of the higher courts with those of the lower they contrast most signally with the decisions rendered by juries in the lower tribunals. While this contrast has a significance in another connection, it casts no shadow on the legality of the decisions of the courts of higher instance. The juries, in great measure, speak for the strained sympathies of the vulgar, which are a matter somewhat apart from the foundations of law and order.(9*)

Popular sentiment, then, does not at all uniformly bear out these decisions of the courts in disputes between property rights and naked mankind, especially not in the more rigorous enforcement of the principle of free contract. This discrepancy serves to show that the vulgar, the laity, from whose numbers the juries are drawn, have not an adequate sense of the principles that lie at the root of the law; which may be due in part to their not realizing how essential a foundation of law, order, and common welfare these principles of natural liberty are. The visible disparity in the distribution of property may make those classes who have little property envious of the wealthy members, and so make them lose interest in the maintenance of the rights of property. But apart from this, the discipline of daily life, from which the common-sense notions of the vulgar are in good part derived, is no longer in full accord with the natural-rights conceptions handed down from the eighteenth century. In other words, the conceptions of natural rights on which the common law rests embody a technically competent formulation of the deliverances of that body of common sense which was inculcated by the discipline of everyday life in the eighteenth century, before the advent of the current situation; whereas the discipline of everyday life under the current technological and business situation inculcates a body of common-sense views somewhat at variance with the received natural-rights notions.

There is apparently something of a divergence between the received notions on this head and the deliverances of latter-day common sense. The divergence is neither well defined nor consistent. The latter-day attitude toward questions of the kind involved is vague, chiefly negative or critical, and apparently fluctuating; but after all there is a somewhat persistent divergence, which may even be said to have a systematic character, so far as it goes. It runs in the direction of a (partial and vacillating) disavowal or distrust of the metaphysics of free contract, and even of natural liberty generally. This uncertainty of allegiance to the received foundations of law and order prevails in unequal degrees among the various classes of the community, being apparently largest and most outspoken among the workmen of the industrial towns, and being, on the whole, less noticeable among the propertied and professional classes and the rural population. The peculiar class distribution of this disintegration of received convictions, as well as its connection with modern industrial conditions, will be taken up again presently in another connection.

The state, that is to say, the government, was once an organization for the control of affairs in the interest of princely or dynastic ends. In internal affairs statecraft was occupied with questions of the dynastic succession, the endeavors and intrigues of the political magnates, fiscal administration directed to finding adequate support for the princely power, and the like. In external politics the objective end was dynastic prestige and security, military success, and the like. Such is still in part the end of political endeavor in those countries, as, e.g., Germany, Austria, or Italy, where the transition to a constitutional government has not been completed. But since the advent of constitutional government and parliamentary representation, business ends have taken the lead of dynastic ends in statecraft, very much in the same measure as the transition to constitutional methods has been effectually carried through. A constitutional government is a business government. It is particularly through the business expedient of parliamentary voting on the budget that any constitutional executive, e.g., is kept within constitutional bounds; and the budget is voted with a main view to its expediency for business ends. The expediency of business enterprise is not questioned, whereas the expediency of an increase of princely power and dignity, with the incidental costs, may be questioned.

Modern governmental policies, looking as they do to the furthering of business interests as their chief care, are of a "mercantile" complexion. They aim to foster trade, as did the mercantile policies of the sixteenth and seventeenth centuries, although since "trade" has come to include much else than foreign commerce, the modern policies look to business in the more comprehensive sense which the term now necessarily has. But these modern mercantile policies, with their tariffs, treaties, interstate commerce regulations, and maxims prohibiting all "restraint of trade," are after all not of the same nature as the mercantile policies of the old French and German statesmen, which they superficially resemble. The old "mercantile system," as it prevailed on the Continent of Europe, was conceived in the interest of the prince, the furthering of commercial advantage being a means to princely power and dignity. (10*) The modern mercantilism under constitutional rule, on the other hand, looks to the prince or to the government as a means to the end of commercial gain. With the transition to constitutional rule and methods, the discretion and autonomy in the case has passed from the hands of the prince into those of the business men, and the interests of the business men have superseded those of the crown.

Representative government means, chiefly, representation of business interests. The government commonly works in the interest of the business men with a fairly consistent singleness of purpose. And in its solicitude for the business men's interests it is borne out by current public sentiment, for there is a naive, unquestioning persuasion abroad among the body of the people to the effect that, in some occult way, the material interests of the populace coincide with the pecuniary interests of those business men who live within the scope of the same set of governmental contrivances. This persuasion is an article of popular metaphysics, in that it rests on an uncritically assumed solidarity of interests, rather than on an insight into the relation of business enterprise to the material welfare of those classes who are not primarily business men. This persuasion is particularly secure among the more conservative portion of the community, the business men, superior and subordinate, together with the professional classes, as contrasted with those vulgar portions of the community who are tainted with socialistic or anarchistic notions. But since the conservative element comprises the citizens of substance and weight, and indeed the effective majority of law-abiding citizens, it follows that, with the sanction of the great body of the people, even including those who have no pecuniary interests to serve in the matter, constitutional government has, in the main, become a department of the business organization and is guided by the advice of the business men. The government has, of course, much else to do besides administering the general affairs of the business community; but in most of its work, even in what is not ostensibly directed to business ends, it is under the surveillance of the business interests. It seldom happens, if at all, that the government of a civilized nation will persist in a course of action detrimental or not ostensibly subservient to the interests of the more conspicuous body of the community's business men. The degree in which a government fails to adapt its policy to these business exigencies is the measure of its senility.

The ground of sentiment on which rests the popular approval of a government for business ends may be summed up under two heads : patriotism and property. Both of these terms stand for institutional facts that have come down out of a past which differed substantially from the present situation. The substance of both is of the nature of unreasoning sentiment, in the sense that both are insisted on as a matter of course, as self-legitimating grounds of action which, it is felt, not only give expedient rules of conduct, but admit of no question as to their ulterior consequences or their value for the life-purposes of the community. The former of these fundamental institutional habits of thought (perhaps better, habits of mind) runs back to the discipline of early barbarism, through the feudal days of fealty to the earlier days of clan life and clannish animosity. It has therefore the deep-rooted strength given by an extremely protracted discipline of predation and servitude. Under modern conditions it is to be rated as essentially an institutional survival, so ingrained in the populace as to make any appeal to it secure of a response irrespective of the material merits of the contention in whose behalf the appeal is made.(11*)

By force of this happy knack of clannish fancy the common man is enabled to feel that he has some sort of metaphysical share in the gains which accrue to the business men who are citizens of the same "commonwealth"; so that whatever policy furthers the commercial gains of those business men whose domicile is within the national boundaries is felt to be beneficial to all the rest of the population.(12*)

The second institutional support of business politics, viz. property, is similarly an outgrowth of the discipline of the past, and similarly, though perhaps in a less degree, out of touch with the discipline of the more recent cultural situation. In the form in which it prevails in the current popular animus, the principle of ownership comes down from the days of handicraft industry and petty trade, as pointed out above. As it is of less ancient and less unbroken descent, so it seems also to be a less secure cultural heritage than the sense of patriotic solidarity. It says that the ownership of property is the material foundation of human wellbeing, and that this natural right of ownership is sacred, after the manner in which individual life, and more especially national life, is sacred. The habits of life and thought inculcated by joint work under the manorial system and by joint rules under the handicraft system have apparently contributed much to the notion of a solidarity of economic interests, having given the notion such a degree of consistency as has enabled it to persist in the face of a visible discrepancy of interests in later, capitalistic times. Under this current, business regime, business gains are the basis of individual wealth, and the (pseudo) notion of joint acquisition has taken the place of the manorial notion of joint work. The institutional animus of ownership, as it took shape under the discipline of early modern handicraft, awards the ownership of property to the workman who has produced it. By a dialectical conversion of the terms, this metaphysical dictum is made to fit the circumstances of later competitive business by construing acquisition of property to mean production of wealth; so that a business man is looked upon as the putative producer of whatever wealth he acquires. By force of this sophistication the acquisition of property by any person is held to be, not only expedient for the owner, but meritorious as an action serving the common good. Failure to bargain shrewdly or to accumulate more goods than one has produced by the work of one's own hands is looked upon with a feeling of annoyance, as a neglect, not only of opportunity, but of duty. The pecuniary conscience commonly does not, of course, go to quixotic lengths in a public spirited insistence on everybody's acquiring more than an aliquot part of the aggregate wealth on hand, but it is felt that he best serves the common good who, other things equal, diverts the larger share of the aggregate wealth to his own possession. His acquiring a defensible title to it makes him the putative producer of it.

The natural-rights basis of ownership is by this paralogism preserved intact, and the common man is enabled to feel that the business men in the community add to the aggregate wealth at least as much as they acquire a title to; and the successful business men are at least as well persuaded that such is their relation to the aggregate wealth and to the material well-being of the community at large. So that both the business men whose gains are sought to be enhanced by business politics and the populace by whose means the business gains are secured work together in good faith towards a well-advised business end, – the accumulation of wealth in the hands of those men who are skilled in pecuniary matters.(13*)

The manner in which business interests work out in government policy may be shown by following up their bearing upon one phase of this policy. An extreme expression of business politics, and at the same time a characteristic trait of the higher levels of national life in Christendom, is the current policy of war and armaments. Modern business is competitive, emulative, and the direction of business enterprise is in the hands of men who are single-minded in their competitive conduct of affairs. They neither are inclined, nor will business competition permit them, to neglect or overlook any expedient that may further their own advantage or hinder the advantage of their rivals. Under the modern situation, as it has taken shape since the industrial revolution,(14*) business competition has become international, covering the range of what is called the world market. In this international competition the machinery and policy of the state are in a peculiar degree drawn into the service of the larger business interests; so that, both in commerce and industrial enterprise, the business men of one nation are pitted against those of another and swing the forces of the state, legislative, diplomatic, and military, against one another in the strategic game of pecuniary advantage. The business interests domiciled within the scope of a given government fall into a loose organization in the form of what might be called a tacit ring or syndicate, proceeding on a general understanding that they will stand together as against outside business interests. The nearest approach to an explicit plan and organization of such a business ring is the modern political party, with its platform, tacit and avowed. Parties differ in their detail aims, but those parties that have more than a transient existence and superficial effect stand for different lines of business policy, agreeing all the while in so far that they all aim to further what they each claim to be the best, largest, most enduring business interests of the community. The ring(15*) of business interests which secures the broadest approval from popular sentiment is, under constitutional methods, put in charge of the government establishment. This popular approval may be secured on the ground of a sound business platform or (in part) on some ground extraneous to business policy proper, such as a wave of national animosity, a popular candidate, a large grain crop, etc. But the only secure basis of an enduring party tenure of the government machinery is a business policy which falls in with the interests or the prejudices of the effective majority.

    In international competition the ultima ratio is, as ever, warlike force, whether the issue be between princes of the grace of God or princes of ownership. It is a favorite maxim of modern politics that trade follows the flag. This is the business man's valuation of national policy and of the ends of national life. So stated, the maxim probably inverts the sequence of facts, but it is none the less a fair expression of the close relation there is between business endeavor and the modern military policies. Diplomacy, if it is to be effective for whatever end, must be backed by a show of force and of a readiness to use it. The definitive argument of those who speak for armaments (in England and America) is that the maintenance of business interests requires the backing of arms. On the Continent of Europe this argument commonly comes second, while patriotic fancy and animosity take the first place.

    Armaments serve trade not only in the making of general terms of purchase and sale between the business men of civilized countries, but they are similarly useful in extending and maintaining business enterprise and privileges in the outlying regions of the earth. The advanced nations of Christendom are proselyters, and there are certain valuable perquisites that come to the business men of those proselyting nations who advance the frontiers of the pecuniary culture among the backward populations. There is commonly a handsome margin of profit in doing business with these, pecuniarily unregenerate, populations, particularly when the traffic is adequately backed with force. But, also commonly, these peoples do not enter willingly into lasting business relations with civilized mankind. It is therefore necessary, for the purposes of trade and culture, that they be firmly held up to such civilized rules of conduct as will make trade easy and lucrative. To this end armament is indispensable.

    But in the portioning out of the trade perquisites that fall to the proselyters any business community is in danger of being overreached by alien civilizing powers. No recourse but force is finally available in disputes of this kind, in which the aim of the disputants is to take advantage of one another as far as they can. A warlike front is therefore necessary, and armaments and warlike demonstrations have come to be a part of the regular apparatus of business, so far as business is concerned with the world market.

    In so far as it is guided by the exigencies of trade, the objective end of warlike endeavor is the peace and security necessary to an orderly development of business. International business relations, it is well said, make for peace; in the sense, of course, that they enforce the pacification of recalcitrant barbarians and lead to contention between civilized nations for a revision of the peace terms. When a modern government goes to war for trade purposes, it does so with a view to reestablishing peace on terms more lucrative to its business men.(16*)

The above inquiry into the nature and causes of the wars of nations has resulted in little else than a recital of commonplaces; the facts and their connection are matters of common notoriety, and probably no one would hazard a question of the sight and obvious inferences drawn in the course of the recital. The excuse for this discursive review of the motives and aims of a war policy is that it gives a basis for an outlook on the present and immediate future of business enterprise.(17*)

The experience of Continental Europe in the matter of armaments during the last half-century, and of all the greater nations during the last two decades, argues that when warlike emulation between states of somewhat comparable force has once got under way it assumes a cumulative character; so that a scale of expenditure for armaments which would at the outset have seemed absurdly impossible comes presently to be accepted as a matter of course. Hitherto the cumulative augmentation of war expenditures and of war animus shows no sign of slackening. One after another, the states that have offered some show of peaceable inclinations have been drawn into the international game of competitive armaments, as they have one after another become ambitious to push the enterprises of their business men in the international markets. An armament is serviceable only if it is relatively large; its absolute magnitude is a matter of no particular consequence for competitive politics. It is its comparative size that counts. Hence the greater the several armaments, the greater the political need of greater armaments, and the prompter the resentment of injuries and the livelier the felt need of offending and of taking offence. A progressively larger proportion of the nation's forces are withdrawn from industry and devoted to warlike ends. In this cumulative diversion of effort to warlike ends a point is presently reached beyond which the question of armament is no longer, What amount of warlike expenditure is needed to extend or maintain business traffic? but rather, What amount will the nation's resources bear? But the progression does not stop at that point; witness the case of Italy, France, and Germany, where the war drain has visibly impaired the industrial efficiency of the several nations concerned, but where the burden still goes on growing, with no stopping-place in sight. England and, more particularly, America are not so near exhaustion, because they have larger resources to draw on as well as a culture and a population more efficient for industrial work. But there is no evident reason why these two should not likewise enter on a policy of emulative exhaustion, and so sacrifice their aggregate industrial and business interest to the furtherance of the "great game."

The question may suggest itself, Why should not the business community, who have a large discretion in international politics and whose aggregate gains are cut into by excessive war expenditures, call a halt when the critical point is reached? There is more than one reason for their failure to do so. War and preoccupation with warlike enterprise breed a warlike animus in the community, as well as a habit of arbitrary, autocratic rule on the part of those in authority and an unquestioning, enthusiastic subservience on the part of the subjects. National animosity and national pride demand more and more of military standing, at the same time that the growing official class needs increasing emoluments and a larger field of employment and display. The cultural effects of the discipline of warfare and armament are much the same whether it is undertaken for drastic or for business ends; in either case it takes on a dynastic complexion and breeds the temperament, ideals, and institutional habits proper to a drastic system of politics. The farther it goes the more it comes to make use of business interests as a means rather than an end, as, e.g., in modern Germany, France, and Italy, and in the Continental states of the sixteenth and seventeenth centuries. The crown, court, bureaucracy, military establishment, and nobility, under whatever designations, gradually come to their own again in such a situation, and affairs again come to turn on questions of the maintenance and dignity of these superior elements of the population.(18*) The objective end of protracted warlike endeavor necessarily shifts from business advantage to dynastic ascendancy and courtly honor. Business interests fall to the position of fiscal ways and means, and business traffic becomes subservient to higher ends, with a fair chance of ultimate exhaustion or collapse through the bankruptcy of the state.

Business enterprise is an individual matter, not a collective one. So long as the individual business man sees a proximate gain for himself in meeting the demands for war funds and materials to maintain the courtly and official establishments that go with military politics, it is not in the nature of the business man to draw back. It is always his profits, not his livelihood, that is involved; the question which touches his profits is the relative gainfulness of alternative lines of investment open to him. So long as the pecuniary inducements held out by the state, in bidding for funds or supplies, overbalance the inducements offered by alternative lines of employment, the business men will supply these demands, regardless of what the ulterior substantial outcome of such a course may be in the end. Funds and business enterprise are now of so pronounced an international or cosmopolitan character that any business man may, even without fully appreciating the fact, lend his aid to the fisc of a hostile power as readily as to a friendly power or to the home government; whereby an equable and comprehensive exhaustion of the several communities involved in the concert of nations is greatly facilitated. Barring accidents and untoward cultural agencies from outside of politics, business, or religion, there is nothing in the logic of the modern situation that should stop the cumulative war expenditures short of industrial collapse and consequent national bankruptcy, such as terminated the carnival of war and politics that ran its course on the Continent in the sixteenth and seventeenth centuries.(19*)

NOTES:

1. Ashley, Economic History and Theory, bk. II, especially ch. III.

2. See Chapter IV above.

3. Cf. e.g., Ashley, "The Economic Atmosphere of America" in Surveys, Historical and Economic, pp. 405 et seq.

4. This date is true for England. For America the discipline favorable to the growth of the natural–liberty dogma lasted nearly a century longer. In America the new, modern, technological and business era can scarcely be said to have set in in good vigor until the period of the Civil War. Hence, with a longer and later training, the preconceptions of natural liberty are fresher and more tenacious in America. For the Continental peoples the case is different again. With them the modern technological and business situation is of approximately the same date as in America, but their training up to the date of the transition to the modern situation was in a much less degree a training in individual initiative, free scattered industry, and petty trade. The Continental peoples for the most part made a somewhat abrupt transition after the middle of the nineteenth century from a stale and dilapidated system of guild and feudalistic prescriptions to the (for them) exotic system of modern technology and business principles.

5. See Chapter II above and Chapter IX below.

6. Under the system of handicraft and petty trade the converse was true. Livelihood was the fundamental norm of business regulations; profits had but a secondary standing, if any.

7. E.g., as to employer's liability for accidents or unsanitary premises, the safeguarding of machinery, age limit of labourers or hour limit of working time, etc.

8. E.g. where a workman's accepting employment on machinery which is not safeguarded as the law requires is construed as an exercise of the indefeasible right of free contract on his part, which thereby exempts the employer from liability for eventual accidents.

In point of legal principle the reluctance to allow or recognize limited liability in joint stock companies, in the English practice prior to the Companies Acts, was of much the same nature as the current reluctance to allow an alienation or abridgment of a workman's individual reSpOnsibility for the terms of his employment and the consequences following from it. It was felt that a pecuniary liability was a personal matter, of which the person was not competent to divest himself under that system of mutual rights and duties in which the members of the community were bound together. Impersonal, collective, and limited liability won its way, as against the system of natural liberty, in this field by sheer force of business expediency. In a conflict of principles between the main proposition and one of its corollaries, the corollary won because the facts had outgrown the primary implication of the main proposition.

9. The common law is of course a formulation of the deliverances of common sense on the points which it touches. But common law, as well as common sense, being a formulation of habits of thought, is necessarily an outgrowth of past rather than of present circumstances, — in this case the circumstances of the eighteenth century, whereas the sympathies of the vulgar, as they appear in jury decisions, are largely the outcome of those modern experiences that are at increasing variance with the foundations of the common law.

It may be remarked by the way that, while the charge of partiality or corruption, often heard as against these higher tribunals, may in a few scattering instances be founded, that is after all not much to the point as regards practical consequences. The greater number of the courts, indeed virtually the entire judiciary, are no doubt above substantial suspicion in the premises. And after all, if they were not incorruptible, — if the common run of the tribunals were corruptly working in the interest of the employers or owners, — that need not seriously affect the outcome as regards the general tenor of the decisions handed down. If they are corrupt or biassed, they will decide in favor of the owners, who can afford to pay, and they will be under the necessity of finding plausible reasons in law for so doing. Such reason can be found only in the metaphysical natural rights basis of the law; and if it can be found by the help of such legal ratiocination, then it is a valid ground of decision, that being the peculiar merit of metaphysical grounds of decision. On the other hand, if the court is a "learned, upright judge," he will look for the grounds of decision in the same place and find them in the same shape. Necessarily so, since the point in dispute is almost invariably a question of the legal rights of property as against the material requirements of comfort or of livelihood; and the rights of property are the foundation of modern law and order, while the requirements of comfort or livelihood passed out of the scope of the law on the abrogation of the outworn system of mandatory prescriptions governing industrial and trade relations in early modern times. Since the disputes in question rarely if ever arise out of a breach of contract on the part of the employer–owner, the decision can ordinarily, in the nature of the case, not go against him, inasmuch as the foundation of economic law and order is the freedom and inviolability of pecuniary contracts. It should, in fact, be nearly a matter of indifference to the "popular" side of this class of litigation whether the courts are corrupt or not. The question has little else than a speculative interest. In the nature of the case the owner alone has, ordinarily, any standing in court. All of which argues that there are probably very few courts that are in any degree corrupt or biassed, so far as touches litigation of this class. Efforts to corrupt them would be a work of supererogation, besides being immoral.

10. This is not true in nearly the same degree for the mercantile policies of England, even in early modern times. In English policy, under the inchoate constitutional system of the mercantilist era, the ulterior (avowed) end is always the (business) advantage of the "commonwealth." The prince comes in rather as second than as first claimant on the solicitude of the mercantilist statesman.

11. The line of descent of the preconception of patriotism or chauvinism, as it finds expression in this lively sense of pecuniary solidarity, may be outlined as follows: Under the clan (gentile or tribal) system out of which the West–European peoples passed into the regime of feudal Christendom, a given group stood together in a union of offence and defence, warlike and economic, on the basis of a putative blood relationship. When the manor or the (essentially servile) mark came to replace the clan group as the economic and civil unit, the bond of putative blood relationship persisted in a slightly modified form and force, the

incidence of the sense of solidarity, the "consciousness of kind," then shifting to the new group unit, with allegiance centring on the feudal head of the group, instead of, as formerly, on the senior line of putative descent. When the state came forward in medieval and early modern times and took over the powers and prerogatives of the head of the manor or the feudal lord, it took over also the incidence of this sense of allegiance, and the sense of solidarity came to cover the larger group of the nation which had succeeded to the autonomy of the manor. Where the line of institutional descent runs through the industrial town, with guild, handicraft, and local government, the transient features of the growth are superficially different but in effect much the same. The discipline of warfare, which kept up the practice of joint action and had the appearance of joint enterprise, served to keep the sense of patriotic solidarity firm and vigorous and enabled it to cover other interests as well as the princely enterprise of warfare and state-making. Wherever unbroken peace prevailed for an appreciable period, so as to affect the growth of traditions, the sense of national solidarity showed symptoms of slackening. For purposes of economic solidarity the commonwealth is conceived after the manner of an overgrown manor. It figures as such, e.g., in English mercantilist writings of the sixteenth to the eighteenth century, as well as in the patriotic trade politics of the present.

12. In passing it may be remarked that the fact of this sense of solidarity being an anachronism must not be taken as implying anything for or against the substantial merits of such a frame of mind.

13. The two complementary sentiments—patriotism and pecuniary solidarity – are found in unequal measure among the several nations of Christendom. The disparity in this respect corresponds roughly with a disparity in past national experience. The Continental peoples, e.g., have, on the whole, a readier and fuller, more unequivocal, patriotic conviction, as they have also had a longer, more severe, and later discipline in the fealty that goes with a system of dynastic warfare and graded servitude; whereas the English-speaking peoples are animated with a more secure conviction that money value is the chief end of serious endeavor and that business solvency is the final attribute of manhood. But in either case the outcome is the primacy of business in the counsels of nations, and its empire is none the less secure for its resting more on one or the other of these two supports.

14. For England the last half of the eighteenth century, for Continental Europe and America the last half of the nineteenth. In colonial commerce the date for both England and the Continent is much earlier.

15. "Ring" is here used as a designation of this loose organization of business interests for the guidance of policy, without implying criticism of the ring or of its aims and methods.

16. Armaments and large military and naval establishments have also a secondary attraction, of a more intimate kind, for enterprising business men, in that they afford opportunities for transactions of a peculiarly lucrative character. One of the parties (the government official) concerned in such transactions has less than the usual incentive to drive a close bargain. His own private gain and loss is not immediately involved, so that he is less given to petty huckstering and close surveillance of the execution of the contracts made. What adds force to this consideration is the fact that military and naval establishments habitually are what the vulgar would call corrupt. The pecuniary interest of the officials does not coincide with that of the establishment There is an appreciable "margin of error" which a sagacious business man may turn to account.

The great business interests are the more inclined to look kindly on an extension of warlike enterprise and armaments, since the pecuniary advantages inure to them, while the pecuniary burden falls chiefly on the rest of the community. It is, to say the least, highly improbable that the business gains which accrue from a well-conducted foreign policy ever, in modern times, equal the cost at which they are secured; but that consideration scarcely enters, since the costs are not paid out of business gains, but out of the industry of the rest of the people. The people, however, are animated with an uncritical persuasion that they have some sort of a residuary share in these gains, and that this residuary share in some manner exceeds the whole of the gains secured.

17. See Chapter X. above.

18. Cf. Hobson, Imperialism, pt. I, ch. VII, pt. II, ch. I, and VII.

19. On the relation of business to warlike expenditure in the sixteenth and seventeenth centuries, cf., Ehrenberg, Zeitalter der Fugger.

Chapter 9. The Cultural Incidence of the Machine Process

So far as regards the non-mechanical factors of culture, such as religion, politics, and even business enterprise, the present is in a very large degree comparable with the scheme of things that prevailed on the Continent of Europe in the seventeenth century. And so far as the working of these cultural factors is undisturbed by forces that were not present in the older days, they should logically again work out in such a situation as came to prevail in Central Europe in the course of the eighteenth century. The modern situation, of course, is drawn on a larger scale; but that is due to the intrusion of a new technology, a different "state of the industrial arts," and not to a substantially altered range of religious, political, or business conceptions. The pitch of squalor that characterized vulgar life in the busier Continental countries at the close of the great era of politics could probably not be reached again, but that again, is due, not to these spiritual factors of cultural growth, but to the altered state of the industrial arts. The factor in the modern situation that is alien to the ancient regime is the machine technology, with its many and wide ramifications.

Business conceptions and business methods were present in vigorous growth in Central Europe in the sixteenth and seventeenth centuries, as they had been in South Europe from a slightly earlier date; although the large sweep of business enterprise is not had until a later date, being conditioned by the machine technology. Business methods and the apparatus of business traffic develop very promptly whenever and wherever the situation calls for them; such is the teaching of economic history.(1*) There is nothing recondite about them, little that has to be acquired by a protracted, cumulative experience running over many generations, such as is involved in technological development. This business development in earlier modern times, together with the accumulations of funded wealth that came of this business enterprise, ran their course to a finish in Continental Europe, leaving no basis for a new start. The new start from which the current situation takes its rise, in Europe and elsewhere, was given to the Continental peoples by the English, ready-made, in the so-called Industrial Revolution. The natural-rights metaphysics, to which the eventual breakdown of the old Continental system owed its specific character, came also from the English.(2*)

In point of blood and cultural descent the population of Great Britain did not differ materially from their neighbors across the Channel or across the North Sea.(3*) But from the beginning of the modern cultural era Great Britain stood outside of the general European situation, by force of its physical isolation. So that during the modern era, down to the close of the eighteenth century, the British community was in the position of an interested third party rather than a participant in the political concert of Europe. The era of "statemaking," so called, is an era in which England interferes, but is, on the whole, not greatly interfered with, so far as her own home affairs are concerned. England, and presently Great Britain, being reduced to law and order under one crown and living in a condition of isolation and (relatively) of internal peace, the cultural growth of that country took a relatively peaceable direction. The dominant note of everyday life was industry and trade, not dynastic politics and war. This national experience gave as its outcome constitutional government and the modern industrial technology, together with the animus and the point of view of the modern materialistic science. The point of departure for the more recent, current situation, therefore, is a twofold one: (1) the British peaceable variant of the Western culture has contributed constitutional methods and natural rights, together with the machine technology brought in under the head of the "industrial revolution"; and (2) there are the patriotic ideals and animosities left as a residue of the warlike political traffic in Continental Europe.

Since the new departure, made on the basis of natural rights and modern industrial and scientific methods, the complex of nations and of international relations is a single, not a twofold one. The stage over which affairs, political, industrial and cultural, run their course is no longer Continental or British, but cosmopolitan, comprising all civilized communities and all civilized interests. So that there is not now, as there was in the sixteenth and seventeenth centuries, an isolation hospital for technology, science, and civil rights, set apart from the general current of cultural development. Whatever the forces at work in the modern situation may eventually bring to pass, therefore, the outcome must touch all communities in the same way and in approximately the same degree. If the outcome is dynastic politics and armament again played to a finish in popular squalor, aristocratic virtues, and universal bankruptcy, there will be no peaceable community of matter–of–fact mechanics and shopkeepers left in reserve from which to make a new cultural and industrial start. The modern technology has, in a manner, cut away the ground out of which it first grew and from which it gathered force to reshape the course of history. It has made it impossible for any community to stand peaceably outside of the great complex of nations.

But within the comprehensive situation of to–day there is this new factor, the machine process. In an earlier chapter (II) the technological character of this machine process has been set forth at some length. The machine process pervades the modern life and dominates it in a mechanical sense. Its dominance is seen in the enforcement of precise mechanical measurements and adjustment and the reduction of all manner of things, purposes and acts, necessities, conveniences, and amenities of life, to standard units. The bearing of this sweeping mechanical standardization upon business traffic is a large part of the subject–matter of the foregoing chapters. The point of immediate interest here is the further bearing of the machine process upon the growth of culture, – the disciplinary effect which this movement for standardization and mechanical equivalence has upon the human material.

This discipline falls more immediately on the workmen engaged in the mechanical industries, and only less immediately on the rest of the community which lives in contact with this sweeping machine process. Wherever the machine process extends, it sets the pace for the workmen, great and small. The pace is set, not wholly by the particular processes in the details of which the given workman is immediately engaged, but in some degree by the more comprehensive process at large into which the given detail process fits. It is no longer simply that the individual workman makes use of one or more mechanical contrivances for effecting certain results. Such used to be his office in the earlier phases of the use of machines, and the work which he now has in hand still has much of that character. But such a characterization of the workman's part in industry misses the peculiarly modern feature of the case. He now does this work as a factor involved in a mechanical process whose movement controls his motions. It remains true, of course, as it always has been true, that he is the intelligent agent concerned in the process, while the machine, furnace, roadway, or retort are inanimate structures devised by man and subject to the workman's supervision. But the process comprises him and his intelligent motions, and it is by virtue of his necessarily taking an intelligent part in what is going forward that the mechanical process has its chief effect upon him. The process standardizes his supervision and guidance of the machine. Mechanically speaking, the machine is not his to do with it as his fancy may suggest. His place is to take thought of the machine and its work in terms given him by the process that is going forward. His thinking in the premises is reduced to standard units of gauge and grade. If he fails of the precise measure, by more or less, the exigencies of the process check the aberration and drive home the absolute need of conformity.

There results a standardization of the workman's intellectual life in terms of mechanical process, which is more unmitigated and precise the more comprehensive and consummate the industrial process in which he plays a part. This must not be taken to mean that such work need lower the degree of intelligence of the workman. No doubt the contrary is nearer the truth. He is a more efficient workman the more intelligent he is, and the discipline of the machine process ordinarily increases his efficiency even for work in a different line from that by which the discipline is given. But the intelligence required and inculcated in the machine industry is of a peculiar character. The machine process is a severe and insistent disciplinarian in point of intelligence. It requires close and unremitting thought, but it is thought which runs in standard terms of quantitative precision. Broadly, other intelligence on the part of the workman is useless; or it is even worse than useless, for a habit of thinking in other than quantitative terms blurs the workman's quantitative apprehension of the facts with which he has to do.(4*)

In so far as he is a rightly gifted and fully disciplined workman, the final term of his habitual thinking is mechanical efficiency, understanding "mechanical" in the sense in which it is used above. But mechanical efficiency is a matter of precisely adjusted cause and effect. What the discipline of the machine industry inculcates, therefore, in the habits of life and of thought of the workman, is regularity of sequence and mechanical precision; and the intellectual outcome is an habitual resort to terms of measurable cause and effect, together with a relative neglect and disparagement of such exercise of the intellectual faculties as does not run on these lines.

Of course, in no case and with no class does the discipline of the machine process mould the habits of life and of thought fully into its own image. There is present in the human nature of all classes too large a residue of the propensities and aptitudes carried over from the past and working to a different result. The machine's regime has been of too short duration, strict as its discipline may be, and the body of inherited traits and traditions is too comprehensive and consistent to admit of anything more than a remote approach to such a consummation.

The machine process compels a more or less unremitting attention to phenomena of an impersonal character and to sequences and correlations not dependent for their force upon human predilection nor created by habit and custom. The machine throws out anthropomorphic habits of thought. It compels the adaptation of the workman to his work, rather than the adaptation of the work to the workman. The machine technology rests on a knowledge of impersonal, material cause and effect, not on the dexterity, diligence, or personal force of the workman, still less on the habits and propensities of the workman's superiors. Within the range of this machine-guided work, and within the range of modern life so far as it is guided by the machine process, the course of things is given mechanically, impersonally, and the resultant discipline is a discipline in the handling of impersonal facts for mechanical effect. It inculcates thinking in terms of opaque, impersonal cause and effect, to the neglect of those norms of validity that rest on usage and on the conventional standards handed down by usage. Usage counts for little in shaping the processes of work of this kind or in shaping the modes of thought induced by work of this kind.

The machine process gives no insight into questions of good and evil, merit and demerit, except in point of material causation, nor into the foundations or the constraining force of law and order, except such mechanically enforced law and order as may be stated in terms of pressure, temperature, velocity, tensile strength, etc.(5*) The machine technology takes no cognizance of conventionally established rules of precedence; it knows neither manners nor breeding and can make no use of any of the attributes of worth. Its scheme of knowledge and of inference is based on the laws of material causation, not on those of immemorial custom, authenticity, or authoritative enactment. Its metaphysical basis is the law of cause and effect, which in the thinking of its adepts has displaced even the law of sufficient reason.(6*)

The range of conventional truths, or of institutional legacies, which it traverses is very comprehensive, being, indeed, all-inclusive. It is but little more in accord with the newer, eighteenth century conventional truths of natural rights, natural liberty, natural law, or natural religion, than with the older norms of the true, the beautiful, and the good which these displaced. Anthropomorphism, under whatever disguise, is of no use and of no force here.

The discipline exercised by the mechanical occupations, in so far as it is in question here, is a discipline of the habits of thought. It is, therefore, as processes of thought, methods of apperception, and sequences of reasoning, that these occupations are of interest for the present purpose; it is as such that they have whatever cultural value belongs to them. They have such a value, therefore, somewhat in proportion as they tax the mental faculties of those employed; and the largest effects are to be looked for among those industrial classes who are required to comprehend and guide the processes, rather than among those who serve merely as mechanical auxiliaries of the machine process. Not that the latter are exempt from the machine's discipline, but it falls upon them blindly and enforces an uncritical acceptance of opaque results, rather than a theoretical insight into the causal sequences which make up the machine process. The higher degree of training in such matter-of-fact habits of thought is accordingly to be looked for among the higher ranks of skied mechanics, and perhaps still more decisively among those who stand in an engineering or supervisory relation to the processes. It counts more forcibly and farthest among those who are required to exercise what may be called a mechanical discretion in the guidance of the industrial processes, who, as one might say, are required to administer the laws of causal sequence that run through material phenomena, who therefore must learn to think in the terms in which the machine processes work.(7*) The metaphysical ground, the assumptions, on which such thinking proceeds must be such as will hold good for the sequence of material phenomena; that is to say, it is the metaphysical assumptions of modern material science, – the law of cause and effect, cumulative causation, conservation of energy, persistence of quantity, or whatever phrase be chosen to cover the concept. The men occupied with the modern material sciences are, accordingly, for the purpose in hand, in somewhat the same case as the higher ranks of those employed in mechanical industry.(8*)

Leaving aside the archaic vocations of war, politics, fashion, and religion, the employments in which men are engaged may be distinguished as pecuniary or business employments on the one hand, and industrial or mechanical employments on the other hand.(9*) In earlier times, and indeed until an uncertain point in the nineteenth century, such a distinction between employments would not to any great extent have coincided with a difference between occupations. But gradually, as time has passed and production for a market has come to be the rule in industry, there has Supervened a differentiation of occupations, or a division of labor, whereby one class of men have taken over the work of purchase and sale and of husbanding a store of accumulated values. Concomitantly, of course, the rest, who may, for lack of means or of pecuniary aptitude, have been less well fitted for pecuniary pursuits, have been relieved of the cares of business and have with increasing specialization given their attention to the mechanical processes involved in this production for a market. In this way the distinction between pecuniary and industrial activities or employments has come to coincide more and more nearly with a difference between occupations. Not that the specialization has even yet gone so far as to exempt any class from all pecuniary care;(10*) for even those whose daily occupation is mechanical work still habitually bargain with their employers for their wages and with others for their supplies. So that none of the active classes in modern life is fully exempt from pecuniary work.

But the need of attention to pecuniary matters is less and less exacting, even in the matter of wages and supplies. The scale of wages, for instance, is, for the body of workmen, and also for what may be called the engineering force, becoming more and more a matter of routine, thereby lessening at least the constancy with which occasions for detail bargaining in this respect recur. So also as regards the purchase of consumable goods. In the cities and industrial towns, particularly, the supplying of the means of subsistence has, in great part, become a matter of routine. Retail prices are in an increasing degree fixed by the seller, and in great measure fixed in an impersonal way. This occurs in a particularly evident and instructive way in the practice of the department stores, where the seller fixes the price, and comes in contact with the buyer only through the intervention of a salesman who has no discretion as to the terms of sale. The change that has taken place and that is still going on in this respect is sufficiently striking on comparison with the past in any industrial community, or with the present in any of those communities which we are in the habit of calling "industrially backward."

Conversely, as regards the men in the pecuniary occupations, the business men. Their exemption from taking thought of mechanical facts and processes is likewise only relative. Even those business men whose business is in a peculiar degree remote from the handling of tools or goods, and from the oversight of mechanical processes, as, for example, bankers, lawyers, brokers, and the like, have still, at the best, to take some cognizance of the mechanical apparatus of everyday life; they are at least compelled to take some thought of what may be called the mechanics of consumption. Whereas those business men whose business is more immediately concerned with industry commonly have some knowledge and take some thought of the processes of industry; to some appreciable extent they habitually think in mechanical terms. Their cogitations may habitually run to pecuniary conclusions, and the test to which the force and validity of their reasoning is brought may habitually be the pecuniary outcome; the beginning and end of their more serious thinking is of a pecuniary kind, but it always takes in some general features of the mechanical process along the way. Their exemption from mechanical thinking, from thinking in terms of cause and effect, is, therefore, materially qualified.

But after all qualifications have been made, the fact still is apparent that the everyday life of those classes which are engaged in business differs materially in the respect cited from the life of the classes engaged in industry proper. There is an appreciable and widening difference between the habits of life of the two classes; and this carries with it a widening difference in the discipline to which the two classes are subjected. It induces a difference in the habits of thought and the habitual grounds and methods of reasoning resorted to by each class. There results a difference in the point of view, in the facts dwelt upon, in the methods of argument, in the grounds of validity appealed to; and this difference gains in magnitude and consistency as the differentiation of occupations goes on. So that the two classes come to have an increasing difficulty in understanding one another and appreciating one another's convictions, ideals, capacities, and shortcomings.

The ultimate ground of validity for the thinking of the business classes is the natural-rights ground of property, − a conventional, anthropomorphic fact having an institutional validity, rather than a matter-of-fact validity such as can be formulated in terms of material cause and effect; while the classes engaged in the machine industry are habitually occupied with matters of causal sequence, which do not lend themselves to statement in anthropomorphic terms of natural rights and which afford no guidance in questions of institutional right and wrong, or of conventional reason and consequence. Arguments which proceed on material cause and effect cannot be met with arguments from conventional precedent or dialectically sufficient reason, and conversely.

The thinking required by the pecuniary occupations proceeds on grounds of conventionality, whereas that involved in the industrial occupations runs, in the main, on grounds of mechanical sequence or causation, to the neglect of conventionality. The institution (habit of thought) of ownership or property is a conventional fact; and the logic of pecuniary thinking− that is to say, of thinking on matters of ownership − is a working out of the implications of this postulate, this concept of ownership or property. The characteristic habits of thought given by such work are habits of recourse to conventional grounds of finality or validity, to anthropomorphism, to explanations of phenomena in terms of human relation, discretion, authenticity, and choice. The final ground of certainty in inquiries on this natural-rights plane is always a ground of authenticity, of precedent, or accepted decision. The argument is an argument de jure, not de facto, and the training given lends facility and certainty in the pursuit of de jure distinctions and generalizations, rather than in the pursuit or the assimilation of a de facto knowledge of impersonal phenomena. The end of such reasoning is the interpretation of new facts in terms of accredited precedents, rather than a revision of the knowledge drawn from past experience in the matter-of-fact light of new phenomena. The endeavor is to make facts conform to law, not to make the law or general rule conform to facts. The bent so given favors the acceptance of the general, abstract, custom-made rule as something real with a reality superior to the reality of impersonal, non-conventional facts. Such training gives reach and subtlety in metaphysical argument and in what is known as the "practical" management of affairs; it gives executive or administrative efficiency, so-called, as distinguished from mechanical work. "Practical" efficiency means the ability to turn facts to account for the purposes of the accepted conventions, to give a large effect to the situation in terms of the pecuniary conventions in force.(11*)

The spiritual attitude given by this training in reasoning de jure, from pecuniary premises to pecuniary conclusions, is necessarily conservative. This species of reasoning assumes the validity of the conventionally established postulates, and is consequently unable to take a sceptical attitude toward these postulates or toward the institutions in which these postulates are embodied. It may lead to scepticism touching other, older, institutions that are at variance with its own (natural-rights) postulates, but its scepticism cannot touch the natural-rights ground on which it rests its own case. In the same manner, of course, the thinking which runs in material causal sequence cannot take a sceptical attitude toward its fundamental postulate, the law of cause and effect; but since reasoning on this materialistic basis does not visibly go to uphold the received institutions, the attitude given by the discipline of the machine technology cannot, for the present, be called a conservative attitude.

The business classes are conservative, on the whole, but such a conservative bent is, of course, not peculiar to them. These occupations are not the only ones whose reasoning prevailingly moves on a conventional plane. Indeed, the intellectual activity of other classes, such as soldiers, politicians, the clergy, and men of fashion, moves on a plane of still older conventions; so that if the training given by business employments is to be characterized as conservative, that given by these other, more archaic employments should be called reactionary.(12*) Extreme conventionalization means extreme conservatism. Conservatism means the maintenance of conventions already in force. On this head, therefore, the discipline of modern business life may be said simply to retain something of the complexion which marks the life of the higher barbarian culture, at the same time that it has not retained the disciplinary force of the barbarian culture in so high a state of preservation as some of the other occupations just named.

The discipline of the modern industrial employments is relatively free from the bias of conventionality, but the difference between the mechanical and the business occupations in this respect is a difference of degree. It is not simply that conventional standards of certainty fall into abeyance for lack of exercise, among the industrial classes. The positive discipline exercised by their work in good part runs counter to the habit of thinking in conventional, anthropomorphic terms, whether the conventionality is that of natural rights or any other. And in respect of this positive training away from conventional norms, there is a large divergence between the several lines of industrial employment. In proportion as a given line of employment has more of the character of a machine process and less of the character of handicraft, the matter-of-fact training which it gives is more pronounced. In a sense more intimate than the inventors of the phrase seem to have appreciated, the machine has become the master of the man who works with it and an arbiter in the cultural fortunes of the community into whose life it has entered.

The intellectual and spiritual training of the machine in modern life, therefore, is very far-reaching. It leaves but a small proportion of the community untouched; but while its constraint is ramified throughout the body of the population, and constrains virtually all classes at some points in their daily life, it falls with the most direct, intimate, and unmitigated impact upon the skilled mechanical classes, for these have no respite from its mastery, whether they are at work or at play. The ubiquitous presence of the machine, with its spiritual concomitant - workday ideals and scepticism of what is only conventionally valid is the unequivocal mark of the Western culture of to-day as contrasted with the culture of other times and places. It pervades all classes and strata in a varying degree, but on an average in a greater degree than at any time in the past, and most potently in the advanced industrial communities and in the classes immediately in contact with the mechanical occupations.(13*) As the comprehensive mechanical organization of the material side of life has gone on, a heightening of this cultural effect throughout the community has also supervened, and with a farther and faster movement in the same direction a farther accentuation of this "modern" complexion of culture is fairly to be looked for, unless some remedy be found. And as the concomitant differentiation and specialization of occupations goes on, a still more unmitigated discipline falls upon ever widening classes of the population, resulting in an ever weakening sense of conviction, allegiance, or piety toward the received institutions.

It is a matter of common notoriety that the modern industrial populations are improvident in a high degree and are apparently incapable of taking care of the pecuniary details of their own life. This applies, not only to factory hands, but also to the general class of highly skilled mechanics, inventors, technological experts. The rule does not hold in any hard and fast way, but it holds with such generality as may fairly be looked for. The present factory population may be compared in this respect with the class of handicraftsmen whom they have displaced, as also with the farming population of the present time, especially the class of small proprietary farmers. The failure of the modern industrial classes on this head is not due to scantier opportunities for saving, whether they are compared with the earlier handicraftsmen or with the modern farmer or peasant; nor is it due to a lack of general intelligence, for a comparison in point of intelligence falls out in favor of the modern industrial workmen. This improvidence is commonly discussed in terms of deprecation, and there is much preaching of thrift and steady habits. But the preaching has no appreciable effect. The trouble seems to be of the nature of habit rather than of reasoned conviction. Other causes may partially explain this improvidence, but the inquiry is at least pertinent how far the absence of property and thrift among them may be traceable to the relative absence of pecuniary training and to the presence of a discipline which is at variance with habits of thrift.

Mere exemption from pecuniary training is not competent alone to explain the patent thriftlessness of modern workmen; the more so since this exemption is but partial and relative. Also, the thriftless classes commonly have an envious appreciation of pecuniary advantages. It is rather the composite effect of exemption from pecuniary training and certain positive requirements of modern life. Among these positive requirements is what has been called the canon of conspicuous waste. Under modern conditions a free expenditure in consumable goods is a condition requisite to good repute.(14*) This conduces to immediate consumption rather than to saving. What is perhaps still more decisive against thrift on the part of workmen is the fact that the modern large organization of industry requires a high degree of mobility on the part of employees. It requires, in fact, that the labor force and the labor units be mobile, interchangeable, distributable, after the same impersonal fashion as the mechanical contrivances engaged are movable and distributable. The working population is required to be standardized, movable, and interchangeable in much the same impersonal manner as the raw or halfwrought materials of industry. From which it follows that the modern workman cannot advantageously own a home. By force of this latter feature of the case he is discouraged from investing his savings in real property, or, indeed, in any of the impediments of living. And the savings-bank account, it may be added, offers no adequate substitute, as an incentive to thrift, in the place of such property as a dwelling-place, which is tangibly and usefully under the owner's hand and persistently requires maintenance and improvement.

The conditions of life imposed upon the working population by the machine industry discourage thrift. But after allowance has been made for this almost physical restraint upon the aquisition of property by the working classes, something is apparently left over, to be ascribed to the moral effect of the machine technology. The industrial classes appear to be losing the instinct of individual ownership. The acquisition of property is ceasing to appeal to them as a natural, self-evident source of comfort and strength. The natural right of property no longer means so much to them as it once did.

A like weakening of the natural-rights animus is visible at another point in the current frame of mind of these classes. The growth of trade-unionism and of what is called the trade-union spirit is a concomitant of industry organized after the manner of a machine process. Historically this growth begins, virtually, with the industrial revolution, coming in sporadically, loosely, tentatively, with no precise assignable date, very much as the revolution does. England is the land of its genesis, its "area of characterization," and the place where it has reached its fullest degree of specification and its largest force;

just as England is the country in which the modern machine industry took its rise and in which it has had the longest and most consistent life and growth. In this matter other countries are followers of the British lead and apparently borrowers of British precedents and working concepts. Still, the history of the trade-union movement in other countries seems to say that the working classes elsewhere have not advisedly borrowed ideals and methods of organization from their British congeners so much as they have been pushed into the same general attitude and line of conduct by the same general line of exigencies and experiences. Particularly, experience seems to say that it is not feasible to introduce the trade-union spirit or the trade-union rules into any community until the machine industry has had time extensively to standardize the scheme of work and of life for the working classes on mechanical lines. Workmen do not take to full-blown trade-union ideals abruptly on the introduction of those modern business methods which make trade-union action advisable for the working class. A certain interval elapses between the time when business conditions first make trade-union action feasible, as a business proposition, and the time when the body of workmen are ready to act in the spirit of trade-unionism and along the lines which the union animus presently accepts as normal for men in the mechanically organized industries. An interval of discipline in the ways of the mechanically standardized industry, more or less protracted and severe, seems necessary to bring such a proportion of the workmen into line as will give a consensus of sentiment and opinion favorable to trade-union action.

The pervading characteristic of the trade-union animus is the denial of the received natural-rights dogmas wherever the mechanical standardization of modern industry traverses the working of these received natural rights. Recent court decisions in America, as well as decisions in analogous cases in England at that earlier period when the British development was at about the same stage of maturity as the current American situation, testify unequivocally that the common run of trade-union action is at variance with the natural-rights foundation of the common law. Trade-unionism denies individual freedom of contract to the workman, as well as free discretion to the employer to carry on his business as may suit his own ends. Many pious phrases have been invented to disguise this iconoclastic trend of trade-union aims and endeavors; but the courts, standing on a secure and familiar natural-rights footing, have commonly made short work of the shifty sophistications which trade-union advocates have offered for their consideration. They have struck at the root of the matter in declaring trade-union regulations inimical to the natural rights of workman and employer alike, in that they hamper individual liberty and act in restraint of trade. The regulations, therefore, violate that system of law and order which rests on natural rights, although they may be enforced by that de facto law and order which is embodied in the mechanical standardization of the industrial processes.

Trade-unionism is an outgrowth of relatively late industrial conditions and has come on gradually as an adaptation of old methods and working arrangements carried over from the days of handicraft and petty trade. It is a movement to adapt, construe, recast, earlier working arrangements with as little lesion to received preconceptions as the new exigencies and the habits of thought bred by them will permit. It is, on its face, an endeavor of compromise between received notions of what "naturally" ought to be in matters of industrial business, on the one hand, and what the new exigencies of industry demand and what the new animus of the workman will tolerate, on the other hand. Trade-unionism is therefore to be taken as a somewhat mitigated expression of what the mechanical standardization of industry inculcates. Hitherto the movement has shown a fairly uninterrupted growth, not only in the numbers of its membership, but in the range and scope of its aims as well; and hitherto it has reached no halting-place in its tentative, shifty, but ever widening crusade of iconoclasm against the received body of natural rights. The latest, maturest expressions of trade-unionism are, on the whole, the most extreme, in so far as they are directed against the natural rights of property and pecuniary contract.

The nature of the compromise offered by trade-unionism is shown by a schedule of its demands: collective bargaining for wages and employment; arbitration of differences between owners and workmen; standard rates of wages; normal working day, with penalized regulation of hours for men, women, and children; penalized regulation of sanitary and safety appliances; mutual insurance of workmen, to cover accident, disability, and unemployment. In all of this the aim of unionism seldom goes the length of overtly disputing the merits of any given article of natural-rights dogma. It only endeavors to cut into these articles, in point of fact, at points where the dogmas patently traverse the conditions of life imposed on the workmen by the modern industrial system or where they traverse the consensus of sentiment that is coming to prevail among these workmen.

When unionism takes an attitude of overt hostility to the natural-rights institutions of property and free contract, it ceases to be unionism simply and passes over into something else, which may be called socialism for want of a better term. Such an extreme iconoclastic position, which would overtly assert the mechanical standardization of industry as against the common-law standardization of business, seems to be the logical outcome to which the trade-union animus tends, and to which some approach has latterly been made by more than one trade-unionist body, but which is, on the whole, yet in the future, if, indeed, it is to be reached at all. On the whole, the later expressions go farther in this direction than the earlier; and the animus of the leaders, as well as of the more wide-awake body of unionist workmen, appears to go farther than their official utterances.

A detail of trade-union history may be cited in illustration of their attitude toward the natural-rights principles that underlie modern business relations. As is well known, trade-unions have somewhat consistently avoided pecuniary responsibility for the actions of their members or officials. They avoid incorporation. Practically an employer has had no recourse in case he suffers from a failure on the part of his union workmen to live up to the terms of an agreement made with the union. In English practice this exemption from pecuniary responsibility has acquired much of the force of law, and indeed was supposed to have gained the countenance of statutory enactment, until, within the past few months, the so-called Taff Vale decision of the House of Lords reversed the views which had come to prevail on this head. This decision, by the most conservative tribunal of the British nation, is too recent to permit its consequences for trade-unionism to be appreciated. But it seems fair to expect that the question which the decision brings home to the unions will be, How is this court-made pecuniary responsibility to be evaded? not, How is it to be lived up to? Patently,(15*) the decision is unexceptionable under common law rules; but, also patently,(16*) it broadly traverses trade-union practice and is wholly alien to the attitude of the trade-unionists.(17*)

The animus shown by the trade-unionists in this shirking of pecuniary responsibility is characteristic of their attitude toward common law rules. The unions and their methods of work are essentially extra-legal. It is only reluctantly, as defendants if at all, that unions are accustomed to appear in court. When they make a move for statutory enactment, as for the enforcement of a normal day or of sanitary and safeguarding regulations, it is prevailingly to criminal law that they turn.

To all this it might, of course, be said that the workmen who make up the trade-union element take the course indicated simply because their selfish interest urges them to this course; that their common necessities and common weakness constrains them to stand together and to act collectively in dealing with their employers; while the fact that their demands have no standing in court constrains them to seek their ends by extra-legal means of coercion. But this objection is little else than another way of saying that the exigencies forced upon the workmen by the mechanically standardized industrial system are extra-legal exigencies – exigencies which do not run in business terms and therefore are not amenable to the natural-rights principles of property and contract that underlie business relations; that they can therefore not be met on common law ground; and that they therefore compel the workmen to see them from another point of view and seek to dispose of them by an appeal to other principles than those afforded by the common law standpoint. That is to say, in other words, these exigencies which compel the trade-unionists to take thought of their case in other terms than those afforded by existing legal institutions are the means whereby the discipline of the machine industry is enforced and made effective for recasting the habits of thought of the workmen. The harsh discipline of these exigencies of livelihood drives home the new point of view and holds the workmen consistently to it. But that is not all that the mechanical standardization of industry does in the case; it also furnishes the new terms in which the revised scheme of economic life takes form. The revision of the scheme aimed at by trade-union action runs, not in terms of natural liberty, individual property rights, individual discretion, but in terms of standardized livelihood and mechanical necessity, – it is formulated, not in terms of business expediency, but in terms of industrial, technological standard units and standard relations.

The above presentation of the case of trade-unionism is of course somewhat schematic, as such a meagre, incidental discussion necessarily must be. It takes account only of those features of trade-unionism which characteristically mark it off from that business scheme of things with which it Comes in conflict. There are, of course, many survivals, pecuniary and others, in the current body of trade-union demands, and much of the trade-union argument is carried on in business terms. The crudities and iniquities of the trade-union campaign are sufficiently many and notorious to require no rehearsal here. These crudities and iniquities commonly bulk large in the eyes of critics who pass an opinion on trade-unionism from the natural-rights point of view; and, indeed, they may deserve all the disparaging attention that is given them. Trade-unionism does not fit into the natural-rights scheme of right and honest living; but therein, in great part, lies its cultural significance. It is of the essence of the case that the new aims, ideals, and expedients do not fit into the received institutional structure; and that the classes who move in trade-unions are, however crudely and blindly, endeavoring, under the compulsion of the machine process, to construct an institutional scheme on the lines imposed by the new exigencies given by the machine process.

The point primarily had in view in entering on this characterization of trade-unionism was that under the discipline of the mechanically standardized industry certain natural rights, particularly, those of property and free contract, are in a degree falling into abeyance among those classes who are most immediately subjected to this discipline. It may be added that other classes also, to an uncertain extent, sympathize with the trade-unionists and are affected with a similar (mild and equivocal) distrust of the principles of natural liberty. When distrust of business principles rises to such a pitch as to become intolerant of all pecuniary institutions, and leads to a demand for the abrogation of property rights rather than a limitation of them, it is spoken of as "socialism" or "anarchism." This socialistic disaffection is widespread among the advanced industrial peoples. No other cultural phenomenon is so threatening to the received economic and political structure; none is so unprecedented or so perplexing for practical men of affairs to deal with. The immediate point of danger in the socialistic disaffection is a growing disloyalty to the natural-rights institution of property, but this is backed by a similar failure of regard for other articles of the institutional furniture handed down from the past. The classes affected with socialistic vagaries protest against the existing economic organization, but they are not necessarily averse to a somewhat rigorous economic organization on new lines of their own choosing. They demand an Organization on industrial as contrasted with business lines. Their sense of economic solidarity does not seem to be defective, indeed it seems to many of their critics to be unnecessarily pronounced; but it runs on lines of industrial coherence and mechanical constraint, not on lines given by pecuniary conjunctures and conventional principles of economic right and wrong.

There is little agreement among socialists as to a programme for the future. Their constructive proposals are ill-defined and inconsistent and almost entirely negative. The negative character of the socialistic propaganda has been made a point of disparagement by its critics, perhaps justly. But their predilection for shifty iconoclasm, as well as the vagueness and inconsistency of their constructive proposals, are in the present connection to be taken as evidence that the attitude of the socialists cannot be expressed in positive terms given by the institutions at present in force. It may also be evidence of the untenability of the socialistic ideals; but the merits of the socialist contentions do not concern the present inquiry. The question here is as to the nature and causes of the socialist disaffection; it does not concern the profounder and more delicate point, as to the validity of the socialist contentions. Current socialism is an animus of dissent from received traditions. The degree and the direction of this dissent varies greatly, but it is, within the socialist scheme of thought, agreed that the institutional forms of the past are unfit for the work of the future.(18*)

The socialistic disaffection has been set down to envy, class hatred, discontent with their own lot by comparison with that of others, and to a mistaken view of their own interests. This criticism may be well enough as far as it goes, but it does not touch socialism in those respects in which it differs from other movements into which this range of motives enters; that is to say, it touches, not the specific traits of socialism, but the common features of popular discontent. History shows many such movements of discontent, pushed on by real or fancied privation and iniquity; and past experience recorded in history should lead us to expect that, under the guidance of such motives and such reasoning as is currently imputed to the socialists by their conservative critics, the malcontents would demand a redistribution of property, a reorganization of ownership on such new lines as would favor the discontented classes. But such is not the trend of socialistic thinking. It looks to the disappearance of property rights rather than their redistribution. The entire range of doctrines covered by the theory of distribution in the received economics is essentially (and characteristically) neglected by the modern socialist speculations.(19*)

The perplexity of those who protest against a supposedly imminent socialistic subversion of property rights is of a twofold kind: (1) The absence of proprietary rights is incomprehensible, and a living together in society without defined ownership of the means of living is held to be impracticable; ownership of goods, in the apprehension of the conservative critics, is involved in the presence of goods. (2) Ownership of the means of living is an inalienable right of man, ethically inevitable; the cancelment of property rights is felt to violate a fundamental principle of morals. All this, of course, proceeds on the assumption that the institution of ownership cannot be abrogated, as being an elemental function of human nature and an integral factor in the order of things in which human life belongs.

To the modern socialist all this is coming to be less and less convincing. In this respect there is a fairly well marked progressive change in the attitude of the professed socialists. Their position is progressively less capable of being formulated as a business proposition; their demands are progressively more difficult to state in the form of a pecuniary claim. The claim to the full product of labor, which once filled a large place in socialistic clamors and had a great carrying force during the earlier three-quarters of the nineteenth century, has gradually fallen into abeyance, both with the agitators and the adherents of the propaganda, during the last generation. To-day this claim is an afterthought in the advocate's presentation of socialism, more frequently than it is a point of departure for the argument, and it is made more of by the proselytes, who have carried the metaphysics of it over from the current common sense of the business community, than by the socialists of confirmed standing. The claim to the full product is an article of natural-rights dogma, and as such it is a reminiscence of the institutional situation from which socialism departs, rather than a feature of the prospective situation to which socialistic sentiment looks.

The like obsolescence of the sense of equity in ownership is visible in the attitude taken by strikers in the large, mechanically organized industries, outside of the ranks of avowed socialism. These strikers are less and less deterred by considerations of vested rights, property rights, owner's interests, and the like. The principle that a man may do what he will with his own is losing its binding force with large classes in the community, apparently because the spiritual ground on which rests the notion of "his own" is being cut away by the latter-day experience of these classes. Abridgment of proprietary discretion, confiscation of proprietary rights, is growing gradually less repugnant to the industrial populace; and the question of indemnity for eventual loss is more and more falling into neglect. With the socialistic element the question is not, what shall be done in the way of readjustment of property claims, but what is to be done to abolish them.(20*)

The question of equity or inequity in the distribution of wealth presumes the validity of ownership rights on some basis or other, or at least it presumes the validity of some basis on which the claims of ownership may be discussed. Ownership is the major premise of any argument as to the equity of distribution, and it is this major premise that is being forgotten by the classes among whom socialistic sentiment is gaining. Equity in this connection seems not to belong in the repertory of socialist concepts. It is at this point – the point of a common ground of argument– that the discrepancy occurs which stands in the way, not only of an eventual agreement between the socialists and their conservative critics, but even of their meeting one another's reasoning with any substantial effect. In the equipment of common–sense ideas on the basis of which the conservatives reason on this matter, there is included the conventional article of ownership, as a prime fact; in the common–sense basis of socialistic thinking this conventional premise has no secure place. There is, therefore, a discrepancy in respect of the metaphysics underlying the knowledge and reasoning of the two parties to the controversy, and the outlook for a common understanding is accordingly vain. No substantial agreement upon a point of knowledge or conviction is possible between persons who proceed from disparate preconceptions.

Still the conservative reformers and the iconoclasts have a good deal in common. The prevalent habit of mind of both classes is a hybrid product of conventional principles and matter–of–fact insight. But these two contrasted grounds of opinion and aspiration are present in unequal degrees in the two contrasted classes; in the conservatives the conventional grounds of finality dominate and bear down the matter–of–fact knowledge of things, while the converse is true of the iconoclasts. Contrasted with earlier times and other cultural regions the consensus, the general drift, of the modern Western culture as a whole is of an iconoclastic character; while the class contrast here in question lies only within the range of this Western cultural consensus. As one or the other of the two contrasted proclivities – recourse to conventional precedents and recourse to matter–of–fact insight – gains and overbalances the other, the general cultural movement will drift toward a more conservative (archaic), conventional position or toward a more iconoclastic, materialistic position. During modern times the cultural drift has set in the latter direction. With due but not large exceptions, the effective body of the modern population has been growing more matter–of–fact in their thinking, less romantic, less idealistic in their aspirations, less bound by metaphysical considerations in their view of human relations, less mannerly, less devout.

The discrepancy between the conservatives and the iconoclasts need not be taken to mean that the two contrasted classes are moving in opposite directions, nor even in widely divergent directions. Neither class can properly be said to be reactionary.(21*) Taken generally, both wings have been moving in the direction of a more impersonal, more matter–of–fact, less conventional point of view. In this composite cultural growth the matter–of–fact habit of mind has on the whole been gaining at the expense of the conventional, and the conventional premises that have been retained have also come to bear more of a matter–of–fact character, – as, e.g., in the supersession of feudalistic or theocratic principles of law by natural rights. So that the position for which the effective body of conservatives now stand is not in substance a very archaic one. It is a more matter–of–fact position, less closely bound by authentic conventions, than the position effectively occupied by the iconoclastic wing a hundred years ago.

Throughout the mod ern cultural complex there is a somewhat variable, scattering shifting of ground to a more matter–of–fact basis. The direction of spiritual growth or change is much the same throughout the general body of the population; but the rate of change, the rate at which matter–of–fact ideals are superseding ideals of conventional authenticity, is not the same for all classes. Hence the class discrepancy here spoken of. The coefficient of change is so much larger in the vulgar, industrial classes as progressively to widen the cultural interval between them and the conservatives in the respect which is here in question. And the resulting discrepancy of institutional aims and ideals may have none the less serious consequences for being due to a differential rate of movement rather than to a divergent cultural trend.

In this differential rate of movement the departure from the ancient landmarks has now gone so far (or is reaching such a point) among the socialistic vulgar as to place their th inking substantially on a plane of material matter of fact, particularly as regards economic institutions. Whereas in the conservative classes the change is not yet large enough to take them off the plane of received conventional truth, particularly as regards economic institutions and such social questions as are of an economic complexion. In the case of the former this change in habit of mind has been so considerable as, in effect, to constitute a change in kind; crude matter of fact has come to be the dominant note of their attitude, and conventional authenticity has been relegated to a subsidiary place; that is to say, the change is of a revolutionary character. In the case of the conservative classes, so far as touches the institutional notions here under inquiry, the corresponding change has not yet gone so far as to amount to a change in kind; it is not of a revolutionary nature. The views current among the respectable classes on these matters still, in effect, run on the ancient levels on which were built up the pecuniary institutions about which the controversy circles. For the present there need be no apprehension that the more respectable classes will reach a mature revolutionary frame of mind. The discipline of their daily life does not, on the whole, favor such a result.

This, in substance, is also the view taken by the socialistic revolutionaries, particularly by those that are of Marxian antecedents. It is a point of conviction with them, though not wholly of reasoned conviction, that the socialistic movement is, in the nature of the case, a proletarian movement, in which the respectable, that is to say the pecuniarily competent, classes can have no organic part even if they try. It is held, in effect, that the well-to-do are, by force of their economic circumstances, incapable of assimilating the socialist ideas. The argument here set forth may serve to enforce this view, but with a difference. Instead of contrasting the well-to-do with the indigent, the line of demarcation between those available for the socialist propaganda and those not so available is rather to be drawn between the classes employed in the industrial and those employed in the pecuniary occupations. It is a question not so much of possessions as of employments; not of relative wealth, but of work. It is a question of work because it is a question of habits of thought, and work shapes the habits of thought. The socialists themselves construe the distinction to be a distinction in respect of habits of thought; and habits of thought are made by habits of life rather than by a legal relation to accumulated goods. This legal relation may count materially in shaping the animus of the several economic classes; but it appears not to be competent of itself to explain the limitations observable in the spread of socialistic sentiment.

The socialistic disaffection shows a curious tendency to overrun certain classes and to miss certain others. The men in the skilled mechanical trades are peculiarly liable to it, while at the extreme of immunity is probably the profession of the law. Bankers and other like classes of business men, together with clergymen and politicians, are also to be held free of serious aspersion; similarly, the great body of the rural population are immune, including the population of the country towns, and in an eminent degree the small farmers of the remoter country districts;(22*) so also the delinquent classes of the cities and the populace of half-civilized and barbarous countries. The body of unskilled laborers, especially those not associated with the men in the skilled mechanical trades, are not seriously affected. The centres of socialistic disaffection are the more important industrial towns, and the effective nucleus of the socialistic malcontents is made up of the more intelligent body of workmen in the highly organized and specialized industries. Not that socialism does not spread in virulent form outside this narrow range, but at a farther remove from the centre of dispersion it appears rather sporadically and uncertainly, while within this field it is fairly endemic. As regards the educated classes, socialistic views are particularly likely to crop out among the men in the material sciences.

The advocates of the new creed have made little headway among the rural classes of Europe, whether peasant farmers or farm laborers. The rural proletariat has hitherto proved virtually impermeable.(23*) The discipline of their daily life leaves their spirit undisturbed on the plane of conventionality and anthropomorphism, and the changes to which they aspire lie within the scope of the conventionalities which have grown out of these circumstances of their life and which express the habit of mind enforced by these circumstances.

Without claiming that this explanation is competent to cover the case of socialism in all its bearings, it may be pointed out that this socialistic bias has effectively spread among the people only within the last quarter of a century, which is also approximately the period since which the machine process and the mechanical standardization of industry has reached its fuller development, both as regards the extent of its field and as regards the extent of its technological requirements; that it is found in vigorous growth only in those communities and particularly among those classes whose life is closely regulated by the machine technology; and that the discipline of this machine technology is peculiarly designed to inculcate such iconoclastic habits of thought as come to a head in the socialistic bias. Socialism, in so far as the term means the subversion of the economic foundations of modern culture, occurs only sporadically and dubiously outside the limits, in time and space, of the discipline of the machine technology. While among those classes whose everyday life schools them to do their habitual serious thinking in terms of material cause and effect, the preconceptions of ownership are apparently becoming obsolescent through disuse and through supersession by other methods of apprehending things.(24*)

But the machine technology not only trains the work men into materialistic iconoclasm, it has also a selective effect. Persons endowed with propensities and aptitudes of a materialistic, matter-of-fact kind are drafted into the mechanical employments, and such are also peculiarly available socialistic material. Aptitude for the matter-of-fact work of the machine technology means, in a general way, ineptitude for an uncritical acceptance of institutional truths, It is probable, therefore, that the apparent facility with which the mechanical employments (and the material sciences) induce a socialistic or iconoclastic bent is to be set down in part to the fact that the human material in these employments is picked material, peculiarly amenable to this discipline. There is a sifting of the working classes, whereby the socialistic and mechanically capable are roughly segregated out from the rest and subjected to the iconoclastic discipline of the mechanical employments and matter-of-fact thinking; while the residue, which is on the whole made up of the persons that are relatively least capable of revolutionary socialism, is at the same time less exposed to the discipline that might fit them for the socialistic movement. This sifting is, of course, a rough one, and leaves many exceptions both ways.

In the light of this consideration, then, it is to be noted: (1) that the dominance of the machine process in modern industry is not so potent a factor for the inculcation of socialistic notions − it does not so irresistibly shape men's habit of mind in the socialistic sense − as the first survey of the facts would suggest; and (2) that the differentiation of occupations involved in modern industrial methods selectively bunches the socialistic elements together, and so heightens their sense of class solidarity and acts to accentuate their bias, gives consistency to their ideals, and induces that boldness of conviction and action which is to be had only in a compact body of men.

But in either case, whether the visible outcome is chiefly due to their selective or to their disciplinary effect, the bearing of the industrial occupations upon the growth of socialism seems equally close and undeniable. The two modes of influence seem to converge to the outcome indicated above, and for the purpose of the present inquiry a detailed tracing out of the two strands of sequence in the case neither can nor need be undertaken.(25*)

With such generality as commonly holds in statements of this kind, it may be said that the modern socialistic disaffection is loosely bound up with the machine industry − spreading where this industry spreads and flourishing where this industry gives the dominant note of life. The correlation between the two phenomena is of such a kind as to leave no doubt that they are causally connected; which means either that the machine industry, directly or indirectly, gives rise to socialism, or that the two are expressions of the same complex of causes. The former statement probably expresses the truth of the case in great part, but the latter need not therefore be false. Wherever and in so far as the increase and diffusion of knowledge has made the machine process and the mechanical technology the tone-giving factor in men's scheme of thought, there modern socialistic iconoclasm follows by easy consequence.

The socialistic bias primarily touches economic institutions proper. But that is not the whole of it. When the term is used without modifying phrase it carries a certain implication touching other than primarily economic matters. The political bias of this unmitigated socialism is always radically democratic, to the extent that these socialists are in a high degree intolerant of any monarchical, aristocratic, or other prescriptive government. The state is doomed in the socialistic view.(26*) The socialist antagonism to the state takes various forms and goes to varying degrees of intemperance, but it is consistently negative. Except in their destructively hostile attitude to existing political organizations, the socialists have nothing consistent to offer on the head of political institutions, less, indeed, latterly than in the earlier days of the propaganda. There seems to be a growing shiftlessness of opinion on this head; one gets the impression that the sense of the socialist malcontents, as near as it may be permissible to use that word in this connection, is that the community can best get along without political institutions.

There is a like departure from the ancient norms touching domestic relations. This is not confined to those portions of the community that avowedly affect socialistic views, although it has, on the whole, gone farthest among the classes among whom the socialistic views prevail. There is a visible weakening of the family ties, a disintegration of the conventions of household life, throughout large classes. The defection is even felt, by sensitive and solicitous persons, to be of such grave proportions as to threaten the foundations of domestic life and morality. This disintegration of the family ties shows itself most alarmingly among the socialistic classes, with whom it all wears such an air of unconcern as argues that in this respect they are incorrigible. To these the conventional form of the household has in good part ceased to appeal as something sacred. It is no longer one of their secure spiritual assets.

What appears to be in jeopardy, should this socialistic defection gain ground, is the headship of the male in the household economy. The family, as it has come down from the medieval past, under the shelter of the church, is of a patriarchal constitution, at least in theory. The man has been vested with discretionary control in domestic affairs. In the earlier days his discretion was very direct and full, comprising corporal coercion. Utterly, after and so far as mastery and servitude have passed off the field and natural rights have come to rule, this direct coercive control has been superseded by a pecuniary discretion; so that the male head of the household is alone competent to exercise a proprietary control of household affairs. This latter-day conventional headship of the man is now in its turn beginning to lose the respect of a good share of the populace. The disintegration of the patriarchal tradition has gone farthest among those industrial classes who are at the same time inclined to socialistic views.

At this point in the institutional structure, as well as at other points where the industrial classes are giving evidence of a loss of spiritual ground, there is little indication of a constructive movement toward any specific arrangement to take the place of the institution whose existence is threatened. There is a loosening of the bonds, a weakening of conviction as to the full truth and beauty of the received domestic institutions, without much of a consensus as to what is to be done about it, if anything. In this, as at other junctures of a similar kind, the mechanically employed classes, trained to matter-of-fact habits of thought, show a notable lack of spontaneity in the construction of new myths or conventions as well as in the reconstruction of the old.

All this disintegration of the spiritual foundations of our domestic institutions spreads with the most telling effect, because most heedlessly, among the population of the industrial towns. But it spreads also outside the limits of the industrial classes; for the habits of life and of thought inculcated by the machine technology are not limited to them, even if these classes are the ones who suffer most and most severely from the machine discipline. The disintegration shows itself, in varying degree, in all modern industrial communities, and it is visible somewhat in proportion as the community is modern and industrial. The machine is a leveller, a vulgarizer, whose end seems to be the extirpation of all that is respectable, noble, and dignified in human intercourse and ideals.

What happens within the narrow range of the institutions of domestic life repeats itself in substance in the larger field of national life and ideals. Fealty to a superior installed by law or custom suffers under the discipline of a life which, as regards its most formative exigencies, is not guided by conventional grounds of validity. And the transmuted form of fealty called patriotism is in much the same insecure case. The new ground of class solidarity and antagonism, for which these extreme spokesmen of the industrial regime stand, is neither ecclesiastic, dynastic, territorial, nor linguistic; it is industrial and materialistic. But in their attitude of heedlessness toward the dynastic and national conventions the socialists are merely the extreme exponents of the spirit of the age in the modern industrial communities.

So, again, as regards the religious life. Men trained by the mechanical occupations to materialistic, industrial habits of thought are beset with a growing inability to appreciate, or even to apprehend, the meaning of religious appeals that proceed on the old-fashioned grounds of metaphysical validity. The consolations of a personal relation (of subservience) to a supernatural master do not appeal to men whose habit of life is shaped by a familiarity with the relations of impersonal cause and effect, rather than by relations of personal dominance and fealty. It does not come as a matter of course for such men to give the catechism's answer to the question, What is the chief end of man? Nor do they instinctively feel themselves to be sinners by virtue of a congenital, hereditary taint or obliquity. Indeed, they can only with great difficulty be seriously persuaded that they are sinners at all. They are in danger of losing the point of view of sin. The relation of status or fealty involved in the concept of sin is becoming alien to their habit of mind. They are therefore slow to realize that their past life has violated such a relation of fealty, on the one hand, and that it is of vital consequence to reestablish such a relation of status by a work of salvation or redemption. The kindly ministrations of the church and the clergy grate on the sensibilities of men so trained, as being so much ado about nothing. The machine, their master, is no respecter of persons and knows neither morality nor dignity nor prescriptive right, divine or human; its teaching is training them into insensibility of the whole range of concepts on which these ministrations proceed.(27*)

Not alone in the direction of growth given to vulgar sentiment and to the vulgar insight into facts is the matter-of-fact discipline of the machine technology apparent, but also in the scope and method of that scientific knowledge that has had the vogue since the advent of the machine industry. Scientific inquiry is directed to a different end and carried out under the guidance of a different range of principles or preconceptions in the modern industrial communities than in earlier days or in cultural centres lying outside the machine's dominion. Modern science is single-minded in its pursuit of impersonal relations of causal sequence in the phenomena with which it is occupied.

The line of descent of this matter-of-fact modern science is essentially British, as is that of the machine technology and of the characteristically modern civil and political institutions. It is true, beginnings of the modern scientific movement were made in Italy in the days of the Renaissance, and Central Europe had its share in the enlightenment; but these early modern risings of the scientific spirit presently ran into the sand, when war, politics, and religion reasserted their sway in the south of Europe. Similar tentative stirrings of matter-of-fact thought were had in Spain and France before and during the early phases of the state-making era; but here, again, war and politics rendered these onsets nearly nugatory, so that the intellectual output was more speculation than science. In the Low Countries something similar holds true, with a larger qualification. The British community made a later and slower start, coming out of barbarism at a later date and with a heavier handicap of physical obstructions. But being, relatively, sheltered from war and politics, the British were able to take up the fund of scientific gains made by the South-European men of workday insight, to turn it to account and to carry it over the era of state-making and so prepare the way for the modern scientific, technological era.

Of course, nothing but the most meagre and sketchiest outline of this matter is practicable in this place, and even that only in its relation to the machine industry during the past one hundred years or so. What is said above of the British lead in modern science may perhaps be questioned, and it is not necessary for the present purpose to insist on its truth; but so much seems beyond hazard as that the lead in the material sciences lay with the British through the early machine age, and that the provenance of this modern scientific research to-day does not extend, in any pronounced degree, beyond those communities that lie within the area of the modern machine industry.

In time and space the prevalence of the modern materialistic science is roughly extensive with that of the machine process. It is, no doubt, related to it both as cause and as effect; but that its relation to modern industry is more that of effect than cause seems at least broadly suggested by the decay which presently overtook scientific research, e.g., in the south of Europe when those peoples turned their attention from material to spiritual and political affairs.(28*)

What is of immediate interest is the change that has come over the scope and method of scientific research since the dominance of the machine process, in comparison with what preceded the coming of the machine age. The beginnings of modern science are older than the industrial revolution; the principles of scientific research (causal explanation and exact measurement) antedate the regime of the machine process. But a change has taken place in the postulates and animus of scientific research since modern science first began, and this change in the postulates of scientific knowledge is related to the growth of the machine technology.

It is unnecessary here to hark back to that scholastic science or philosophy that served as an intellectual expression of the ecclesiastical and political culture of the Middle Ages. Its character, as compared with later science, is sufficiently notorious. By the change from scholastic knowledge to modern science, to the extent to which the change was carried through, the principle (habit of mind) of adequate cause was substituted for that of sufficient reason. The law of causation as it is found at work, in the maturer science of the eighteenth and early nineteenth centuries, comprises two distinguishable postulates: (1) equality (quantitative equivalence) of cause and effect; and (2) similarity (qualitative equivalence) of cause and effect. The former may, without forcing it, be referred to commercial accountancy as its analogue in practical life and as the probable cultural ground out of which the habit of insisting on an inviolable quantitative equivalence gathered consistency. The ascendancy of the latter seems in a similar manner to be referable to the prevalence of handicraft as its cultural ground. Stated negatively, it asserts that nothing appears in the effect but what was contained in the cause, in a manner which suggests the rule that nothing appears in the product of handicraft but what was present in the skill of the artificer. "Natural causes," which are made much of in this middle period of modern science, are conceived to work according to certain "natural laws." These natural laws, laws of the "normal course" of things, are felt to tend to a rational end and to have something of a coercive force. So that Nature makes no mistakes, Nature does nothing in vain, Nature takes the most economical course to its end, Nature makes no jumps, etc. Under this law of natural causation every effect must have a cause which resembles it in the particular respect which claims the inquirer's attention. Among other consequences of this view it follows that, since the details as well as the whole of the material universe are construed to show adaptation to a preconceived end, this "natural order" of things must be the outcome of preexistent design residing in the "first cause," which is postulated by virtue of this imputed design and is designated the "Great Artificer." There is an element of conation in this original modern postulate of cause and effect. The shadow of the artificer, with his intelligence and manual skill is forever in the background of the concepts of natural law. The "cause" dealt with in a given case is not thought of as an effect; and the effect is treated as a finality, not as a phase of a complex sequence of causation. When such a sequence is under inquiry; as in the earlier, pre-Darwinian theories of evolution, it is not handled as a cumulative sequence whose character may blindly change from better to worse, or conversely, at any point; but rather as an unfolding of a certain prime cause in which is contained, implicitly, all that presently appears in explicit form.

In the conception of the causal relation as it may be seen at work a hundred years ago, cause and effect are felt to stand over against one another, so that the cause controls, determines the effect by transmitting its own character to it. The cause is the producer, the effect the product. Relatively little emphasis or interest falls upon the process out of which the product emerges; the interest being centred upon the latter and its relation to the efficient cause out of which it has come. The theories constructed under the guidance of this conception are generalizations as to an equivalence between the producing cause and the effect-product. The cause "makes" the effect, in much the same sense as the craftsman is apprehended to make the article on which he is engaged. There is a felt distinction between the cause and the environing circumstances, much as there is between the workman on the one hand and his tools and materials on the other hand. The intervening process is simply the manner of functioning of the efficient cause, much as the workman's work is the functioning of the workman in the interval between the inception and the completion of the product. The effect is subsequent to the cause, as the workman's product is subsequent to and consequent upon his putting forth his productive efficiency. It is a relation of before and after, in which the process comes in for attention as covering and accounting for the time interval which, in analogy with workmanlike endeavor, is required for the functioning of the efficient cause.(29*)

But as time passes and habituation to the exigencies of the machine technology gains in range and consistency, the quasi-personal, handicraft conception of causation decays, – first and most notably in those material, inorganic sciences that stand in the closest relation to the mechanical technology, but presently also in the organic sciences, and even in the moral sciences. The machine technology is a mechanical or material process, and requires the attention to be centred upon this process and the exigencies of the process. In such a process no one factor stands out as unequivocally the efficient cause in the case, whose personal character, so to speak, is transfused into the product, and to whose workings the rest of the complex of causes are related only as subsidiary or conditioning circumstances. To the technologist the process comes necessarily to count, not simply as the interval of functioning of an initial efficient cause, but as the substantial fact that engages his attention. He learns to think in terms of the process, rather than in terms of a productive cause and a product between which the process intervenes in such a manner as to afford a transition from one to the other. The process is always complex; always a delicately balanced interplay of forces that work blindly, insensibly, heedlessly; in which any appreciable deviation may forthwith count in a cumulative manner, the further consequences of which stand in no organic relation to the purpose for which the process has been set going. The prime efficient cause falls, relatively, into the background and yields precedence to the process as the point of technological interest.

This machine technology, with its accompanying discipline in mechanical adaptations and object-lessons, came on gradually and rose to a dominating place in the cultural environment during the closing years of the eighteenth and the course of the nineteenth century; and as fast as men learned to think in terms of technological process, they went on at an. accelerated pace in the further invention of mechanical processes, so that from that time the progress of inventions has been of a cumulative character and has cumulatively heightened the disciplinary force of the machine process. This early technological advance, of course, took place in the British community, where the machine process first gained headway and where the discipline of a prevalent machine industry inculcated thinking in terms of the machine process. So also it was in the British community that modern science fell into the lines marked out by technological thinking and began to formulate its theories in terms of process rather than in terms of prime causes and the like. While something of this kind is noticeable relatively early in some of the inorganic sciences, as, e.g., Geology, the striking and decisive move in this direction was taken toward the middle of the century by Darwin and his contemporaries.(30*) Without much preliminary exposition and without feeing himself to be out of touch with his contemporaries, Darwin set to work to explain species in terms of the process out of which they have arisen, rather than out of the prime cause to which the distinction between them may be due.(31*) Denying nothing as to the substantial services of the Great Artificer in the development of species, he simply and naively left Him out of the scheme, because, as being a personal factor, He could not be stated and handled in terms of process. So Darwin offered a tentative account of the descent of man, without recourse to divine or human directive endeavor and without inquiry as to whence man ultimately came and why, or as to what fortune would ultimately overtake him. His inquiry characteristically confines itself to the process of cumulative change. His results, as well as his specific determination of the factors at work in this process of cumulative change, have been questioned; perhaps they are open to all the criticisms levelled against them as well as to a few more not yet thought of; but the scope and method given to scientific inquiry by Darwin and the generation whose spokesman he is has substantially not been questioned, except by that diminishing contingent of the faithful who by force of special training or by native gift are not amenable to the discipline of the machine process. The characteristically modern science does not inquire about prime causes, design in nature, desirability of effects, ultimate results, or eschatological consequences.

Of the two postulates of earlier modern science, – the quantitative equivalence and the qualitative equivalence of cause and effect, – the former has come practically to signify the balanced articulation of the process of cumulative change; the endeavor of the Positivists to erect this canon of quantitative equivalence into the sole canon of scientific truth, and so to reduce scientific theory to a system of accountancy, having failed. The latter thesis, that like causes produce like effects, or that the effect is, in some sense, of the same character as the cause, has fallen into decay as holding true only in such tenuously general terms as to leave it without particular force. The scientists are learning more and more consistently to think in the opaque, impersonal terms of strains, mechanical structures, displacement, and the like; terms which are convertible into the working drawings and specifications of the mechanical engineer.

The older preconceptions are, of course, not wholly eliminated from the intellectual apparatus of scientific research and generalization. The cultural situation whose discipline gives the outcome is made up of inherited traditional notions at least as much as of the notions brought in by the machine process. Even among the scientific adepts there has been no complete break with the past; necessarily not, since they are, after all, creatures of their own generation. Many of them, but more especially those who are engaged in upholding the authentic results of scientific research, are somewhat prone to make much of the definitive results achieved, rather than of the process of research in which these results are provisional appliances of work. And many of these, together. with the great part of those well-meaning persons who exploit the sciences for purposes of edification, such as clergymen and naturalistic myth-makers, still personify the process of cause and effect and find in it a well-advised meliorative trend. But that work of research which effectually extends the borders of scientific knowledge is nearly all done under the guidance of highly impersonal, mechanical, morally and aesthetically colorless conceptions of causal sequence. And this scientific work is carried out only in those communities which are in due contact with the modern mechanically organized industrial system, – only under the shadow of the machine technology.

In the nature of the case the cultural growth dominated by the machine industry is of a sceptical, matter-of-fact complexion, materialistic, unmoral, unpatriotic, undevout. The growth of habits of thought, in the industrial regions and centres particularly, runs in this direction; but hitherto there has enough of the ancient norms of Western Christendom remained intact to make a very respectable protest against that deterioration of the cultural tissues which the ferment of the machine industry unremittingly pushes on. The machine discipline. however, touches wider and wider circles of the population, and touches them in an increasingly intimate and coercive manner. In the nature of the case, therefore, the resistance opposed to this cultural trend given by the machine discipline on grounds of received conventions weakens with the passage of time. The spread of materialistic, matter-of-fact preconceptions takes place at a cumulatively accelerating rate, except in so far as some other cultural factor, alien to the machine discipline, comes in to inhibit its spread and keep its disintegrating influence within bounds.

NOTES:

1. The perfected system of business principles rests on the historical basis of free institutions, and so presumes a protracted historical growth of these institutions; but a highly efficient, though less perfect, business system was worked out in a relatively short time by the South and Central European peoples in early modern times on the basis of a less consummate system of rights. – Cf. Ehrenberg, Zeitalter der Fugger; Sombart, Kapitalismus, vol. II. ch. VIII, XIV, XV.

2. See Chapter IV, above.

3. Cf. Keane, Man, Past and Present, ch. XIV; W.Z. Ripley, Races of Europe; Lapouge, L'Aryen; Montelius, Les temps prehistoriques en Bubde, etc.; Andreas Hansen, Menneskesloegtens Aelde.

4. If, e.g., he takes to myth making and personifies the machine or the process and imputes and benevolence to the mechanical applications, after the manner of current nursery tales and pulpit oratory, he is sure to go wrong.

5. Such expressions as "good and ill," "merit and demerit," "law and order," when applied to technological facts or to the outcome of material seience, are evidently only metaphorical expressions, borrowed from older usage and serviceable only as figures of speech.

6. Tarde, Psychologic Economique, vol. I. pp. 122-131, offers a characterization of the psychology of modern work, contrasting, among other things, the work of the machine workman with that of the handicraftsman in respect of its psychological requirements and effects. It may be taken as a temperate formulation of the cent commonplaces on this topic, and seems to be fairly wide of the mark.

7. For something more than a hundred years past this change in the habits of thought of the workman has been commonly spoken of as a deterioration or numbing of his intelligence. But that seems too sweeping a characterization of the change brought on by habituation to machine work. It is safe to say that such habituation brings a change in the workman's habits of thought, – in the direction, method, and content of his thinking, – heightening his intelligence for some purposes and lowering it for certain others. No doubt, on the whole, the machine's discipline lowers the intelligence of the workman for such purposes as were rated high as marks of intelligence before the coming of the machine, but it appears likewise to heighten his intelligence for such purposes as have been brought to the front by the machine. If he is by nature scantily endowed with the aptitudes that would make him think effectively in terms of the machine process, if he has intellectual capacity for other things and not for this, then the mining of the machine may fairly be said to lower his intelligence, since it hiders the full development of the only capacities of which he is possessed. The resulting difference in intellectual training is a difference in kind and direction, not necessarily in degree. Cf. Schmoller, Grundriss der Volkswirtschaftslehre, vol. I. secs. 85-86, 132; Hobson, Evolution of Modern Capitalism, ch. IX. secs. 4 and 5; Cooke Taylor, Modern Factory System, pp. 434-435; Sidney and Beatrice Webb, Industrial Democrocy, e.g. pp. 327 et seq.; K. Th. Reinhold, Arbeit und Werkzeug, ch. X. (particularly pp. 190-198) and ch. XI (particularly pp. 221-240).

8. Cf. J.C. Sutherland, "The Engineering Mind" Popular Science Monthly, January 1903, pp. 254-256.

9. Cf. "Industrial and Pecuniary Employments" especially pp. 198-218.

10. As G.F. Steffen has described it: "Those who hire out their labor power or their capital or their land to the entrepreneurs are as a rule not absolutely passive as seen from the point of view of business enterprise. They are not simply inanimate implements in the hands of the entrepreneurs. They are, enterprising implements, (foretagaade verktyg) who surrender their undertaking functions only to the extent designated in the contract with the entrepreneur." – Ekonomisk Tidskrift, vol. V. p. 256.

11. Cf., on the other hand, Reinhold, Arbeit und Werkzeug, ch. XII and XIV, where double dealing is confused with workmanship, very much after the manner familiar to readers of expositions of the "wages of superintendence," but more broadly and ingeniously than usual.

12. Individual exceptions are, of course, to be found in all classes, but there is, after all, a more or less consistent, prevalent class attitude. As is well known, clergymen, lawyers, soldiers, civil servants, and the like, are popularly held to be of a conservative, if not reactionary temper. This vulgar apprehension may be faulty in detail, and especially it may be too sweeping in its generalizations; but there are, after all, few persons not belonging to these classes who will not immediately recognize that this vulgar appraisement of them rests on substantial grounds, even though the appraisement may need qualification. So, also, a conservative animus is seen to pervade all classes more generally in earlier times or on more archaic levels of culture than our own. At the same time, in those early days and in the more archaic cultural regions, the structure of conventionally accepted truths and the body of accredited spiritual or extra-material facts are more comprehensive and rigid, and the thinking on all topics is more consistently held to tests of authenticity as contrasted with tests of sense perception. On the whole, the number and variety of things that are fundamentally and eternally true and good increase as one goes outward from the modern West-European cultural centres into the earlier barbarian past or into the remoter barbarian present.

13. See Chapter II above.

14. Cf. Theory of the Leisure Class, especially ch. IV and V.

15. As, e.g., Mr W.G.S. Adams cogently points out in a recent number of the Journal of Political Ecomnomy (December 1902).

16. As Mr. Webb shows (Industrial Democracy, 1902, pp. xxivxxxvi).

17. The historical explanation of this House of Lords reversal of trade-union practice is probably to be found in the conservative, or rather reactionary, trend given to British sentiment by the imperialist policy of the last two or three decades, accentuated by the experiences of the Boer War. The Boer War seems to mark a turning-point in the growth of sentiment and institutions. Since the seventies the imperialist interest, that is to say, the dynastic interest, has been coming into the foreground among the interests that engage the attention of the British community. It seems now to have definitively gained the first place, and may be expected in the immediate future to dominate British policy both at home and abroad. Concomitantly, it may be remarked, the British community has been slowing down, if not losing ground, in industrial animus, technological efficiency, and scientific spirit. Cf. Hobson, Imperialism, part II ch. I and III.

18. All this applies to anarchism as well as to socialism; similarly to several minor categories of dissentients. In their negative proposals the socialists and anarchists are fairly agreed. It is in the metaphysical postulates of their protest and in their constructive aims that they part company. Of the two, the socialists are more widely out of touch with the established order. They are also more hopelessly negative and destructive in their ideals, as seen from the standpoint of the established order. This applies to the later socialists rather than to the earlier, and it applies, of course, only to the lower-class, "democratic" socialists, not to the so-called state and Christian socialists.

Anarchism proceeds on natural-rights ground, and is accordingly in touch with the postulates of the existing property arrangements to that extent. It is a more unmitigated working out of the same postulates. It is a system of "natural liberty" unqualified to the extent even of not admitting prescriptive ownership. Its basis is a (divinely instituted) order of nature, the keynote of which is an inalienable freedom and equality of the individual, quite in the eighteenth-century spirit. It is in this sense an offshoot of the Romantic school of thought. Anarchism is a de jure seheme, which takes no account of mechanical exigencies but rests its case altogether on anthropomorphic postulates of natural rights. It is, from the natural-rights standpoint, substantially sound, though senselessly extreme.

What may be called the normal socialism, socialism of the later, more dangerous, and more perplexing, kind, does not build on the received metaphysical basis of the "natural order." It demands a reconstruction of the social fabric, but it does not know on what lines the reconstruction is to be carried out. The natural rights of the individual are not accepted as the standard (except by certain large bodies of neophytes, especially rural American, who are carrying under socialist mottoes the burden of animosities and preconceptions that once made populism), but nothing definite is put in the place of this outworn standard. The socialists of the line, in so far as there is any consensus among them, profess that the mechanical exigencies of the industrial system must decide what the social structure is to be, but beyond this vague generality they have little to offer. And this mechanical standardization can manifestly afford no basis for legislation on civil rights. Indeed, it is difficult to see how any seheme of civil rights, much or little, can find a place in a socialistic reorganization.

19. The "scientific socialism" of Marx and Engels as promulgated during the third quarter of the nineteenth century was not of this negative character. It was a product of Hegelianism blended with the conceptions of natural rights, its chief count being the "claim to the full product of labor." This socialism never made serious inroads among the working classes outside of Germany – the home of Hegelianism. Even in that country the most vigorous growth of socialistic sentiment came after Hegelianism had begun to yield to Darwinian methods of thought, and this later growth has been progressively less Marxian and less positive. Marxism is now little more than a pro forma confession of faith. Avowed socialism is practically taking on the character described above, except so far as it has grown opportunist and has sought affiliation with the liberal democratic movement and the reformers.

20. Where members of the well-to-do classes avow socialistic sentiments and ideals it commonly turns out to be a merely humanitarian aspiration for a more "equitable" redistribution of wealth, a readjustment of the seheme of ownership with some improved safeguarding of the "reasonable" property claims of all members of the community. What "socialist" reform commonly means to this contingent of well-to-do irregulars is some seheme of equal rights of ownership for all. Whereas to socialists of the line equal rights of ownership is as idle a proposition as an equal right of citizens to sell their votes. Instead of a reform of ownership the socialists contemplate the traceless disappearance of ownership.

21. Unless it be in the latest extremes of conservatism, such as is shown in the recent of dynastic politics in Germany, Tory policy in England, and predatory political ideals in America.

22. Socialistic notions are apprently making some inroads among the rural population of the American prairie region, where a mechanically organized and standardized method of farming prevails, with a large use of mechanical appliances.

23. So striking has been the failure of the German socialists, for instance, in their attempts upon the integrity of the farming community, that they have latterly changed their tactics, and instead of attempting to convert the peasants to a full socialistic programme, they have turned to measures of compromise, in which the characteristic and revolutionary features of the socialistic programme are softened beyond recognition, if not suppressed. The habits of life, and therefore the habits of thought, of the peasant farmers move on the ancient leveis of handicraft, pecuniary management, personal consequence, and preseriptive custom.

24. If this account of the class limitation of the socialist bias is accepted, it has an immediate bearing upon a question which is latterly engaging the attention of the advocates of socialism. The question is as to the part played by propertyless office employees and by the business men whom the modern consolidations of business reduce to the position of salaried managers and superintendents. With a faith prompted by their own hopes rather than by observed facts or by the logic of events, the spokesmen for socialism are strongly inclined to claim this "business proletariat" as a contingent which the course of economic development is bound to throw into the socialist camp. The facts do not in any appreciable degree

countenance such an expectation. The unpropertied classes employed in business do not take to socialistic vagaries with such alacrity as should inspire a confident hope in the advocates of socialism or a serious apprehension in those who stand for law and order. This pecuniarily disfranchised business population, in its revulsion against unassimilated facts, turns rather to some excursion into pragmatic romance, such as Social Settlements, Prohibition, Clean Politics, Single Tax, Arts and Crafts, Neighborhood Guilds, Institutional Church, Christian Science, New Thought, or some such cultural thimblerig. The work of the captain of industry in curtailing the range of individual discretion in business and in reducing the lesser undertakers to the rank of clerks and subalterns need not be looked upon as unavoidably furthering the spread of the socialistic bias, except in so far as the change results in throwing the men affected by it out of the pecuniary or business occupations and subjecting them to the discipline of the mechanical industry. At the most, apparently, the change from an independent to a dependent business life serves to weaken the men's interest in the question of property; it does not appear that it throws them into an attitude of substantial distrust or iconoclasm. Their interest in this particular institution slackens through the loss of that emulative motive on which pecuniary endeavor proceeds, but their faith in its intrinsic fitness is not thereby shaken, nor are they thrown into the ranks of the chronic dissentients. The training given by their life continues prevailingly to run on conventional grounds; that is to say, on grounds of legal relation, solvency, and the like. Accountants and office employees are nearly as conservative as clergymen and lawyers, and their being so is apparently due to the fact that their experience runs on much the same ground of conventional finality.

    25. Connected with this apparent selective action which the modem specialization of occupations exerts, there is a further, and at first sight more singular, point of disparity between the socialists and the conservatives; and this difference has also a curious correlation with the distribution of the machine industry. In a degree, – slight and uncertain, perhaps, but searcely to be mistaken, – the socialists and the conservatives are apparently of different racial antecedents. It has been seen above that the propaganda is most vital and widespread in the industrial towns, as contrasted with the agricultural country. But if the researches of such students as Ammon, Ripley, Lapouge, Closson, and others that might be named, are taken at their face value, it appears that the towns differ perceptibly from the open country in point of race; and that the migration from the country into the industrial towns has a selective effect of such a kind that a larger proportion of one racial stock than of another resorts to the towns. The towns, in those countries where data are available, show a larger admixture of the dolicho–blond stock than the open country. This seems to argue that the dolicho–blond stock, or the racial mixture of the towns in which there is a relatively large admixture of the dolicho–blond, is perceptibly more efficient in the machine industries, more readily inclined to think in materialistic terms, more given to radical innovation, less bound by convention and prescription. This generalization is strengthened by the fact that the more dolicho–blond regions are also, on the whole, more socialistic than those in which this element is less in evidence. At the same time they are industrially in advance of the latter in the matter of machine industry; and they are also Protestant (irreligious) rather than Catholic.

    26. This, of course, does not hold for the inoffensive pseudo–socialistic diversions set afoot by various well–meaning politicians and clergmen, known by various qualifying designations, such as "State," "Christian," "Catholic," etc., and desired to act as correctives of the socialistic distemper.

    27. The cultural era of Natural Rights, Natural Liberty, and Natural Religion reduced God to the rank of a "Great Artificer," and the machine technology is, in turn, relegating Him to that fringe of minor employments and those outlying industrial regions to which the handicraftsmen have been retired.

    28. There is a similar suggestion in the relative (slight but perceptible) decline of scientific animus in England since the English community has turned its attention and aspirations to imperialistic feats of prowess more than to industrial matters.

29. Compare, however, Sombart, Kapitalismus, especially vol. I. ch. VIII and XV. Sombart finds the modern seientific concept of cause and effect to be essentially an outcome of the discipline of accountancy enforced by business traffic. So that he makes business enterprise rather than mechanical industry accountable for the rise of modern science and for the matter-of-fact character which distinguishes this science. In this view there is, no doubt, a large and valuable element of truth. To the end of a mathematical formulation of causal phenomena as well as a tenacious grasp of the principle of quantitative equivalence, the accountancy enfoxed by the petty trade of early modern times, as well as by commercial traffic proper, appears to have given the most effective training. In so far as this element of quantitative equivalence, simply, has dominated the growth of science, it has given, as its most perfect product, Positivism. Positivism flourished at its best and freest in France, where the modern economic culture was commercial rather than mechanical. And when the machine discipline seriously invaded France, Positivism languished and died. But modern seience is not a calculus simply. It deals not with calculations of quantitative equivalence only, but with efficient causes, active relations, creative foxes. The concept of efficient cause is not a derivative of accountancy, nor is it formed in the image of accountancy. But this generic concept of efficient cause, the kinetic concept, antedates Positivism and has outlived it. In its earlier (eighteenth-century) phase this concept shows close relationship with the notion of workmanship, in its later (nineteenth-century) use it has much in common with the notion of mechanical efficiency.

30. Darwin, of course, does not stand alone. He is the great exponent of a mass movement which involves a shifting of the point of view and of the point of interest in seientific research and speculation.

31. This is the substance of Darwin's advance over Lamarck, for instance.

Chapter 10. The Natural Decay of Business Enterprise

Broadly, the machine discipline acts to disintegrate the institutional heritage, of all degrees of antiquity and authenticity – whether it be the institutions that embody the principles of natural liberty or those that comprise the residue of more archaic principles of conduct still current in civilized life. It thereby cuts away that ground of law and order on which business enterprise is founded. The further cultural bearing of this disintegration of the received order is no doubt sufficiently serious and far-reaching, but it does not directly concern the present inquiry. It comes in question here only in so far as such a deterioration of the general cultural tissues involves a setback to the continued vigor of business enterprise. But the future of business enterprise is bound up with the future of civilization, since the cultural scheme is, after all, a single one, comprising many interlocking elements, no one of which can be greatly disturbed without disturbing the working of all the rest.

In its bearing on the question in hand, the "social problem" at large presents this singular situation. The growth of business enterprise rests on the machine technology as its material foundation. The machine industry is indispensable to it; it cannot get along without the machine process, But the discipline of the machine process cuts away the spiritual, institutional foundations of business enterprise; the machine industry is incompatible with its continued growth; it cannot, in the long run, get along with the machine process. In their struggle against the cultural effects of the machine process, therefore, business principles cannot win in the long run; since an effectual mutilation or inhibition of the machine system would gradually push business enterprise to the wall; whereas with a free growth of the machine system business principles would presently fall into abeyance.

The institutional basis of business enterprise the system of natural rights – appears to be a peculiarly instable affair. There is no way of retaining it under changing circumstances, and there is no way of returning to it after circumstances have changed. It is a hybrid growth, a blend of personal freedom and equality on the one hand and of prescriptive rights on the other hand. The institutions and points of law under the natural–rights scheme appear to be of an essentially provisional character. There is relatively great flexibility and possibility of growth and change; natural rights are singularly insecure under any change of circumstances. The maxim is well approved that eternal vigilance is the price of (natural) liberty. When, as now, this system is endangered by socialistic or anarchistic disaffection there is no recourse that will carry the institutional apparatus back to a secure natural–rights basis. The system of natural liberty was the product of a peaceful regime of handicraft and petty trade; but continued peace and industry presently carried the cultural growth beyond the phase of natural rights by giving rise to the machine process and the large business; and these are breaking down the structure of natural rights by making these rights nugatory on the one hand and by cutting away the spiritual foundations of them on the other hand. Natural rights being a by–product of peaceful industry, they cannot be reinstated by a recourse to warlike habits and a coercive government, since warlike habits and coercion are alien to the natural–rights spirit. Nor can they be reinstated by a recourse to settled peace and freedom, since an era of settled peace and freedom would push on the dominance of the machine process and the large business, which break down the system of natural liberty.

When the question is cast up as to what will come of this conflict of institutional forces – called the Social Problem – it is commonly made a question of remedies: What can be done to save civilized mankind from the vulgarization and disintegration wrought by the machine industry?

Now, business enterprise and the machine process are the two prime movers in modern culture; and the only recourse that holds a promise of being effective, therefore, is a recourse to the workings of business traffic. And this is a question, not of what is conceivably, ideally, idyllically possible for the business community to do if they will take thought and act advisedly and concertedly toward a chosen cultural outcome, but of what is the probable cultural outcome to be achieved through business traffic carried on for business ends, not for cultural ends. It is a question not of what ought to be done, but of what is to take place.

Persons who are solicitous for the cultural future commonly turn to speculative advice as to what ought to be done toward holding fast that which is good in the cultural heritage, and what ought further to be done to increase the talent that has been intrusted to this generation. The practical remedy offered is commonly some proposal for palliative measures, some appeal to philanthropic, aesthetic, or religious sentiment, some endeavor to conjure with the name of one or another of the epiphenomena of modern culture. Something must be done, it is conceived, and this something takes the shape of charity organizations, clubs and societies for social "purity", for amusement, education, and manual training of the indigent classes, for colonization of the poor, for popularization of churches, for clean politics, for cultural missionary work by social settlements, and the like. These remedial measures whereby it is proposed to save or to rehabilitate certain praiseworthy but obsolescent habits of life and of thought are, all and several, beside the point so far as touches the question in hand. Not that it is hereby intended to cast a slur on these meritorious endeavors to save mankind by treating symptoms. The symptoms treated are no doubt evil, as they are said to be; or if they are not evil, the merits of that particular question do not concern the present inquiry. The endeavors in question are beside the point in that they do not fall into the shape of a business proposition. They are, on the whole, not so profitable a line of investment as certain other ventures that are open to modern enterprise. Hence, if they traverse the course of business enterprise and of industrial exigencies, they are nugatory, being in the same class with the labor of Sisyphus; whereas if they coincide in effect with the line along which business and industrial exigencies move, they are a work of supererogation, except so far as they may be conceived to accelerate a change that is already under way. Nothing can deflect the sweep of business enterprise, unless it be an outgrowth of this enterprise itself or of the industrial means by which business enterprise works.

Nothing can serve as a corrective of the cultural trend given by the machine discipline except what can be put in the form of a business proposition. The question of neutralizing the untoward effects of the machine discipline resolves itself into a question as to the cultural work and consequences of business enterprise, and of the cultural value of business principles in so far as they guide such human endeavor as lies outside the range of business enterprise proper. It is not a question of what ought to be done, but of what is the course laid out by business principles; the discretion rests with the business men, not with the moralists, and the business men's discretion is bounded by the exigencies of business enterprise. Even the business men cannot allow themselves to play fast and loose with business principles in response to a call from humanitarian motives. The question, therefore, remains, on the whole, a question of what the business men may be expected to do for cultural growth on the motive of profits.

Something they are doing, as others are, from motives of benevolence, with a well-advised endeavor to maintain the cultural gains of the past and to make the way of life smoother for mankind in the future. But the more secure and substantial results to be looked for in this direction are those that follow incidentally, as byproducts of business enterprise, because these are not dependent on the vagaries of personal preference, tastes, and prejudices, but rest on a broad institutional basis.

The effects of business enterprise upon the habits and temper of the people, and so upon institutional growth, are chiefly of the nature of sequelae, It has already been noted that the discipline of business employments is of a conservative nature, tending to sustain the conventions that rest on natural-rights dogma, because these employments train the men engaged in them to think in terms of natural rights. It is unnecessary to return to this topic here, except to notice that, in its severer, more unmitigated form, this discipline in pecuniary habits of thought falls on a gradually lessening proportion of the population. The absolute number of business men, counting principals and subordinates, is, of course, not decreasing, The number of men in business pursuits, in proportion to the population, is also apparently not decreasing; but within the business employments a larger proportion are occupied with office routine, and so are withdrawn from the more effectual training given by business management proper. If such a decrease occurs in any country, it is almost certainly not to be found in any other country than America.

This business discipline is somewhat closely limited both in scope and range. (1) It acts to conserve, or to rehabilitate, a certain restricted line of institutional habits of thought, viz. those preconceptions of natural rights which have to do with property. What it conserves, therefore, is the bourgeois virtues of solvency, thrift, and dissimulation. The nobler and more spectacular aristocratic virtues, with their correlative institutional furniture, are not in any sensible degree fortified by the habits of business life. Business life does not further the growth of manner and breeding, pride of Caste, punctilios of "honor," or even religious fervor. (2) The salutary discipline of business life touches the bulk of the population, the working classes, in a progressively less intimate and less exacting manner. It can, therefore, not serve to correct or even greatly to mitigate the matter-of-fact bias given these classes by the discipline of the machine process.

As a direct disciplinary factor the machine process holds over the business employments, in that it touches larger classes of the community and inculcates its characteristic habits of thought more unremittingly, And any return to more archaic methods of industry, such as is sometimes advocated on artistic grounds, seems hopeless, since business interests do not countenance a discontinuance of machine methods, The machine methods that are corrupting the hearts and manners of the workmen are profitable to the business men, and that fact seems to be decisive on the point. A direct, advised return to handicraft, or any similar discontinuance of the machine industry, is out of the question; although something in the way of a partial return to more primitive methods of industry need not be impracticable as a remote and indirect consequence of the working of business enterprise.

The indirect or incidental cultural bearing of business principles and business practice is wide-reaching and forceful. Business principles have a peculiar hold upon the affections of the people as something intrinsically right and good. They are therefore drawn on for guidance and conviction even in concerns that are not conceived to be primarily business concerns. So, e.g., they have permeated the educational system, thoroughly and intimately. Their presence, as an element of common sense, in the counsels of the "educators" shows itself in a naive insistence on the "practical" whenever the scheme of instruction is under advisement. "Practical" means useful for private gain. Any new departure in public instruction, whether in the public schools or in private endowed establishments, is scrutinized with this test in mind; which results in a progressive, though not wholly consistent, narrowing of instruction to such learning as is designed to give a ready application of results rather than a systematic organization of knowledge. The primary test is usefulness for getting an income. The secondary test, practically applied where latitude is allowed in the way of "culture" studies, is the aptness of the instruction in question to fit the learners for spending income in a decorous manner. Hence quasi-scholarly accomplishments. Much of the current controversy as to the inclusion or exclusion of one thing and another from the current curriculum of secondary and higher schools might be reduced to terms of one or the other of these two purposes without doing violence to the arguments put forth and with a great gain in conciseness and lucidity.

There is also a large resort to business methods in the conduct of the schools; with the result that a system of scholastic accountancy is enforced both as regards the work of the teachers and the progress of the pupils; whence follows a mechanical routine, with mechanical tests of competency in all directions. This lowers the value of the instruction for purposes of intellectual initiative and a reasoned grasp of the subject-matter. This class of erudition is rather a hindrance than a help to habits of thinking. It conduces to conviction rather than to inquiry, and is therefore a conservative factor.

In the endowed schools there is, moreover, an increasing introduction of business men and business methods into the personnel and the administrative work. This is necessarily so since these schools are competitors for students and endowments. The policy of these schools necessarily takes on some thing of the complexion of competitive business; which throws the emphasis on those features of school life that will best attract students and donors. The features which count most directly in these directions are not the same as would count most effectively toward the avowed ends of these schools. The standards which it is found Operative to live up to are not the highest standards of scholarly work. Courtesy as well as expediency inclines these schools to cultivate such appearances and such opinions as may be expected to find favor with men of wealth. These men of wealth are business men, for the most part elderly men, who are, as is well known, prevailingly of a conservative temper in all cultural matters, and more especially as touches those institutions that bear on business affairs.

A more far-reaching department of the educational system, though not technically rated as such, is the periodical press, both newspapers and magazines. This is a field of business enterprise, and business principles may be expected to work more consistently and to a more unqualified result in this field than in the school system, where these principles come in incidentally.

The current periodical press, whether ephemeral or other, is a vehicle for advertisements. This is its raison d'etre, as a business proposition, and this decides the lines of its management without material qualification. Exceptions to the rule are official and minor propagandist periodicals, and, in an uncertain measure, scientific journals. The profits of publication come from the sale of advertising space. The direct returns from sales and subscriptions are now a matter of wholly secondary consequence. Publishers of periodicals, of all grades of transiency, aim to make their product as salable as may he, in order to pass their advertising pages under the eyes of as many readers as may be. The larger the circulation the greater, other things equal, the market value of the advertising space. The highest product of this development is the class of American newspapers called "independent." These in particular – and they are followed at no great interval by the rest edit all items of news, comment, or gossip with a view to what the news ought to be and what opinions ought to be expressed on passing events.(1*)

The first duty of an editor is to gauge the sentiments of his readers, and then tell them what they like to believe. By this means he maintains or increases the circulation. His second duty is to see that nothing is said in the news items or editorials which may discountenance any claims or announcements made by his advertisers, discredit their standing or good faith, or expose any weakness or deception in any business venture that is or may become a valuable advertiser. By this means he increases the advertising value of his circulation.(2*) The net result is that both the news columns and the editorial columns are commonly meretricious in a high degree.

Systematic insincerity on the part of the ostensible purveyors of information and leaders of opinion may be deplored by persons who stickle for truth and pin their hopes of social salvation on the spread of accurate information. But the ulterior cultural effect of the insincerity which is in this way required by the business situation may, of course, as well be salutary as the reverse. Indeed, the effect is quite as likely to be salutary, if "salutary" be taken to mean favorable to the maintenance of the established order, since the insincerity is guided by a wish to avoid any lesion of the received preconceptions and prejudices. The insincerity of the newspapers and magazines seems, on the whole, to be of a conservative trend.

The periodical press is not only a purveyor of news, opinions, and admonitions; it also supplies the greater part of the literature currently read. And in this part of its work the same underlying business principles are in force. The endeavor is to increase the circulation at any cost that will result in an increased net return from the sale of the advertising space. The literary output of the magazines is of use for carrying the advertising pages, and as a matter of business, as seen from the standpoint of the business man's interest, that is its only use.

The standards of excellence that govern this periodical literature seem fairly to be formulated as follows: (1) In each given case it must conform to the tastes and the most ready comprehension of the social strata which the particular periodical is designed to reach; (2) it should conduce to a quickened interest in the various lines of services and commodities offered in the advertising pages, and should direct the attention of readers along such lines of investment and expenditure as may benefit the large advertisers particularly. At least it must in no way hamper the purposes of the advertisers. Nothing should go in a popular magazine which would cast a sinister shadow over any form of business venture that advertises or might be induced to advertise.(3*)

Taken in the aggregate, the literary output is desired to meet the tastes of that large body of people who are in the habit of buying freely. The successful magazine writers are those who follow the taste of the class to whom they speak, in any aberration (fad, mannerism, or misapprehension) and in any shortcoming of insight or force which may beset that class. They must also conform to the fancies and prejudices of this class as regards the ideals – artistic, moral, religious, or social – for which they speak. The class to which the successful periodicals turn, and which gives tone to periodical literature, is that great body of people who are in moderately easy circumstances. Culturally this means the respectable middle class (largely the dependent business class) of various shades of conservatism, affectation, and snobbery. (4*)

On the whole, the literature provided in this way and to this end seems to run on a line of slightly more pronounced conservatism and affectation than the average sentiment of the readers appealed to. This is true for the following reason. Readers who are less conservative and less patient of affectations, snobbery, and illiberality than the average are in the position of doubters and dissentients. They are less confident in their convictions of what is right and good in all matters, and are also not unwilling to make condescending allowances for those who are less "advanced," and who must be humored since they know no better; whereas those who rest undoubting in the more conservative views and a more intolerant affectation of gentility are readier, because more naive, in their rejection of whatever does not fully conform to their habits of thought.

So it comes about that the periodical literature is, on the whole, somewhat more scrupulously devout in tone, somewhat more given to laud and dilate upon the traffic of the upper leisure class and to carry on the discussion in the terms and tone imputed to that class, somewhat more prone to speak deprecatingly of the vulgar innovations of modern culture, than the average of the readers to whom it is addressed. The trend of its teaching, therefore, is, on the whole, conservative and conciliatory. It is also under the necessity of adapting itself to a moderately low average of intelligence and information; since on this head, again, it is those who possess intelligence and information that are readiest to make allowances; they are, indeed, mildly flattered to do so, besides being the only ones who can. It is a prime requisite to conciliate a large body of readers.

This latter characteristic is particularly evident in the didactic portion of the periodical literature. This didactic literature, running on discussions of a quasi-artistic and quasi-scientific character, is, by force of the business exigencies of the case, designed to favor the sensibilities of the weaker among its readers by adroitly suggesting that the readers are already possessed of the substance of what purports to be taught and need only be fortified with certain general results. There follows a great spread of quasi-technical terms and fanciful conceits. The sophisticated animal stories and the half-mythical narratives of industrial processes which now have the vogue illustrate the results achieved in this direction.

The literary output issued under the surveillance of the advertising office is excellent in workmanship and deficient in intelligence and substantial originality. What is encouraged and cultivated is adroitness of style and a piquant presentation of commonplaces. Harmlessness, not to say pointlessness, and an edifying, gossipy optimism are the substantial characteristics, which persist through all ephemeral mutations of style, manner, and subject-matter.

Business enterprise, therefore, it is believed, gives a salutary bent to periodical literature. It conduces mildly to the maintenance of archaic ideals and philistine affectations, and inculcates the crasser forms of patriotic, sportsmanlike, and spendthrift aspirations.

The largest and most promising factor of cultural discipline – most promising as a corrective of iconoclastic vagaries – over which business principles rule is national politics. The purposes and the material effects of business politics have already been spoken of above, but in the present connection their incidental, disciplinary effects are no less important. Business interests urge an aggressive national policy and business men direct it. Such a policy is warlike as well as patriotic. The direct cultural value of a warlike business policy is unequivocal. It makes for a conservative animus on the part of the populace. During war time, and within the military organization at all times, under martial law, civil rights are in abeyance; and the more warfare and armament the more abeyance. Military training is a training in ceremonial precedence, arbitrary command, and unquestioning obedience. A military organization is essentially a servile organization. Insubordination is the deadly sin. The more consistent and the more comprehensive this military training, the more effectually will the members of the community be trained into habits of subordination and away from that growing propensity to make light of personal authority that is the chief infirmity of democracy. This applies first and most decidedly, of course, to the soldiery, but it applies only in a less degree to the rest of the population. They learn to think in warlike terms of rank, authority, and subordination, and so grow progressively more patient of encroachments upon their civil rights. Witness the change that has latterly been going on in the temper of the German people.(5*)

The modern warlike policies are entered upon for the sake of peace, with a view to the orderly pursuit of business. In their initial motive they differ from the warlike dynastic politics of the sixteenth, seventeenth, and eighteenth centuries. But the disciplinary effects of warlike pursuits and of warlike preoccupations are much the same what ever may be their initial motive or ulterior aim. The end sought in the one case was warlike mastery and high repute in the matter of ceremonial precedence; in the other, the modern case, it is pecuniary mastery and high repute in the matter of commercial solvency. But in both cases alike the pomp and circumstance of war and armaments, and the sensational appeals to patriotic pride and animosity made by victories, defeats, or comparisons of military and naval strength, act to rehabilitate lost ideals and weakened convictions of the chauvinistic or dynastic order. At the same stroke they direct the popular interest to other, nobler, institutionally less hazardous matters than the unequal distribution of wealth or of creature comforts. Warlike and patriotic preoccupations fortify the barbarian virtues of subordination and prescriptive authority. Habituation to a warlike, predatory scheme of life is the strongest disciplinary factor that can be brought to counteract the vulgarization of modern life wrought by peaceful industry and the machine process, and to rehabilitate the decaying sense of status and differential dignity. Warfare, with the stress on subordination and mastery and the insistence on gradations of dignity and honor incident to a militant organization, has always proved an effective school in barbarian methods of thought.

In this direction, evidently, lies the hope of a corrective for "social unrest" and similar disorders of civilized life. There can, indeed, be no serious question but that a consistent return to the ancient virtues of allegiance, piety, servility, graded dignity, class prerogative, and prescriptive authority would greatly conduce to popular content and to the facie management of affairs. Such is the promise held out by a strenuous national policy.

The reversional trend given by warlike experience and warlike preoccupations, it is plain, does not set backward to the regime of natural liberty. Modern business principles and the modern scheme of civil rights and constitutional government rest on natural-rights ground. But the system of natural rights is a halfway house. The warlike culture takes back to a more archaic situation that preceded the scheme of natural rights, viz. the system of absolute government, dynastic politics, devolution of rights and honors, ecclesiastical authority, and popular submission and squalor. It makes not for a reinstatement of the Natural Rights of Man but for a reversion to the Grace of God.

The barbarian virtues of fealty and patriotism run on national or dynastic exploit and aggrandizement, and these archaic virtues are not dead. In those modern communities whose hearts beat with the pulsations of the world-market they find expression in an enthusiasm for the commercial aggrandizement of the nation's business men, But when once the policy of warlike enterprise has been entered upon for business ends, these loyal affections gradually shift from the business interests to the warlike and dynastic interests, as witness the history of imperialism in Germany and England. The eventual outcome should be a rehabilitation of the ancient patriotic animosity and dynastic loyalty, to the relative neglect of business interests. This may easily be carried so far as to sacrifice the profits of the business men to the exigencies of the higher politics.(6*)

The disciplinary effect of war and armaments and imperialist politics is complicated with a selective effect. War not only affords a salutary training, but it also acts to eliminate certain elements of the population. The work of campaigning and military tenure, such as is carried on by England, America, or the other civilizing powers, lies, in large part, in the low latitudes, where the European races do not find a favorable habitat. The low latitudes are particularly unwholesome for that dolicho-blond racial stock that seems to be the chief bearer of the machine industry. It results that the viability and the natural increase of the soldiery is perceptibly lowered. The service in the low latitudes, as contrasted with Europe, for instance, is an extrahazardous occupation. The death rate, indeed, exceeds the birth rate. But in the more advanced industrial communities, of which the English and American are typical, the service is a volunteer service; which means that those who go to the wars seek this employment by their own choice. That is to say, the human material so drawn off is automatically selected on the basis of a peculiar spiritual fitness for this predatory employment; they are, on the whole, of a more malevolent and vagabond temper, have more of the ancient barbarian animus, than those who are left at home to carry on the work of the home community and propagate the home population. And since the troops and ships are officered by the younger sons of the conservative leisure class and by the buccaneering scions of the class of professional politicians, a natural election of the same character takes effect also as regards the officers. There results a gradual selective elimination of that old-fashioned element of the population that is by temperament best suited for the old-fashioned institutional system of status and servile organization.(7*)

This selective elimination of conservative elements would in the long run leave each succeeding generation of the community less predatory and less emulative in temper, less well endowed for carrying on its life under the servile institutions proper to a militant regime. But, for the present and the nearer future, there can be little doubt but that this selective shaping of the community's animus is greatly outweighed by the contrary trend given by the discipline of warlike preoccupations. What helps to keep the balance in favor of the reversional trend is the cultural leaven carried back into the home community by the veterans. These presumptive past masters in the archaic virtues keep themselves well in the public eye and serve as exemplars to the impressionable members of the community, particularly to the less mature.(8*)

The net outcome of the latter-day return to warlike enterprise is, no doubt, securely to be rated as fostering a reversion to national ideals of servile status and to institutions of a despotic character. On the whole and for the present, it makes for conservatism, ultimately for reversion.

The quest of profits leads to a predatory national policy. The resulting large fortunes call for a massive government apparatus to secure the accumulations, on the one hand, and for large and conspicuous opportunities to spend the resulting income, on the other hand; which means a militant, coercive home administration and something in the way of an imperial court life a dynastic fountain of honor and a courtly bureau of ceremonial amenities. Such an ideal is not simply a moralist's day-dream; it is a sound business proposition, in that it lies on the line of policy along which the business interests are moving in their own behalf. If national (that is to say dynastic) ambitions and warlike aims, achievements, spectacles, and discipline be given a large place in the community's life, together with the concomitant coercive police surveillance, then there is a fair hope that the disintegrating trend of the machine discipline may be corrected. The regime of status, fealty, prerogative, and arbitrary command would guide the institutional growth back into the archaic conventional ways and give the cultural structure something of that secure dignity and stability which it had before the times, not only of socialistic vapors, but of natural rights as well. Then, too, the rest of the spiritual furniture of the ancient regime shall presumably he reinstated; materialistic scepticism may yield the ground to a romantic philosophy, and the populace and the scientists alike may regain something of that devoutness and faith in preternatural agencies which they have recently been losing. As the discipline of prowess again comes to its own, conviction and contentment with whatever is authentic may return to distracted Christendom, and may once more give something of a sacramental serenity to men's outlook on the present and the future.

But authenticity and sacramental dignity belong neither with the machine technology, nor with modern science, nor with business traffic. In so far as the aggressive politics and the aristocratic ideals currently furthered by the business community are worked out freely, their logical outcome is an abatement of those cultural features that distinguish modem times from what went before, including a decline of business enterprise itself.(9*)

How imminent such a consummation is to be accounted is a question of how far the unbusinesslike and unscientific discipline brought in by aggressive politics may be expected to prevail over the discipline of the machine industry. It is difficult to believe that the machine technology and the pursuit of the material sciences will be definitively superseded, for the reason, among others, that any community which loses these elements of its culture thereby loses that brute material force that gives it strength against its rivals. And it is equally difficult to imagine how any one of the communities of Christendom can avoid entering the funnel of business and dynastic politics, and so running through the process whereby the materialistic animus is eliminated. Which of the two antagonistic factors may prove the stronger in the long run is something of a blind guess; but the calculable future seems to belong to the one or the other. It seems possible to say this much, that the full dominion of business enterprise is necessarily a transitory dominion. It stands to lose in the end whether the one or the other of the two divergent cultural tendencies wins, because it is incompatible with the ascendancy of either.

NOTES: 1. "Ought", is of course here used to denote business expediency, not moral restraint.

2. As a side line, which affords play for the staff's creative talent, whatever is exceptionally sensational at the same time that it is harmless to the advertisers' interests should, in newspaper slang be "played up".

3. Business enterprises that are not notable advertisers may be roundly eken to task, as, e.g., the Standard Oil Company or the American Sugar Refining Company; and, indeed, it may be shrewd management to abuse these concerns, since such abuse redounds to the periodical's reputation for popular sympathy and independence.

4. "Snobbery" is here used without disrespect, as a convenient term to denote the element of strain involved in the quest of gentility on the Part of persons whose accustomed social sending is less high or less authentic than their aspirations.

5. Cf., e.g., Maurice Lair, l'Imperialism allemand, especially ch. II and III. The like change of sentiment is visible in the British community. Cf. Hobson, Imperialism, especially pt II, ch. I and III.

6. Cf., e.g., Hobson, Imperialism, p. II, chap. VII.

7. The selective effect of warfare, both ancient and modern, has been discussed by various writers. Protracted wars Or a warlike policy always have some such effect, no doubt, and in old times this has shown itself to be a serious cultural factor. It is commonly regarded that the selection results in an elimination of the "best" human material. Perhaps the most cogent spokesman for this view is D.S. Jordan, The Blood of the Nation. The "best" in this case must be taken to mean the best for the prupose, not necessarily for other purposes. In such a case as the Chinese or the Jewish peoples, e.g., a very long–continued, though not in both cases a close, selective elimination of the peace–dturbing elements has left a residue that is highly efficient ("good") in certain directions, but not good war material. The case of the North–European peoples, however, in the present juncture is somewhat different from these. Racially, the most efficient war material among them seems to be those elements that contain an appreciable admixture of the dolicho–blond stock. These elements at the same time are apparently, on the whole, also the ones most generally endowed with industrial initiative and a large, aptitude for the machine technology and scientific research. Selective elinination by war and military tenure in the case of these peoples should, therefore, apparently lower both their fighting capacity and their industrial and intellectual capacity; so that, by force of this double and cumulative effect, the resulting national decline should in their case be comprehensive and relatively precipitate.

8. With the complement of archaic virtues that invests these adepts there is also associated a fair complement of those more elemental vices that are growing obsolete in the peaceable civilized communities. Such debaucheries, extravagances of cruelty, and general superfluity of naughtiness as are nameless or impossible in civil life are blameless matters of course in the service. In the nature of the case they are inseparable from the service. The service commonly leaves the veterans physical, intellectual, and moral invalids (as witness the records of the Pension Office). But these less handsome concomitants of the service should scarcely be made a point of reproach to those brave men whose devotion to the flag and the business interests has led them by the paths of disease and depravity. Nor are the accumulated vices to be lightly condemned, since their weight also falls on the conservative side; being archaic and authenticated, their cultural bearing is, on the whole, salutary.

9. See Chapter VIII, pp. 347–350.